CASCADIA: THE ELUSIVE UTOPIA

D1021821

PRAISE FOR
Cascadia: The Elusive Utopia

෴

*"The conventional wisdom of the 'left coast' as a
Godless land whose inhabitants are dedicated to the pursuit of
self-indulgence is boldly confronted in Douglas Todd's
amazing new volume on the diverse spiritual character of
Cascadia. Todd's engrossing introduction plus essays from
some of North America's top thinkers reveal a region that
transcends national boundaries and traditional concepts for a
description of religion and spirituality. Read this book
and you'll gain a new perspective on a magical land where the
dance between Heaven and Earth, though wide ranging
and complex, shares a common melody."*

—ANGUS REID, CEO OF ANGUS REID STRATEGIES
AND FOUNDER OF ANGUS REID GLOBAL MONITOR

෴

*"*Cascadia: The Elusive Utopia *demonstrates how the
character of a place shapes and nourishes the civil society that
lives there. Editor Douglas Todd has assembled some of
the region's best thinkers, essayists and poets to bring this
region's unique story to print. The writers show how the
Pacific Northwest's stunning wilderness and intricate ecology
have inspired modern environmental movements,
a self-reliant secular spirituality, ethnic pluralism and rugged
independence. This cauldron of creative social change
has been the birthplace of Greenpeace, recycling laws, a whale
sanctuary and innovative companies such as Microsoft
and Amazon. As this volume reveals, something
special is going on in Cascadia."*

—REX WEYLER, AUTHOR OF *GREENPEACE: THE INSIDE STORY*
AND *THE JESUS SAYINGS.*

CASCADIA

THE ELUSIVE UTOPIA

Exploring the Spirit of the Pacific Northwest

EDITOR

DOUGLAS TODD

RONSDALE PRESS

CASCADIA: THE ELUSIVE UTOPIA
Copyright © 2008 held by the authors herein

All rights reserved. No part of this publication may be reproduced, stored in a re-trieval system, or transmitted, in any form or by any means, without prior written permission of the publisher, or, in Canada, in the case of photocopying or other reprographic copying, a licence from Access Copyright (The Canadian Copyright Licensing Agency).

RONSDALE PRESS
3350 West 21st Avenue
Vancouver, B.C., Canada
v6s 1G7

Typesetting: Julie Cochrane, in Utopia 10.5 pt on 15.5
Cover Design & Photography: Julie Cochrane
Index: Bookmark Editing & Indexing
Paper: Ancient Forest Friendly Silva (FSC) — 100% post-consumer waste

Ronsdale Press wishes to thank the following for their support of its publishing program: the Canada Council for the Arts, the Government of Canada through the Book Publishing Industry Development Program (BPIDP), and the Province of British Columbia through the Book Publishing Tax Credit Program and the British Columbia Arts Council.

Library and Archives Canada Cataloguing in Publication

   Cascadia: the elusive Utopia: exploring the spirit of the Pacific
Northwest / Douglas Todd, editor.

Includes bibliographical references and index.
ISBN 978-1-55380-060-6

   1. Spirituality — Northwest, Pacific. 2. Northwest, Pacific — History.
3. Northwest, Pacific — Economic conditions. 4. Bioregionalism — Northwest,
Pacific. 5. Northwest, Pacific — In literature. 6. Human ecology — Northwest,
Pacific. 7. Sacred space — Northwest, Pacific. 8. Landscape — Northwest, Pacific.
9. Utopias. I. Todd, Douglas

BL2520 C38 200   204'.09795   C2008-904737-0

At Ronsdale Press we are committed to protecting the environment. To this end we are working with Markets Initiative (www.oldgrowthfree.com) and printers to phase out our use of paper produced from ancient forests. This book is one step towards that goal.

Printed in Canada by Marquis Book Printing, Quebec, Canada

To my mother, Mary,
and my uncle, George Fox,
both of whom love this deep-green
place and taught me to be
curious about it

And always: to my beloved sons,
Nate, Thomas and Devin

ACKNOWLEDGEMENTS

∾

I am grateful to Jack Shadbolt, the adventurous Cascadian painter, and his wife, arts writer Doris Shadbolt, for the generous donation that led to my 2006 fellowship at Simon Fraser University, without which this project would not have been born. The Shadbolts were devoted to the people, land and spirit of the West Coast. I think they would be pleased with our vision for Cascadia. I also thank SFU's former dean of arts and social sciences, the dynamic John Pierce, for putting together the Jack and Doris Shadbolt Fellowship in the Humanities, which aims to strengthen connections between academia and the wider community. A tip of the hat as well to Anne-Marie Feenberg-Dibon, head of SFU's Institute for the Humanities, who cheerfully backed this project from the beginning.

Many of the Canadian and American thinkers who collaborated on this book have been my intellectual heroes. I cannot thank them enough for their original and heartfelt contributions to this interdisciplinary effort, which illustrates the bridge-building I would like to see take place more often among creative Cascadians. The editors of the *Vancouver Sun*, where I work, have also been supportive, including by offering photos. Without listing all their names, I offer warm appreciation to my family members and friends who encouraged me in putting together this book.

At Ronsdale Press, publisher Ronald Hatch has been a pleasure to work with, combining grace and rigour. Exacting Julie Cochrane has made the book visually inviting. Finally, for her commitment to helping edit and weave together this complex project, my great thanks go to Trish Graham, of the Institute for the Humanities, who along the way became a friend.

CONTENTS

Introduction

DOUGLAS TODD

"Oregon is California's Canada."

— US POLITICAL SATIRIST
STEPHEN COLBERT

POPULAR CULTURE HAS tuned into the unique character of Cascadia: the rich, wet and spectacularly mountainous region this book defines as Oregon, Washington and British Columbia. Late-night TV comedian Stephen Colbert, who mocks right-wing ideology at the same time as he pretends to be one of its chief exponents, has a regular shtick in which he highlights how progressive values among "the tie-dyed tree-hugging wusses" of Oregon reflect the pink-tinged hues of liberal-left Canada.

Even the veteran lawyer played by William Shatner in the TV show *Boston Legal* sees Cascadia as a utopian home of the divine, remarking, "God lives in British Columbia." His jest reflects the belief, widely held outside Cascadia, that the region is intimately connected to nature, leery of tradition-bound institutions and open to experimenting with novel expressions of freedom. Cascadia may be a so-called secular place where fewer people than anywhere else in North America consider themselves institutionally "religious," but they certainly think of themselves as "spiritual," often experiencing sacredness in the imposing landscapes.

Then there are those semi-humorous bumper stickers found on cars in the region, which read, "Keep the US Out of Cascadia!" They are warning the imperialistic eastern establishment of a long-held separatist sensibility among many of the Pacific Northwest's Americans and Canadians. Their prickly attitude goes something like this: if outside government and corporate forces would just stop meddling, Cascadia would be able to evolve into something truly idyllic.

Up until the last 150 years, the relatively few people who lived in or thought about what we now call Cascadia considered it a cohesive bioregion, as do many of the contributors to this book. To some extent that remains the mindset of the region's aboriginals, who practised their nature-revering spirituality while hunting, fishing and trading along its north-south valleys and inter-connecting coastline. They certainly did not conceive of invisible boundaries on maps. In a different way, a borderless vision was shared by early European explorers and trappers. They include Columbia River explorer David Thompson and Captain George Vancouver, one of those credited with "discovering" this land off the northern Pacific Ocean in the 1790s.

Soon after, in 1803, US President Thomas Jefferson dispatched the famous Lewis and Clark expedition to the region, in part to solidify the majestic terrain between what is now northern California and Alaska into an independent entity to be called "The Republic of the Pacific." As historian Jean Barman explains in Chapter 4, there were several times during the nineteenth century when expansionist Americans almost had their wish of claiming what is now the west coast of Canada. But the British Empire, working through the Hudson's Bay Company, did just enough to claim for itself a portion of this wild and bountiful region now known as Cascadia, which through the early 1800s was being called "The Oregon Territory."

The international border, featuring in recent years often-intimidating customs guards, was not created at the 49th parallel until 1846, when Britain and the US felt pressured to accept a compromise to avoid warfare. Despite the pronouncements of radical environmentalists, some popular talk-show hosts, urban planners and intellectual travel writers, few people with their feet planted in the world of *realpolitik* would suggest the US-Canada border is going to disappear anytime soon, making way for a proud new, independent Cascadian nation. But that has not stopped many people from dreaming about all the things — seen and unseen — that continue to tie together the landscape, people and futures of Oregon, Washington and B.C.

The aim of this book is to explore deeply that elusive utopia. To dig into Cascadia's seemingly unlimited possibilities, this volume brings together fourteen of the region's most able essayists, religion scholars, bioregionalists, literary analysts, historians, philosophers, theologians, ethicists, political scientists and poets. With the addition of two carefully selected Cascadian "outsiders," from Toronto and Connecticut, the contributors to this book are almost evenly sorted between those born in the US and those born in Canada, with two carrying dual citizenship. (One other was raised largely in Latin America until arriving in Canada in his teens.) I believe Americans and Canadians in Cascadia have been missing out by failing to learn about each other's insights. The people of Cascadia have many common values, worries and sensibilities, but the international border has often proved a barrier to sharing innovative responses to the region's problems and possibilities. In this book, you would be hard-pressed to find a more gifted and well-suited binational group of people with whom to probe — imaginatively, realistically and even romantically — the cultural promise and spiritual character of this remarkable place.

Before the reader goes much further, take note that *Cascadia:*

The Elusive Utopia defines "spirituality" very broadly — as the way that humans create for themselves ultimate meaning, values and purpose. Along with the unusually high number of Cascadians who like to say "I'm spiritual but not religious," the authors agree that one does not have to adhere to a religion to be spiritual. Contributors to the volume may go one step further: we assume that atheists, who live in record numbers in Cascadia, can and are making profound contributions to this region's particular sense of spirituality and place.

THE GEOGRAPHIC, CULTURAL AND ECONOMIC TIES CONNECTING CASCADIA

Before turning to the crucial role that spirituality is playing in shaping public life in Cascadia — the subject at the heart of this book — it is worth taking a look at the more commonly discussed links among residents of Washington, Oregon and B.C. These factors have customarily made both residents of the region and a surprisingly large number of outsiders wax eloquent about their dreams for Cascadia.

Perhaps the most distinctive feature of Cascadia, which is also known as the Pacific Northwest, is that its rugged geography is impossible to ignore. Even the origins of the name Cascadia emerge from the natural world, which is so passionately revered in the region. The term "Cascadia" is historically credited to early nineteenth-century Scottish botanist David Douglas, after whom the mighty Douglas fir, one of the tallest trees in the world, is named. Hunting for plants near the mouth of the Columbia River in the 1820s, Douglas was struck by the region's many glorious "cascading" rivers and waterfalls. Since then, the name has been applied to the Cascade Mountain Range, the Pacific Ocean's Cascadia subduction zone (tectonic plates which frequently visit earthquakes upon one and all) and the Cascade Volcanic Arc, part of the Pacific Rim of Fire.

Unlike in less physically endowed corners of the world, Cascadia's geography is so grand it is inescapable. Cascadia boasts the imposing Cascade and Coastal mountain ranges, with many of their peaks as volcanic and changeable as the region's residents. These daunting mountains, with their bears and wolves, are in view of the region's three major metropolises: Seattle, Portland and especially Vancouver (where one of the city's most impressive spectacles, the Cascade's perpetually snow-capped Mount Baker, actually rises up from US soil to the south). Also impossible to disregard are Cascadia's waterways: the Pacific Ocean, bringing temperate weather; and its thundering rivers, particularly the take-your-breath-away Columbia, which runs through and has helped define all three political jurisdictions. The region's waters, in turn, are famous for salmon, the legendary and threatened species that some people believe should be the symbol of Cascadia.

Those who champion the supremacy of salmon mythology for the Pacific Northwest, however, will have to battle with earlier defenders of the concept of an independent Cascadia, who have customarily held up the Douglas fir tree as the region's archetype, displayed on their only slightly tongue-in-cheek rebel "Cascadia nation" flag (affectionately known as "the Doug"). As both evergreens and salmon decline in abundance, threats to these awe-inspiring expressions of raw wilderness are causing many to mount the ramparts to try to preserve this edge of the continent, or at least parts of it, as a glimpse of unspoiled Eden. Then again, as religious historian Eleanor Stebner writes persuasively in Chapter 11, perhaps the region needs a human-constructed symbol, like the Peace Arch at the Blaine international border crossing, which reflects the goodwill, idealism and communitarianism that those who have settled in Cascadia can bring to creating a model future for this binational, multi-spiritual land.

Setting aside the spectacular wilderness, however, Cascadia has an inter-connected urban culture, and not only because sidewalk coffee cafes are *de rigueur*, and fashion (typified by water-repellant fleece clothing) is ultra-casual compared to the pinstriped East. The city dwellers of Cascadia live surprisingly close to each other.

Cascadia's three major metropolises house almost half the region's almost 14 million people (6 million in Washington, 4.25 million in B.C. and 3.5 million in Oregon). A resident of Vancouver can drive to Seattle in one-quarter the time it takes to motor to the nearest major Canadian city, Calgary — the oil-industry-run, Conservative-party-backing prairie metropolis nicknamed "Cowtown," a tag that suggests just how culturally removed it is from the West Coast, a.k.a. "Lotusland" or the "Left Coast."

On the so-called profane level of economics, Washington, Oregon and B.C. produce hundreds of billions of dollars worth of goods and services each year — which would make the combined region one of the world's top economies. Promoters on both sides of the border highlight the benefits of the "two-nation vacation," with more than 40 million people flying or driving across the Washington state/B.C. border each year, clogging customs. In late 2007, B.C. and Washington State officials revealed their plans to introduce similar high-tech licence plates to let drivers cross the border without long delays. Business and community leaders in Vancouver and Seattle began consulting in 2006 on making a joint bid to host either the World Cup of Soccer or the Summer Olympics. In Chapter 2, pollster Andrew Grenville reveals that the residents of B.C. and Washington are the most favourable in North America to an open international border. Whether Canadian or American, his polling suggests, Cascadians like each other.

Politicians on both sides of the border have worked with influential think-tanks, particularly Seattle's Discovery Institute Cascadia Center, to emphasize the importance of expanding high-speed train connections between Vancouver and Seattle, as well as other commuter and trade links within Cascadia. In 2001, provincial and state politicians formed the Pacific Northwest Economic Region (PNER) to foster regional and economic co-operation. However, the PNER stretches the definition of Cascadia to include Alberta, Idaho and Alaska, which this book avoids because of its lack of bioregional and cultural cohesiveness. When it comes to corporate life, Cascadia is known worldwide for its long-time lumber and airplane (Boeing) industries, as well as lifestyle-related newcomers expanding the reach of coffee (Starbucks), computers (Microsoft), on-line marketing (Amazon), co-operative banking (VanCity Savings Credit Union), sports shoes (Nike) and ecotourism.

Many note there is a cultural kinship among many Cascadians, especially those on the highly populated coast, which includes a comfort with individuality and freedom. At a socio-economic level, household incomes in B.C., Washington and Oregon are higher than each country's average. Real estate prices tend to stay strong in Portland, Seattle and Vancouver even while they flatten out in most of the rest of North America. Residents are the most highly educated on the continent, with more than 26 percent holding bachelor's degrees. When it comes to entertainment, the residents of Vancouver provide 40 percent of the funding for Seattle's arts-oriented public TV station, KCTS, and tens of thousands of Canadians frequently attend Seattle Mariners baseball games and rock festivals at the Columbia River Gorge in central Washington. Virtually every Cascadian seems proud of homegrown Jimi Hendrix, whose utterly groundbreaking guitar style seemed to rise out of the region's wildness. And Washingtonians and Oregonians often dash up to B.C. to ski at Whistler, visit their recreational properties or revel in Vancouver's exotically cosmopolitan urban life, which overflows with Chinese, Japanese, Indian, Korean, aboriginal, Vietnamese and European restaurants, not to mention those experimenting with culinary "fusion."

Part of the romantic appeal of this pluralistic region is that utopian dreams for it never quite die. At the most audacious level, some organizations remain devoted to the vision of unifying the Pacific Northwest, culturally and perhaps even politically. The websites of politico-enviro groups such as Cascadian Bioregionalism, the Cascadian National Party and Team Cascadia include variations on the Cascadian evergreen flag and rally cries to form "the Republic of Cascadia." At the height of his fame, B.C.'s top talk-show host, a former cabinet minister and political centrist named Rafe Mair, was one of those predicting a political entity called Cascadia would exist by 2010.

The most famous symbol of this mythical free-standing state is Ernest Callenbach's legendary futuristic 1975 novel, *Ecotopia*. Although the boundaries of Callenbach's *Ecotopia* do not actually include B.C., the book describes the Pacific Northwest as a newly separated ecologically sensitive country with a female president and free love. Author Joel Garneau followed *Ecotopia* with a more grounded 1981 book, *The Nine Nations of North America*, which used the novel's title to describe the US and Canadian west coast as a unified geographic and cultural entity, noted for environmental sensibilities and high quality of life. Timothy Egan's 1990 Cascadian classic, *The Good Rain*, magnificently captured how the region is coming of age, promising to reveal to the world tantalizing new ways of doing things. In his best-selling 1998 book, *An Empire Wilderness: Travels into America's Future*, noted intellectual Robert Kaplan enthusiastically championed the notion of B.C. leaving a dismantled Canada to join Washington and Oregon to create a superior culture. Naive or not, Cascadia has a way of inspiring grand visions.

CASCADIANS' DISTINCTIVE SPIRITUALITY SHAPES PUBLIC LIFE

This book is uniquely devoted to an aspect of Cascadia that rarely, if ever, receives discussion: the surprisingly crucial way that religion and spirituality influences the binational region's public life.

Connecticut religion scholar Mark Silk, senior editor of the sweeping eight-book "Religion by Region" project, maintains in Chapter 5 that religious differences may make up the strongest influence on regional public life in North America. Many of us agree. And in few places would this be more relevant than in Cascadia.

How do the forces of informal spirituality and organized religion, impacted by an overpowering landscape, influence what people believe, feel, do and imagine in Cascadia? They influence Cascadians' sense of morality, values, politics, ecology and social justice. They shape what it means to be a citizen in this fast-changing, hybrid region, which is continually inventing itself. They create a spirituality of place, which some have called Cascadia's "geography of wonder."

The power of religion and spirituality is felt in a paradoxical way in Cascadia. This book is not about how one dominant religion shapes the people of the region, as it does in evangelical Protestant Texas, Muslim Iran or Catholic Mexico. Instead, it focuses on the question: What ramifications stream from the residents of Cascadia being the least institutionally religious on the continent?

Readers will discover that the answers revolve around Cascadians' unusually strong sense of being "secular but spiritual," which feeds a kinship with nature and a yearning for a fresh future, a kind of non-sectarian version of what Silk calls a "New Cascadian Jerusalem."

In this book, Cascadia's leading thinkers reflect on how spirituality, in the broadest sense, shapes the people of the region. While recognizing institutional religion has had an important part to play in Cascadian history and life, they explore how most residents resist organized religion. The contributors show how this relates to Cascadians' anti-institutional attitudes, often-bewildering ethnic pluralism, somewhat European sensibilities, liberal-left leanings, secessionist defiance of central governments (in Washington, D.C., and Ottawa), future-orientedness, artistic and literary ties to a sacred sense of place, intense focus on health and healing, and willingness to experiment with something, anything, new in this "new" land.

Cascadia: The Elusive Utopia examines why this frontier region, on the edge of the continent, has for more than 150 years drawn thousands of people who are determined to create their own paradise on Earth. They have come to follow everyone from a charismatic socialist Finn and a theosophist named Brother Twelve to a Rolls-Royce-loving Indian yogi and a former Tacoma housewife

J.Z. Knight, who claims to channel a thirty-thousand-year-old war-rior called Ramtha. The book includes the unique research of poll-ster Andrew Grenville, who shows how the people who move to and live in Cascadia are more devoted than most to individual freedom, whether it is in regards to spirituality, abortion, marijuana, euthana-sia, homosexuality or politics. Readers will also learn that many of those who answer "None" when asked to name their religion, still have deep spiritual concerns, some of which dovetail with the more traditionally religious, some of which decidedly do not.

Readers will learn about the many connections between Casca-dians' individualistic and nature-based forms of spirituality and how the region gave birth to ecological movements such as Green-peace, the continent's earliest bottle recycling laws (in B.C. and Oregon), radical farmland protection laws and old-growth forest legislation. Could there also be a tie between Cascadians' distrust of traditional institutions and their being among the first in North America to organize mass protests against globalization?

What is more, since the people who claim "no religion" have turned into one of the fastest growing and largest cohorts in both the US and Canada through most of the 1990s, could what is going on in Cascadia indicate the future direction of the continent?

Although this book reflects on how Cascadia could be in a prime position to foster creative social change, it will not ignore the dark-er side of life in Oregon, Washington and B.C. While there is some-thing to be said for Cascadians being future-directed, some of the book's writers suggest that the downside is a tendency toward a lack of collective memory, which contributes to people in Cascadia lacking roots and succumbing to extreme individualism. Culturally and politically, as well, all three political jurisdictions have not escaped polarization — between extremists of the left and right, as well as between the liberal coastal population and more conserva-tive interior residents. The center, as W.B. Yeats might say, has trou-ble holding in Cascadia.

There are fringe apocalyptics who make their homes in the region's corners, where various New Age proponents sometimes match them for flakiness. Authoritarianism is hardly unknown, either, whether among hard-headed politicians, tough union leaders, bully-boy business people, Christian clergy, ethnic-based Eastern religious groups and the large military cohort in Washington State. The rapacious face of capitalism, particularly in regard to resource extraction, often seems as strong in Cascadia as anywhere else, provoking activists, artists and writers to stand up for the land, the sea and their creatures. Paradoxically, the region's many champions of freedom can often foster a kind of hyper-individualism, leading to a harsh lack of concern for the common good. Yet the contributors to this book strive to bridge the often unhelpful gap between what some observers have called the region's abundance of "right-wing bigots and left-wing loonies." They suggest there is a third way.

This third Cascadian way centers on the potential for constructing a new consensus on ecological issues. The region has experienced rapid old-forest devastation and overfishing and, especially in Washington and Oregon, urban sprawl. The most visible blemish on the region's natural wonders may be the supposedly efficient Interstate-5 Highway, which slashes through the coastal region like a scar, splitting up Seattle, Portland and expanding suburbs. (In Canada, the extension of the I-5 mercifully ends, literally, at the border of the City of Vancouver.)

What do all these challenges say about the possibility for change in Cascadia? Many believe that, while Cascadia may not be the launching point for a global revolution, there is a spiritually informed mindset of optimism, inventiveness, tolerance and ferment here that suggests the region could become a model for measured progressive transformation, especially regarding how people of the planet interact with nature.

LOW RELIGIOSITY, BUT HIGH SPIRITUALITY
The valleys and mountainsides of the Pacific Northwest are home to the least institutionally religious people in North America. Until this book came into being, few observers have noted that residents of

Washington and Oregon are almost as vigilant as British Columbians in shunning organized religion. Before we explore the major cultural, moral and political ramifications of this unusual link among Cascadians, I will introduce some key polling numbers.

Canadians are far less formally religious than their American cousins, but in no province in Canada is wariness about religion stronger than in B.C. A rising number of British Columbians, 36 percent, told Canadian census takers in 2001 they have "no religion" (almost double the Canadian average of 19 percent). In Oregon, 21 percent told a comprehensive 2001 American Religious Identification Survey (ARIS) they have "no religion," compared to 14 percent across the US. And in Washington State, the religious "Nones" (those who answer "None" when asked to name their religion) make up 25 percent of all residents. Like British Columbians, the people of Washington and Oregon are the least conventionally religious in their country.

These numbers, however, do not show the full extent of Cascadians' relative lack of loyalty to formal religion. When pollsters have probed whether residents of B.C., Washington and Oregon who say they are affiliated with a religion actually ever bother attending one of its institutions, the percentage of those who end up having virtually no connection with organized religion almost doubles — to about 60 percent.

Paradoxically, however, this does not mean Cascadia is teeming with atheists or even agnostics. Only 14 percent of British Columbians say they are atheists, says pollster Reginald Bibby. Most of the religious Nones, as they are often called, are expanding the definition of what it means to be religious, or, as many of them prefer, "spiritual." At least two-thirds of religious Nones tell pollsters in Canada and the US they believe in God. More than half of the Nones in Canada say they have "spiritual needs," according to ARIS. These are some of the reasons that Mark Shibley, one of our Oregonian contributors, came up with the helpful term, "secular but spiritual."

The "secular but spiritual" cohort is unusually strong in Cascadia. And through the 1990s the same cohort has made up the fastest-growing major "religious" group on the continent — expanding rapidly in Canada and doubling in the last decade in the US. Given such developments, I join some contributors to this book in wondering: Are the people of Cascadia at the forefront of a North American spiritual trend?

Then there is established religion. Despite its struggles in Cascadia, institutional religion is not irrelevant. It is becoming more ecumenical, interfaith and experimental to meet the needs of the region's independent-minded, secularized residents. Organized religion's active adherents are relatively small compared to the rest of the continent but, as Andrew Grenville points out in Chapter 2, more than two-thirds of Cascadians continue to believe, at least in a private, apparently vague way, in traditional Christian beliefs. Many people who are actively involved in religious institutions are making significant cultural, political and ecological contributions in Cascadia. Their numbers may be smaller compared to the rest of North America, but scholar Patricia O'Connell Killen, from Washington State, spells out in statistical detail in Chapter 3 that about one out of four Cascadians at least once a month attend institutional forms of Christianity, and to a lesser extent Buddhism, Judaism, Sikhism, Islam and Hinduism. While many Cascadian Christians are conservative on social and moral issues, Patricia O'Connell Killen, Sallie McFague, a dual American-Canadian citizen living in Vancouver, and Gail Wells, of Oregon, stress that many other Catholics, as well as Methodists, Anglicans, Episcopalians, United Church of Canada members, Lutherans, evangelicals, Jews, Sikhs and Buddhists in Cascadia lean to the liberal side of the spectrum and have been on the front lines of progressive social change and environmental consciousness raising.

Despite so many similarities across the border, it is worth noting, however, two key religious differences between B.C., on one hand, and Washington and Oregon, on the other. The two American states

of Cascadia have a much larger, and generally more politically conservative, evangelical Christian population (25 percent of all residents) than Cascadia's Canadian province (where only about 10
percent are evangelical). Another significant imbalance relates to
those connected to Asian religions. Only 1.2 percent of the people in
Washington and Oregon identify as belonging to an Asian religion,
such as Sikhism, Hinduism, Buddhism or Islam. In B.C., the figure
rises to more than 8 percent. In Greater Vancouver, the percentage
following Eastern religions has more than doubled in the past
decade to a hard-to-ignore 13 percent.

WHY MANY CASCADIANS SHUN ESTABLISHED RELIGION

Although religion and spirituality are not as dead in secularized
Cascadia as many media commentators like to suggest, and Christian missionaries and churches, especially, had a major role to play
in the development of the region, the question still needs to be
asked: Why is such an exceptionally large percentage of people in
Cascadia either antagonistic or indifferent toward faith institutions?

Some thinkers believe it has something to do with our rugged
geography, and our global position — on the edge of what is often
wryly called "civilization." The daunting geography scattered the
European settlers who moved into Cascadia. The reasons explored
by Patricia O'Connell Killen and Mark Wexler relate to how early
settlers in this resource-rich region, much like aboriginals, were
forced to move to survive, to find the best places to log, fish and
mine. Restless mobility and a boom-and-bust economy, either in
mining or more recently computers, have not been conducive to
the creation of lasting communities, where formal religion could
put down lasting roots.

Cascadia's geography-inspired mobility continues today. The
recent census showed an astonishing 60 percent of the residents of
Metro Vancouver were not born in B.C. Some 36 percent were actually born outside Canada, typically in East and South Asia. This rare

phenomenon makes the city one of the most "cosmopolitan" in the world (often drawing comparisons with Toronto and London, England). Washington and Oregon do not have as many foreign-born residents as B.C., at just 10 percent of the population. But the two northwestern states have grown phenomenally through recent in-migration and now house a wide multicultural population (with fewer blacks and Hispanics than the US national average but with more Asians and aboriginals).

Cascadians' tendency to be on the move physically leads to a psychological mobility. Many may have limited loyalty to the region, thinking often of their far-away birthplace or international business connections. Certainly, fewer Cascadians bother to sign up with institutions, religious or otherwise. The region's mobility and ethnic diversity means that no single religion has ever come to dominate. Cascadians do not realize how rare this is. With no religion reigning supreme in the region, Patricia O'Connell Killen makes a compelling argument that many Cascadians lose an incentive to define themselves religiously, either by joining the reigning religious body — or by actively opposing it. In other words, Cascadians spend a lot of time wondering exactly who they are. Spiritually speaking, most Cascadians drift, albeit often rather contentedly. Those who do commit to a religious path, whether conservative or progressive, tend to be passionate about it, since they have made a choice that counters the dominant ethos.

Cascadia's location on the proverbial edge of the continent has also contributed to its lack of formal religiosity. Many among the flood of people moving to the region, the last western frontier, want to get away from the restrictions and perceived oppressions of their past, including the religion of their parents. Compared to other North Americans, Cascadians tend to rely on their feelings to guide them when it comes to spirituality. British Columbians appear to have the greatest receptiveness of all Canadians to unstructured experiences of divinity. While most Americans and Canadians from a Christian background use traditional language about Jesus and heaven to describe their beliefs, British Columbians are more likely to opt for open-ended expressions of spirituality. For instance, Andrew Grenville has shown that more than 41 percent of British Columbians claim to have had "a religious or mystical experience," compared to the Canadian average of just 29 percent. Such spiritual individualism is a hallmark of Cascadian life.

SEARCHING FOR UTOPIA

The mountains, remote inlets and try-anything attitude of many people in Cascadia have provided fertile ground for spiritual, utopian ventures. Countless people have flocked to the region believing that this was their last chance to create a paradigmatic society. Even the comic strip *Doonesbury* has picked up on idealism about the Pacific Northwest, depicting its main character as blown away by the region's fabulous coffee, excellent public schools and polite workplaces.

In Cascadia's eclectic culture — in which no single religion, or in many regions no single ethnicity (including generically European), dominates — scores of new religions have attempted to set down roots, and occasionally succeeded. The largely unattached people of Cascadia are often lured to new forms of spirituality. A short list of major utopian experiments, each involving networks of thousands of people, who have made a home in Cascadia includes the Bhagwan Shree Rajneesh's world famous, contentious and short-lived 1980s Oregon commune, which emphasized spiritual and sexual permissiveness; the persecution-escaping Mennonites and more radical Doukhobors, tens of thousands of whom tried to establish pacifist, egalitarian, anti-materialistic communities in B.C.; the Mormon polygamists who for fifty years have maintained extensive settlements on the rural B.C. — Washington border; the thriving Yasodhara ashram in the Kootenays, which spreads yoga culture globally, and the New Age community near Elm, Washington, centered on a thirty-thousand-year-old warrior named "Ramtha," which recently produced a much-discussed documentary on science and religion, *What the Bleep Do We Know!?*

This list does not include thousands of smaller utopian-minded communities, many of which have blossomed and died. Those able to merge their dreams with the harsh real world have hung on, and some even flourish today. They are devoted to wildly diverging alternative ways of living in the world — including neo-paganism (Wicca), back-to-the-land philosophies, Buddhism, religious apocalypticism, Eastern orthodoxy, sexual liberation, the merging of science and religion, yoga, Christian ecology, socialism, organic farming, feminine aspects of divinity, egalitarian gender relations, shared ownership of property, celibacy, the power of silence and spiritual healing.

Cascadia's utopian sensibility has not just been for fringe radicals, either. The pretty town of Ashland, Oregon, has turned into the latest New Age mecca for North America, becoming the home of Neale Donald Walsch, Jean Houston and other big-name spiritual teachers. Mark Shibley, who lives and teaches in Ashland, says well-off baby boomers from across the US are "cashing out" of their successful businesses and professions to move to the city in the Mediterranean-like hills of southern Oregon, where they can well afford to raise children in a safe setting, shop at boutiques, pursue inner peace and enjoy the arts (the city is home to a legendary Shakespeare festival).

One could also argue that a utopian impulse was behind many now-almost-mainstream Cascadian creations, including Vancouver-born Greenpeace, Bainbridge Island's Positive Futures Network, Cortes Island's Hollyhock retreat center, Puget Sound's Whidbey Institute for Earth, Spirit and the Human Future, Washington's Sustainable Northwest, Seattle's Sightline Institute, SFU's Wosk Centre for Dialogue, Portland's Mercy Corps, Seattle-based World Vision, Olympia's experimental Evergreen State College, EcoTrust and scores of other forward-thinking non-profit organizations. As well, some of the often-innovative environmental policies created by politicians in Cascadia have had a utopian element, leading to the West Coast being called the Left Coast.

Spiritual idealism certainly had much to do with the reason that a

Canadian-raised gold seeker, Oswald West, became the Democratic governor of Oregon in 1911 and, fueled by firm Christian principles, decided to protect forever its seemingly endless beach coastline for public enjoyment. It may also have had something to do with why, in 1971, Oregon activists, inspired in part by a B.C. politician, made their state the first jurisdiction in North America to bring in refundable bottle recycling laws. Utopianism, in addition, led Oregon and B.C., also in the early 1970s, to be among the first in North America to establish tough farmland-protection policies. At the same time, B.C. legislated state-run auto insurance, which has managed to survive many subsequent right-wing provincial governments. And in recent years Vancouver politicians have set up safe-injection sites for drug addicts, while leading the charge for the de-criminalization of soft drugs.

In the Pacific Northwest, idealism has become a way of life for many, a kind of shared civil, or secular, religion — based on reverence for nature and hope for the future. Even though many people who live in or come to Cascadia have hopes of creating the last paradise on Earth, contributor Philip Resnick is one of those a tad sceptical about the region's utopian impulses. In his challenging Chapter 6, Resnick says a regional utopian streak combined with a sense of being marginalized on the continent can have downsides. An obsession about the future can lead to a rejection of traditional, sometimes more communitarian, values. While some utopians look eagerly to a wonderful future, they can also often lack a sense of collective memory and roots. Utopians, in addition, sometimes live up to a West Coast stereotype of extremism and flakiness. In other words, they are almost as known for being willing to champion radical forms of winner-take-all neo-conservatism (as exemplified by Vancouver's influential right-wing Fraser Institute, or Portland's cigar-smoking reactionary radio show host, Lars Larson, who is now one of the US's most popular) as they are for fighting for novel forms of egalitarian living or environmental sensitivity.

Still, there is nothing wrong with trying to realize social ideals while also facing difficult reality, as both Philip Resnick and George Bowering, Canada's first official poet laureate, seem determined to attempt in their poems at the end of this book. The contributors have not given up hoping the people of Cascadia could come to be admired for a kind of tempered utopianism.

NATURE RELIGION AND ENVIRONMENTALISM ARE ALIVE

"We don't have the galleries and cathedrals of Europe here. We have wilderness and we still have to find some ways to preserve that," says John Mikes, of Canadian River Expeditions. In some ways, Mikes was talking about the eco-tourist potential of the Pacific Northwest. But his remark also reflects a spiritual impulse that is very much alive in Cascadia. We do not have many awe-inspiring religious edifices to draw visitors to Cascadia. But we do have awe-inspiring wilderness.

It is a west coast cliché, but when many residents of Cascadia want to find God, peace of mind or just relief from stress, they go for a walk in the forest or on the beach. However loosely, spirituality and nature are inextricably linked in the public's mind, and this is true for many of those who also attend religious institutions but take frequent breaks from the pews to venture out into the great outdoors.

Call it a civil religion.

Civil religion is everywhere. It's made up of public events, rituals and iconic individuals that bind a society together under the rubric of something deemed sacred. Civil religion is a non-sectarian way to articulate and ground our vision of reality, of the way things are and should be. Some say the values of Thanksgiving and even baseball add up to civil religions. Many in this book, especially Sallie McFague, maintain there is absolutely nothing wrong in a pluralistic Cascadia highlighting an environmental civil religion — which reminds people how interconnected they are with the Earth and its creatures, and which urges ethical practices.

Certainly one of the most distinctive cultural values to emerge from Cascadia is an informal, non-sectarian, virtually universal reverence for nature. In the Pacific Northwest, where traditional religion does not pervade the cultural landscape, nature religion is ubiquitous — in literature, in the leisure rituals of city dwellers, in environmental movement ethics, in aboriginal culture and even in progressive religious institutions. Public signs of nature religion in Cascadia include bumper stickers and T-shirts reading, "May the Forest Be with You" and "Tree-Hugging Dirt Worshipper." As well as being avid hikers, gardeners, sailors, birders, windsurfers and fishers, the people of Cascadia think of themselves as protectors and stewards of the environment. Mark Shibley has called this rampant environmentalism a religious system, "not simply because it is sometimes dogmatic and moralistic, but rather because its rituals and core beliefs distinguish between things sacred (wilderness) and things profane (all else, often including people)."

Philip Resnick and Mark Silk suggest most of Cascadia's public intellectuals share ecological awareness as a passion, or at least a mutual concern. And the visual art we most treasure in Cascadia's galleries and the stories we read by its most cherished writers are invariably suffused with nature reverence. The popular visual artists, such as B.C. painters Emily Carr and Jack Shadbolt and Washington's glass-blowing Dale Chihuly, continually employ images of nature to symbolize transformation, power and mythology. Literary specialist Nicholas O'Connell writes in *On Sacred Ground: The Spirit of Place in Pacific Northwest Literature* that the most important contribution that Pacific Northwest writers have made to North American literatures is the way they are "articulating a more spiritual relationship with landscape."

In Chapter 10, Paulo Lemos Horta offers his "literary map" of Cascadia. He illustrates how world-renowned writers in Washington, Oregon and B.C., particularly Jack Hodgins and Gina Ochsner, find a spiritual glow in the humbling, sometimes threatening, landscape. Some writers, Horta says, have adapted "magic realism" to highlight Cascadian dreams of utopia and spirituality in this supposed "secular" region, to capture a sense of "the divine brushing against the natural." On one Cascadian author, however, Patricia O'Connell Killen and Philip Resnick have surprisingly different perspectives: B.C.'s future-oriented Douglas Coupland. In the best-selling *Life After God*, Coupland popularized the quintessentially Cascadian notion that people in their thirties and forties who did not attend religious institutions are now searching for the sacred in rivers and on mountaintops.

In his definitive lead chapter, Mark Shibley says Cascadia's large secular-but-spiritual cohort breaks down into at least three world views, each with its own approaches to nature. The first group engages with New Age spiritualities, emphasizing discovering one's true self and sacred nature through such phenomenally popular books of Oregon's Neale Donald Walsch, author of *Conversations with God*, and Vancouver's Oprah-Winfrey-promoted Eckhart Tolle, author of *The Power of Now* and *A New Earth*. Another group is apocalyptic. It includes hard-core anti-government white supremacists and survivalists. Like some hardcore environmentalists in Cascadia, survivalists have a sense of apocalypse: they fear that soon all of the region's wilderness and beauty will be destroyed by unbridled capitalism and corrupt governments.

The third major secular-but-spiritual group, according to Shibley, is made up of those who intentionally follow nature religion. People with this Earth-revering sensibility may be more dominant than those who adhere to institutional religion in Oregon, Washington and B.C. This group is drawn to North American aboriginal spirituality and the way it has developed methods of living respectfully off the land. Contributor Mike Carr, a bioregionalist who is not institutionally religious, sees efforts to protect bioregions such as Cascadia as a counter-globalization movement with a spiritual and aboriginal component, which enthusiastically welcomes rituals based on nature.

Many people who attend Christian and other religious institutions in Cascadia are also passionate about Earth-centered spirituality. These people are admirers of aboriginal land stewardship and noted progressive Christian eco-theologians such as Matthew Fox, Thomas

Berry and Vancouver's Sallie McFague. Her rousing Chapter 9 champions an emerging philosophical world view called panentheism, which maintains divinity is both embedded in nature, but also transcends it. McFague, an American who has taken out dual Canadian-US citizenship, says the environmentally sensitive residents of the bountiful Pacific Northwest may be developing a healthy civil religion, open to everyone. Stressing an issue that is important to many contributors, McFague writes about how Cascadia's city dwellers must treat the environment as a "garden," while placing special emphasis on enhancing the "second nature" that exists in urban centers. After all, says McFague, it is in cities that most of the population of Cascadia (and the planet) lives, including the poor.

What about Cascadia's conservative Protestants, led in the US for much of the early twenty-first century by President George W. Bush, who has been judged more of a friend of the oil industry than the environment? Many evangelical Christians tend to be less pro-environment than the rest of the Cascadian population because they hold the unfortunate belief the Earth will be destroyed in a cosmic cataclysm and they, the "saved," will be delivered into divine bliss. But there are indications that many of Cascadia's evangelicals have not given up on the planet. Some have been on the front lines to protection creation, like ecological thinker Loren Wilkinson, who teaches at Vancouver's evangelical Regent College, and Washington State's dynamic Peter Illyn, director of Restoring Eden: Christians for Environmental Stewardship.

Although generally welcoming the nature-rooted religion that pervades Cascadia, some contributors, such as Mark Shibley and Gail Wells, are concerned that more than a few Earth-worshippers who want only to "conserve" nature may have turned into unhelpful purists. Many doctrinaire conservationists may be inadvertently promoting policies that protect roughly 10 percent of the land as parks but allow the rest to be ravaged by marketplace forces. This book values wilderness protection, but strongly advocates philosophies and policies that will help humans respectfully live *with* nature, particularly in urban centers.

CASCADIAN SPIRITUALITY INFLUENCES MORALITY

Cascadians approach personal moral issues with an anti-establishment mindset. Compared to most other North Americans they are less patriarchal, deferential and trusting of those with power — particularly of those who try to dominate through religious control.

Pollster Michael Adams, who compares Canadian and US values in books such as *Sex in the Snow* and *Fire and Ice*, says British Columbian baby-boomers are the most likely in Canada to be "autonomous rebels" who prize individuality and are sceptical of traditional authority. In the US, Adams writes, it is mainly residents of the Pacific Northwest (and New England) who reflect this anti-patriarchal moral mindset.

In his entertaining, fun and revealing "map" of the values and beliefs of Cascadians, Andrew Grenville shows in Chapter 2 how the people of Cascadia are more liberal, more libertarian, more laissez-faire, more live-and-let-live — particularly in regards to hot-button issues related to sexual politics. Suggesting a lack of religious "original sin" theology, Grenville's polling also shows an unusually confident sense of do-it-yourself optimism, hinting at utopianism, among the people of Cascadia.

On the political front, many observers have correctly noted that a loosely liberal-libertarian stream runs through Cascadian politics on both sides of the border. Most of Washington and Oregon's governors have been Democrats, and the Republicans who sometimes obtain power are usually of the "progressive" kind. There is no doubt that polarized politics can rear its head in Cascadia, including in battles between the region's secularists and evangelicals, but even most of B.C.'s conservative premiers, like evangelical W.A.C. Bennett in the 1960s, have been populists. Apart from partisan politics and personal morality, does Cascadia have a distinct approach to business and economics? Washington State has shown an amazing degree of lifestyle-changing entrepreneurship (Starbucks and Microsoft) that extends into the social sector, with the creation of global non-profits such as World Vision, the Bill and Melinda Gates Foundation and the Casey family foundations. In a remarkably original chapter on "workplace spirituality" in Cascadia, business ethicist Mark Wexler develops the provocative thesis Cascadians are largely caught in an unrecognized competition between the communitarian, nature-revering spirituality associated with the non-profit and eco-sensitive sector — symbolized by Greenpeace and Recreational Equipment Inc. (REI) — and the innovative values of global leaders in the high-tech, knowledge industry (illustrated by Microsoft, Electronic Arts and Amazon).

When it comes to the long-time moral wedge issue, same-sex marriage, Andrew Grenville's tailored polling shows Cascadians are significantly more likely than those outside the region to agree that "homosexuals should have the same rights as other Americans and Canadians." Cascadians have pushed the edges of personal morality in other ways. Washington, Oregon and B.C. have the highest divorce rates on the continent. B.C., following the Canadian lead, has permitted abortion for decades, and Washington and Oregon are among two of the relatively few US states that allow unrestricted access to abortion. Cascadians are also more likely to smoke marijuana. Boasting some marijuana cafes, Vancouver is becoming known as "Vansterdam," with British Columbians at the forefront of efforts to decriminalize marijuana possession and provide government-approved safe-injection sites for drug addicts. Famously, in 1994, Oregon became the first jurisdiction in North America to permit physician-assisted suicide. Washington State's former governor, Booth Gardner, campaigned more recently for a similar openness to legal euthanasia.

THE EFFECT OF ABORIGINAL AND ASIAN
SPIRITUALITY ON CASCADIAN LIFE

One important aspect of Cascadia that sets it apart from most of North America is its aboriginal population, which is not only larger per capita than across the rest of the continent, but far more culturally influential, maintaining a deep mythic presence in the region's culture.

Almost 5 percent of British Columbians are aboriginal, higher than the Canadian average. The proportion of North American aboriginals in Washington and Oregon is lower than in B.C. but higher than the US average (according to the North American Religious Atlas). However, Cascadians' fascination with aboriginal customs, issues and spirituality goes far beyond these numbers.

Aboriginal art, design and traditions are a mainstay of Cascadia's tourist industry, with monumental aboriginal sculpture, art and mythology, for instance, welcoming newcomers at Vancouver International Airport. In Canada and the US Pacific Northwest, through numerous often-divisive court cases, the non-aboriginal population has struggled with what it means for a people to have collective, not just individual, rights. The public of B.C., Washington and Oregon has in recent decades had to confront what it means to be fair to aboriginals in relation to land claims, environmental protection, timber and salmon harvesting, colonialism and aboriginal control of education. Aboriginals have often been supported in their rights battles by Cascadia's mainline religious organizations.

Most aboriginals in the region practise a syncretistic mix of Christianity and pan-aboriginal rituals, such as the sweat lodge, healing circle and vision quest. Still, many European and other newcomers are drawn to the ways that aboriginals have for thousands of years, as Jean Barman shows in Chapter 4, revered the region's trees, mountains, bears, salmon, eagles and orcas and tried to live in respectful harmony with the land. Although Gail Wells cogently suggests aboriginal spirituality has been often romanticized, its acceptance in public schools and ecological circles is a sign of how it resonates today through the entire population. In chapter 12, Aboriginal writer Eli Enns gives us an inside feel for the transformative power of traditional spiritual customs and "medicine." Bioregionalist Mike Carr urges all to adopt an aboriginal-influenced sense of kinship with nature and its creatures.

While Cascadians on both sides of the border have adopted similar approaches to aboriginal culture and spirituality, one of the differences between British Columbians and the residents of Oregon and Washington may reside in the contrasting demographic strengths of Asian immigrants and their newly imported religions. People of Asian descent are influential in Washington and Oregon, but especially so in B.C. They make up one in five people across the province, compared to one in twenty in Washington and Oregon (a figure slightly higher than the US average). The percentage of British Columbians who practise an "Asian" religion is 8 percent, or more than quadruple that in the US Pacific Northwest. In Greater Vancouver, it is much higher again — at 13 percent.

But how does that religious devotion play out in their morality and politics? Some immigrants who follow Asian religions, such as Buddhism, Hinduism and Sikhism, are socially conservative on sex-related issues to do with marriage, divorce and homosexuality. Nevertheless, since many Asian immigrants have benefited from liberal values such as multiculturalism, human rights and affirmative action — and many, especially Muslims, are appalled at US imperialism — my research suggests Cascadians of Asian origin may tend to be liberal-left on social and economic policy. At the least, in Washington, Oregon and B.C., the Asian presence has contributed to residents feeling positive about multiculturalism and embracing "secularized" Asian spiritual methods. This was borne out through my research, which suggested that British Columbians are more than twice as likely as other North Americans to practise the Eastern spiritual disciplines of yoga or meditation as routes to individual health and healing.

MELDING VISIONS FOR CASCADIA

One of the goals of *Cascadia: The Elusive Utopia* is to highlight the different ways that Cascadians who are either institutionally religious or who consider themselves secular but spiritual are trying to effect creative social transformation in ways that protect liberty, respect human dignity and nature, and advance the commonweal.

In the long run in Cascadia, things — as fear-mongers from all sides constantly warn us — could go badly. The ecology could be further destroyed, cities could become less liveable and the social fabric ripped apart by fear and greed. But given the spiritual openness in Cascadia and the predilection of its hybrid community for trying something new, the potential for positive change seems strong. There are reasons to maintain some trust in Cascadians' two major civil religions — the one that centers on respecting nature, and the other revolving around residents' fervent desire to forge a better future.

What can we expect from the unusually large number of Cascadians who are not affiliated with organized religion, but consider themselves "spiritual"? They may be rebellious individualists, but some contributors suggest many believe personal growth should have a social and ecological dimension. Even in Cascadian New Age spirituality, which focuses on discovering one's authentic inner self, most practitioners express concern for the environment. Even though they are not as numerically strong as in other parts of North America, what about the roughly one out of four people in Cascadia who remain actively involved in an institutional religion? Are these religious institutions in danger of losing their voice — a voice that was heard strongly during the civil rights movement and in opposition to the Vietnam War? Patricia O'Connell Killen, Sallie McFague and Gail Wells continue to find hope in how the region's mainline Protestants, Catholics and Jews, sometimes joined by Buddhists, Muslims and the non-religious, were key to supporting mass protests against the World Trade Organization in Seattle in 1999, campaigning against nuclear submarine bases, supporting Central American refugees, protecting the Columbia River, pressing for reduced energy consumption, demonstrating in favour of Third World debt-forgiveness and organizing huge protests in 2002 against the Iraq war.

For their part, non-religious environmental bioregionalists such as Mike Carr are convinced Cascadian sustainability is the best alternative to "the homogenizing trends of corporate globalization." Mike Carr, Peter Drury and other contributors are captured by the secular-but-spiritual dream set down by Sightline Institute founder Alan Durning of Seattle in the book series, *Cascadia Scorecard*. As Durning says, "Cascadia retains a larger share of its ecosystems intact than any other part of the industrial world and has helped set the conservation agenda for the continent. . . . But there is a broader challenge to which Cascadia is just beginning to rise: gradually but fundamentally realigning the human enterprise so that the region's economies and their supporting ecosystems both can thrive."

Cascadians such as Philip Resnick, an avowed secularist, does not use obviously spiritual language, but he holds out hope that independent-minded Cascadians will not drop out of social engagement to become merely self-seeking and eccentric. He envisions a humble Cascadian world view, which includes a tolerance for difference and willingness to live simply, which balances a healthier respect for the wisdom of the past with residents' always strong yearning for the future, for a better tomorrow.

To lead readers into these different visions, which are in many ways complementary, the chapters of *Cascadia: The Elusive Utopia* have been structured into four sections: spirituality, history, nature and culture. Nevertheless, this is a book that takes pride in being cross-disciplinary. So, even though the authors may emphasize one of these themes in their chapters, none of them felt restricted by "disciplinolatry." The reader will see virtually all effortlessly blend together ecology, politics, spirituality, popular culture, history, morality, economics, religion, literature and geography. The final sections of the book offer some poetic contemplations about Cascadia from George Bowering and Philip Resnick. Following my Afterword are the contributors' lively profiles, which include some heartfelt remarks about their connection to this place.

In such a diverse place as Cascadia it will not be easy to find common ground about the best way to advance. A buoyant future for Cascadia cannot be taken for granted. But there are encouraging developments emerging in the region, from which the rest of the world could possibly learn. The contributors to this book believe that heartening social transformation is occurring, albeit incrementally, in Cascadia. They are mature utopians who know the human struggle will never end. Yet even while they are working towards something better, they celebrate that some of the longed-for future is already here — Cascadia's residents are every day creating glimmers of beauty and goodness.

Part One

⁓

CASCADIAN RELIGION,
SPIRITUALITY
AND VALUES

CHAPTER 1

∽

The Promise and Limits
of Secular Spirituality
in Cascadia

MARK A. SHIBLEY

WE CASCADIANS RELISH the idea that our character and culture distinguish us from other North Americans. Ernest Callenbach's Ecotopian vision may have over-reached but, we believe, Cascadia *is* an extraordinary home-place, a geographic region where people are reimagining human/nature relationships and inventing the social organizations and cultural practices needed to sustain those visions. According to William James, this is religious work, and the question asked is: What ultimately does it mean to be human in this place, and how shall we organize ourselves in relationship to one another and the Earth? Yet one must recognize that Cascadia is a relatively "unchurched" region, with much of this cultural creativity occurring in secular but spiritual realms outside conventional religious institutions. This essay describes some of that variegated spiritual terrain, exploring its promise and limitations in the cultural evolution of our region.

THE SPIRITUAL LANDSCAPE

As noted in Douglas Todd's introduction, the defining feature of our cultural landscape is that fewer people in Oregon, Washington and British Columbia affiliate with a religious congregation than in any other North American region, and more people in Cascadia answer "None" when asked their religious identification. Yet beliefs and practices regarding sacred things pervade our region, particularly ideas that elevate the self and revere the natural world.

The data are striking: according to the American Religious Identification Survey (ARIS), 14 percent of the US population claims no religious identity, but in Oregon and Washington, about one-quarter of the population is a self-identified None, and a majority in those two states (63 percent) is not affiliated with a religious congregation (Kosmin, Mayer and Keysar). Similarly, the 2001 Canadian census found that more than a third of British Columbians have "no religion," and only 20 percent are tied to religious institutions. In this light, the region is often dismissed as a relatively secular anomaly in North America. Since most Cascadians do not go to church, it is assumed the region is not significantly religious. That is false: people throughout Cascadia cultivate spiritual lives outside traditional religious institutions — the secular but spiritual realm. Our best estimates suggest that only 5 to 7 percent of the population of Oregon and Washington and 14 percent of the B.C. population, is atheist, or fundamentally irreligious (Kosmin, Mayer and Keysar). ARIS data show that even Nones in those areas believe in God (67 percent) and miracles (69 percent) (Kosmin, Mayer and Keysar).

Most Cascadians, therefore, have spiritual inclinations. My recent research explores what is sacred to the people in this region who claim no religious preference, where and how they experience the sacred, and the difference their spiritual convictions and practices make in the public life of the region. Briefly put, there are three clusters of spirituality shaping our region's future. One is the apocalyptic millennialism of a loose set of anti-government groups, such as Patriots, white supremacists, the Militia, and various kinds of survivalists. Much more prevalent in the US than in Canada, these groups are now less potent than they were in the 1980s and '90s, but they remain poised to exploit the simmering resentment of rural Northwesterners who feel colonized and neglected. A second and more important feature of the cultural landscape is a constellation of New Age spiritualities including neo-paganism, channelling, metaphysics and the "New Spirituality" literature (e.g., *Conversations with God* and *The Power of Now*). While we grow our own gurus here — J.Z. Knight began channelling Ramtha in the Puget Sound area and Neale Donald Walsch started his conversations with God in southern Oregon — other spiritual entrepreneurs like Eckhart Tolle (Vancouver, B.C.) and Jean Houston (Ashland, Oregon) have relocated to this region because they perceive an open religious marketplace. Third and most central to our regional ethos is Earth-based spirituality, which is expressed in a variety of ways in regional literature, in the secular environmental movement, in rituals of leisure, in indigenous cultural traditions and even in conventional religious institutions. For many in Cascadia, the Earth is sacred.

None of these spiritual practices is unique to Cascadia, but in the absence of a dominant religion, they define regional culture and identity more substantially than they do elsewhere. Put differently, "alternative spirituality" is more center-culture than counter-culture in our region. As is characteristic of new religions, there are dualistic and millenarian tendencies in all three forms of Cascadian spirituality, but these impulses are often balanced by more inclusive, collaborative and pragmatic efforts to engage and transform the social world. Given their prominence, this chapter explores the character and role of self and Earth-based spirituality in particular.

SACRED SELF

From the outside, metaphysics, channelling and other New Age practices are often thought to be fringe activities explored by relatively few facile and loosely connected individuals. From the inside, these practices lead to authentic spiritual experience and are not religious in the ordinary sense, in that they reject the strictures of traditional religious institutions. In our region, this variety of spiritual practice is most usefully thought of as a form of popular religion because it is a *common* way in which Cascadians construct meaningful lives and experience the sacred, and because those practices bind people together and take on institutional form.

As sociologist Robert Wuthnow has shown, small groups and web-based connections are the grassroots structure of North American spirituality today (Wuthnow). In the Pacific Northwest, New Spirituality leaders like Walsch have elaborate websites that move ideas and link followers in local "Wisdom Groups" for conversations with God and each other. Tolle's website organizes people into *The Power of Now* study groups, of which there are dozens in our region. Followers of Nordic gods in the Puget Sound area congregate in "kindreds." Neo-pagans in Oregon come together in "groves." These and other new spirituality house-groups are plentiful in Cascadia, and there are also communities in this alternative vein, large and small, that look and act more like conventional religious organizations than upstart spirituality groups.

The Aquarian Tabernacle Church in Everett, Washington, for instance, is an accredited Wiccan congregation that owns property, holds regular worship, performs weddings and offers pastoral counselling. The twenty-thousand-student public University of Victoria became in 1998 one of the first, if not the first, university in North America to officially approve a Wiccan as chaplain. The Living Enrichment Center, before it imploded due to financial mismanage-. ment, was a New Spirituality mega-church (3,000 weekly adherents, and weekly televised broadcasts), with a sprawling campus on the I-5 corridor south of Portland — a one-stop spiritual shopping center. And communities like WICCA (Women in Conscious Creative

Action) in Eugene, Oregon, a mature and durable organization facilitating women's spirituality, are commonplace in our region. In Vancouver, Banyen Books has been specializing since the early 1970s in what used to be called "New Age" books. The bookstore now stretches for almost half a city block on the main street of the upscale beachside neighbourhood of Kitsilano. These organizations illustrate how the unconventional spiritual explorations of individuals can, over time, grow, institutionalize, and become an ordinary feature of the religious landscape. In Cascadia alternative spirituality is popular religion.

In large part, this folk religion is directed toward nurturing transcendent experience for individuals, and thus it privileges practice over doctrine, but there are clear ideological dimensions to this activity with implications for community building. Underlying these diverse spiritual practices is a belief that the self is sacred; everyone is God, or as Shirley MacLaine famously said, "I am God." These practices are driven by a protean impulse. To uncover one's authentic self involves, among other things, shedding the dogma and expectations of "exclusivist organized religion," to use Walsch's terms (Personal Interview). This cluster of beliefs and practices is fundamentally a spirituality of self-development designed to empower individuals over dominant cultural institutions. Social transformation, its practitioners hold, will follow personal transformation as a matter of course. But what contribution can a radically individualized religion make to Cascadia's version of the "good society"? Is there a sufficiently outward orientation to balance the inward focus?

Like evangelical Protestantism over the last quarter century, New Spirituality has grown in North America by meeting the spiritual, psychological and social needs of *individuals*. Personal salvation/ transformation is at the center of these religious movements, and like some evangelical entrepreneurs, some New Spirituality leaders have begun to envision a purpose-driven life centered on the common good that undergirds individual prosperity. Southern California's Rick Warren, for instance, pastor of one of the largest evangelical congregations in North America, has made headline news in recent years for turning some of his ministry's considerable resources toward lessening hunger, homelessness and HIV. From Cascadia, Neale Donald Walsch has launched Humanity's Team — "a global civil rights movement for the soul" — to address social problems. Yet the New Spirituality strategy for alleviating human conflict and suffering often boils down to linking individuals to a set of support groups and self-development seminars designed to liberate them from the core beliefs of their cultural traditions. Social change, they hope, will follow individual enlightenment. But New Spirituality, judging from the websites of key movement leaders, offers no particular strategy for building a local or global sustainable culture.

The initial success and subsequent failure of a regional event illustrates the limits of New Spirituality as *public* religion in Cascadia, or any place. In 2004, a World Wellness Weekend was organized in Ashland, Oregon, a New Spirituality festival headlined by Deepak Chopra and Bernie Siegel. That event drew many thousands of participants from all over the region, exceeding organizers' expectations. By contrast, World Wellness Weekend 2005, which featured Robert Kennedy Jr. and Martin Luther King III, drew crowds that numbered only in the hundreds. New Spirituality gurus, it turned out, were a much bigger draw for spiritual explorers than environmental and civil rights leaders who spoke about electoral politics rather than enlightenment principles. In fact, survey data show that secular but spiritual Cascadians are more ideologically liberal but less likely to vote or affiliate with a political party than others in the region (Kosmin, Mayer and Keysar). A spirituality that frees individuals from cultural traditions can spur innovation, but paradoxically, the self-centered focus may also inhibit the construction of a new public order since civic institutions by definition constrain individual freedom.

Perhaps the most interesting expression of the New Spirituality emanating from Cascadia today is what has come to be called Spiritual Cinema. Hollywood director Stephen Simon (*What Dreams*

May Come and *Indigo*), filmmaker William Arntz (*What the Bleep Do We Know!?*), and international peace troubadour James Twyman (*Indigo*) have collaborated with Walsch, J.Z. Knight and other Cascadian gurus to cultivate a new cinematic genre. According to the Spiritual Cinema Circle website, Southern Oregon has become an international hub for this effort to "awaken your sense of joy and wonder; inspire love and compassion; and evoke a deeper connection with the universe." These films that preach to the New Spirituality choir, had mixed box-office success, and were roundly criticized by film critics across North America (for example, the reviews of *Conversations with God* in the *Oregonian, Seattle Post-Intelligencer* and the *San Francisco Chronicle*) as being vacuous vessels of divine light.

In sum, New Spirituality thrives in Cascadia because there is space for it in the cultural landscape, and because it nourishes wondering souls. Yet many of its chief practitioners are focused more on facilitating self development than social change. Instead of reinventing civil society, most New Spirituality entrepreneurs are endeavouring to shape popular culture by facilitating personal enlightenment through books and films, retreats and support groups. It is not clear how these efforts will amount to sustainable new practices for our common life, but one element of New Spirituality that resonates deeply in Cascadia is Earth reverence.

SACRED NATURE

Earth-based spirituality — pervasive beliefs and practices regarding sacred nature — is the other indigenous form of Cascadian folk religion. In the absence of a dominant conventional religion, this "nature religion," a term coined by historian Catherine L. Albanese, plays a fundamental role in the region's public life. Albanese observes:

> [N]ature religion . . . is a useful construct . . . because it throws light
> on certain aspects of our history that we have only haphazardly
> seen — or even failed to see — religiously. By thinking of these

manifestations as nature religion, we begin to discover the links and connections among them, we gain a sense of their logic, and we come to sense their power. (Albanese)

This Cascadian folk religion, which I explore systematically elsewhere (Shibley), has ritualistic, experiential, mythic and communal dimensions. Here I'll simply illustrate something of the texture and importance of nature religion in this region.

In the Pacific Northwest, religious experience — the charged and creative moment of encounter with the sacred — is rooted historically in contact with the landscape. That is certainly true in Native American culture, and Euro-American explorers and settlers, too, found the vast and imposing geography of Cascadia both overwhelming and awe-inspiring, by turns a savage wilderness and the Garden of Eden. *The Journals of Lewis and Clark*, for instance, show a preoccupation with the physical grandeur of the country, experienced in light of what would later be called "Manifest Destiny" and in the frontier myths explorers carried with them (O'Connell). Even today, Northwesterners find moments of mystical illumination in contact with nature.

The prototypical religious experience of nature in the American West is the mountain epiphany, embodied in the adventures of John Muir, who, writing of a sojourn into the wild, said: "I will touch naked God" (Hoagland). In frequent wilderness treks, from the Sierra Mountains of northern California to the glaciers and waterways of southeast Alaska, Muir sought after religious experience. Mountains and valleys became cathedrals. Here is an excerpt of Muir's writing on Yosemite that illustrates his religious world view:

> No pain here, no dull empty hours, no fear of the past, no fear of the future. These blessed mountains are so compactly filled with God's beauty, no petty personal hope or experience has room to be. Drinking this champagne water is pure pleasure, so is breathing the living air, and every movement of limbs is pleasure, while the body seems to feel beauty when exposed to it as it feels the campfire or sunshine, entering not by the eyes alone, but equally through all one's flesh like

radiant heat, making a passionate ecstatic pleasure glow not explainable. . . . Perched like a fly on this Yosemite dome, I gaze and sketch and bask, oftentimes settling down into dumb admiration without definite hope of ever learning much, yet with the longing, unresting effort that lies at the door of hope, humbly prostrate before the vast display of God's power, and eager to offer self-denial and renunciation with eternal toil to learn any lesson in the divine manuscript. (Cronon, 69–90)

Muir's romantic experience of the landscape as welcome ecstasy helped transform public perceptions of frontier wilderness in the late nineteenth century. His public testimony was pivotal in turning America's Christian impulse to subjugate godless nature to the celebration of God in nature, an ethos that now pervades Cascadia. Muir preached a wilderness preservation ethic with evangelical zeal, believing that wild nature was an expression of God. Ultimately, Muir became the patron saint of the twentieth-century wilderness preservation movement — the political expression of an ethic and spirituality that makes wild nature sacred, and he paved the way for successive generations of Cascadians to experience the sacred in nature (Thomas, 120-124).

The spirituality and activism of Chant Thomas exemplifies this sensibility in the mythical "State of Jefferson," a mostly rural region of legendarily independent-minded people in Cascadia's southernmost province, stretching from the Pacific Ocean to Oregon's Crater Lake, and south to Mount Shasta in northern California. A self-described "environmental activist, naturalist and wilderness guide," Thomas is one of the urban refugees that went "back to the land" in the 1970s. He now runs an environmental education program and spiritual retreat center on his remote southern Oregon ranch. During the late 1980s and early '90s he became a prominent local activist in the conflict over public land management. For Thomas, nature is sacred, and our public life — land management policies — ought to reflect that belief.

In an essay titled "The Sacred Tree," Thomas recalls a chance encounter with a ponderosa pine tree in terms tantamount to a born-again experience, in the vernacular of nature religion. On the verge of despair following a broken marriage, he recalls setting off at dawn one cold November morning to wander in the wilderness surrounding his home, in search of hope. This is what he found:

> I looked up, realizing the fog had ended, and stepped into early morning sunshine. I looked out over a sea of blinding white clouds, with snowy ridges rising all around and crowding the brilliant blue sky. Immediately in front of me, beyond the fallen dragon snag, rose a massive flat-topped Pine like a green apparition silhouetted against the snowy slopes above.
>
> The ancient Pine beckoned me closer. Somehow I worked my way around the dragon snag which spanned the entire width of the narrow ridge top. Approaching the Pine, I stepped between the boughs which reached the ground, pausing to hold those on either side. A deeply spiritual feeling coursed through my being, not unlike the hush I felt as a young altarboy entering the cathedral for my First Communion.
>
> Stepping forward I instinctively hugged the tree, my long arms covering only a small fraction of the trunk's diameter. The beautiful brown pussle-bark was already warm from the morning sun. I slipped to the ground, curling against the tree in a deep carpet of pine needles. The spirit of the tree relaxed me into my deepest sleep in a week. . . . Like myself, several friends returned to the Pine to sit there for a few days and nights, fasting, praying and singing to the tree with flute or drum. Soon the ancient Pine became known to many as the "Sacred Tree." (Thomas)

In his essay, Thomas goes on to argue that the area surrounding the Sacred Tree, which is federal land, deserves protection (wilderness designation) not just because of the unique ecological character of the Klamath-Siskiyou region but because this particular place has become a sacred site ("place of power") for those he calls "new natives," like himself. He further writes,

> This power, inherent in wilderness landscape, is the legacy of creation, a resource far more valuable than the commodity value of timber or minerals.

On my next pilgrimage to the Sacred Tree I'll be thinking about a bumper sticker given to me by a Baptist minister at a recent forest conference. It reads: "If you love the Creator, take care of the Creation." For the Sacred Tree and the [surrounding] wilderness, caring equals defending. (Thomas)

The folkways and legitimating myths of the unofficial region in southern Oregon and northern California that locals proudly dub the State of Jefferson — which also shape the broader region of Cascadia — are being remade by New Natives like Thomas. In Cascadian nature religion, experiencing sacred Earth is personally redemptive, and it leads to an ethical imperative: wilderness preservation becomes a guiding principle for public policy.

A culminating event in the cultural evolution of the State of Jefferson was the establishment of the Cascade-Siskiyou National Monument, designated by President Clinton in 2000 as a "place of wonder." Bruce Babbitt, Clinton's Secretary of the Interior, said of the Cascade-Siskiyou National Monument, "[This is] a priceless natural landscape that [has] remained almost untouched by exploitation, development and urban sprawl" (Cole and Brinckman, *Oregonian*, A01). The White House press release announcing National Monument designation, which gave the Cascade-Siskiyou region some protection from environmental destruction, describes a geological and ecological treasure — "one of the most biological distinctive and diverse places on Earth." Conservation groups and their staff scientists talked about "botanical richness," evolutionary "relic species," an "ecological land-bridge" linking distinct bioregions, and an irreplaceable "reservoir of genetic diversity."

Yet for all the scientific claims, one of the most striking features of the pitched battles among residents of the State of Jefferson leading up to Clinton's announcing creation of the Cascade-Siskiyou National Monument was the use of religious metaphor. In the end, Dave Willis, the chief citizen-proponent for preserving the Cascade-Siskiyou landscape, spoke of the proposed Cascade-Siskiyou National Monument as "a kind of Noah's Ark," with the broader bioregion "the loading dock to the ark" (Cole, *Oregonian*, A11).

Conservation groups advocating for the Cascade-Siskiyou National Monument used this resonant religious symbol frequently, and it was echoed in news media.

For most of two decades Willis worked to protect the landscape of what was to become the Cascade-Siskiyou National Monument, which surrounds his rural home. When the *Oregonian* probed Willis on his stewardship devotion, he responded, "I think God wants us to care about all creation" (Cole, *Oregonian*). In a sense, conflict over the Cascade-Siskiyou National Monument was a struggle for the soul of the mythical State of Jefferson. Public debate was often acrimonious because opposing groups disagreed over core values — the rights of nature versus the rights of property owners — and what they understood to be most sacred. But Cascade-Siskiyou National Monument supporters far outnumbered the opposition at public meetings around the Rogue Valley in the summer of 2000. Rural folk adhering to old frontier ethics were a remnant voice. Whatever else it meant in national politics, the establishment of the Cascade-Siskiyou National Monument symbolized the ascendance of a new cultural script for Earth reverence in this local region.

Notwithstanding the ecological justifications for new natural resource policies, the idea of wilderness — symbolized by the Cascade-Siskiyou National Monument designation — is the spiritual core of an emergent new culture. Ironically, this romantic principle bears more continuity with American religious and cultural history than secular environmentalists would care to admit. Historian William Cronon put it this way:

> Wilderness fulfills the old romantic project of secularizing Judeo-Christian values so as to make a new cathedral not in some petty human building but in God's own creation, Nature itself. Many environmentalists who reject traditional notions of the Godhead and who regard themselves as agnostics or even atheists nonetheless express feelings tantamount to religious awe when in the presence of wilderness — a fact that testifies to the success of the romantic proj-

ect. Those who have no difficulty seeing God as the expression of our human dreams and desires nonetheless have trouble recognizing that in a secular age Nature can offer precisely the same sort of mirror. Thus it is that wilderness serves as the unexamined foundation on which so many of the quasi-religious values of modern environmentalism rest. (Cronon, 69–90)

Nowhere is this more evident than in Cascadia. New Natives have fashioned and now inhabit new sacred space. Nature religion provides the most potent symbolic touchstones for public debate about the management of natural resources.

In the summer of 2001, a *Time* cover story, "The War over the West," featured conflict over the Cascade-Siskiyou National Monument (Ressner). The reporter's description of the Monument's landscape illustrates how pervasive the interpretative framework of nature religion has become in popular culture. It is more prosaic than Muir's writing on Yosemite but no less romantic. Ressner wrote:

> . . . take a hike up picturesque Soda Mountain, where the Western Cascade Mountains meet the Siskiyou range, and you'll begin to sense what's really at stake here. The place is nothing less than a panoramic Eden, a province where glorious forests of Douglas fir, white oak, sugar pine and rainbow swirls of butterflies abound. Spotted owls and peregrine falcons swoop through the skies, while rare, colourful wildflowers dot the ground below. (Ressner, 26–28)

One key point of contention now is whether the historic practice of cattle grazing should continue within the Cascadia-Siskiyou National Monument landscape under the new management regime. On that issue, the Klamath-Siskiyou Wildlands Center, a leading local conservation group asks rhetorically, "Would you graze cows in the Sistine Chapel?" The Cascadia-Siskiyou National Monument and public land in the broader region are as much a mythical as a physical reality, and while these cultural dynamics are conspicuous on the landscape in the State of Jefferson, similar issues and dynamics have played out all over Cascadia in recent decades.

Region-wide conflict over logging and spotted owl habitat, which came to a head in the early 1990s, for instance, was the pivotal event in the culture clash between the old and the new Pacific Northwest. This was followed in the mid-1990s by the region-wide salmon crisis and the debate over the breaching of four Snake River dams along the Washington-Idaho border. Then came the restoration of whale hunting in Puget Sound by the Makah Indians, and in recent years the B.C. government's agreement with aboriginal and environmentalists to protect from rapacious logging the vast north coastal habitat of the rare Kermode bear, which has increasingly come to be known as the "Spirit Bear" because of its ghostly white appearance. Of course, environmental advocates on all these issues make arguments for the preservation of nature that put forth scientific claims, but their pleas hinge on striking a resonant moral and spiritual chord in the populace, and increasingly they do. Their success at doing so could explain why B.C. Premier Gordon Campbell announced in 2006 that the "Spirit Bear" would be the province's official animal — and also urged that it become the mascot of Vancouver's 2010 Winter Olympics. These are cultural struggles about the nature of nature and what it means to live in Cascadia. The idea of sacred nature is at the heart of this cultural transformation. However, nature religion, like self spirituality, can be a problematic script for sustainability.

SUSTAINABLE CASCADIA

Northwestern migrants, from homesteaders in the mid-nineteenth century to back-to-the-land utopians in the late twentieth century, have always imagined the frontier to be culturally empty, a place of limitless possibility, with their task being to pour meaning in the vacuum. In this way, Cascadians are hopeful and forward looking; they stand ready to invent new and better traditions. So it is unsurprising that this region is an incubator of alternative spirituality, and as with John Muir and the New Natives, the most profound experiences come from encounters with nature, the deepest meanings forged in mythical narratives about wilderness and the last frontier. What then will self and Earth-based spirituality contribute to a sustainable Cascadian culture?

These perspectives and practices offer a needed critique of the dominant culture. Religious traditions can be oppressive and alienating, and our high consumption economy has depleted the resource base and altered ecological systems in undesirable ways. Yet both New Spirituality and Nature Religion, as described in this chapter, contain flawed assumptions about human nature that will limit their value as cornerstones of a sustainable Cascadian culture.

The desire not to be shackled by inherited traditions is understandable, but New Spirituality's preoccupation with uncovering the "authentic self" by peeling away the "socialized mode of being" misunderstands human *social* nature. We do not live and cannot survive independently of others. The self is a product of history. Humans change relationships, explore and cultivate new ways of thinking and living, but the meaning we make in our lives is made in relationship to place and others. Culture is the shared current of human history. Too often, New Spirituality is an effort to escape from history and obligation rather than a vehicle for thoughtfully engaging and shaping history. Insofar as New Spirituality remains largely egocentric, it will not contribute much to the crafting of new folkways in Cascadia since sustainability is about building just and enduring communities in healthy and resilient environments.

The core ideas and practices of Nature Religion, as expressed in our regional literature and the venerable campaigns to "save" nature, fail to provide a firm foundation for sustainable culture because they offer no path to a future of viable living *in* the natural systems that sustain human life. Much Earth-based spirituality in Cascadia laments paradise lost but, paradoxically, retains the dualism that separates humans from nature. In their pining for Eden, advocates of Nature Religion make wilderness sacred, causing human civilization to become profane. Moral action then becomes the preservation of wilderness, which is by definition where people are absent. The idea of wilderness has been a potent and a useful perspective from which to critique human/nature relations in the twentieth century, but sustainability will require less romantic and more practical symbols of nature (perhaps the garden, as writer Michael Pollan suggested in *Second Nature*).

Portland writer and nature lover David Oates, in his book, *Paradise Wild: Reimagining American Nature*, blazes a trail beyond the wilderness mythology. Forging a more sustainable culture, he argues, involves the religious work of rethinking the sacred symbols that idolize nature and keep humans apart from it. He suggests celebrating the wildness throughout creation rather than worshipping the wilderness in a few remnant places. Oates argues:

> A sacred space is a metaphor: it says Eden, but is not Eden. If it burns or gets bulldozed, Eden is not threatened. Though we are rightly distressed when an Eden is felled, the right response is to rebuild the temple, consecrate it, and get right back into the business of metaphoring, of playing both sides of the street. Of course, that game . . . requires making lots of decisions — where to use, where to rest, where to make sacred. Everywhere is not church (we don't want Christmas every day) so outside the symbolic park-Edens, we will probably need to follow Ashworth's advice after all: finding the right forests, doing what must be done. Enlisting that army of environmentalists with chainsaws, but leaving the place intact. . . .
>
> When Black Elk, in his last years, retold the vision he had received as a child on his sacred peak in the Dakotas, he added an aside that has rung in my heart for many years. Harney Peak was the holy center of the Lakota ritual world, he said, "but anywhere is the center of the world." That two-mindedness is what I'm after. We will all continue to choose our sacred spaces. But at the same time we must be realizing that they are symbols, that they speak for everywhere. Otherwise, we are fundamentalists, we are idolators, we are dullard literalists not getting the joke, the flirt, the joy. (Oates)

This post-wilderness perspective is beginning to gain traction in the Pacific Northwest, and, just in time, for the challenges ahead will be significant: Cascadia's population is growing; the built environment will continue to expand; agricultural and forestlands will come under greater development pressure; transportation problems in urban areas will become more acute; energy use will increase; rural economies will continue to struggle; and more and more people will head to the mountains, rivers and ocean beaches to find recreation, rest and renewal. In this light, the primary cultural challenge will be to cultivate a Cascadian world view, with attendant rituals, that will enable a growing population — including a steady stream of utopian migrants — to engage the natural world with wisdom and maturity, not merely romance. Can Cascadians learn to revere and restore their natural environment while using it as the vital resource base that it is? There are hopeful signs throughout the region.

One example is the Positive Futures Network (PFN), based on Bainbridge Island, Washington. PFN is an independent, nonprofit organization dedicated to supporting people's active engagement in creating a just, sustainable, and compassionate world. Author David Korten and the other founders were acting on their belief that humanity has reached a turning point where only creative change can meet the "unprecedented threats to Earth's ecosystems and our social fabric." People like Korten are crafting new ideas, new ways of living, new forms of community in the hope of transforming what they see as an unjust and unsustainable world. Following the founding of the eco-activist organization Greenpeace in Vancouver in 1971, many non-profit organizations in this vein, with local and global reach, were launched in Cascadia in the 1980s and '90s — such as EcoTrust, Sustainable Northwest, The Whidbey Institute, The Sightline Institute, The Western Canada Wilderness Committee, The Green Party of B.C. (which won 12 percent of the vote in the 2001 provincial election) and Vancouver's internationally influential David Suzuki Foundation, to name a few. They consistently offer a vision of sustainability that links healthy environments to healthy communities, very often anchored in a spiritual language of care, compassion, honour, justice and restoration (see

Appendix). Remarkably, these grassroots efforts in the non-profit sector led the way for serious new sustainability policy and practice in the public sector. The cities of Vancouver, Seattle and Portland, and many smaller municipalities, have in the last decade established Departments of Sustainable Development and in 2001 Oregon passed the Sustainability Act. The principles governing public life in Cascadia are shifting perceptively in a direction that tries to remake the human place in nature.

In sum, there will be a spiritual dimension to any new set of cultural practices that are ecologically and socially sound because core values, when expressed communally in belief and ritual, take on religious form by symbolizing the sacred. What are Cascadia's emerging sacred symbols? The same old ones, re-imagined: salmon, Mt. Baker (or Rainier, or Hood), a giant cedar tree, Crater Lake, an orca pod, the Columbia River, an old-growth forest. The basic features of the landscape will not change, but the meaning must evolve. The romantic myth — nature as wilderness — that came of age in the resource conflicts that closed the last century will serve no better than Manifest Destiny in forging a sustainable relationship between humans and nature.

In *The Left Hand of Eden*, William Ashworth, a Cascadian writer and lifelong environmental activist proclaims, "Protect nothing; venerate everything." A new Cascadia will not idolize salmon. It will take what it needs and no more, give thanks, distribute the bounty equitably, and make sure the rivers run clean with abundant fish for many generations to come.

APPENDIX: MISSION STATEMENT OF SUSTAINABLE NORTHWEST

(Editor's note: The 2008 mission statement of Portland-based Sustainable Northwest, one of Cascadia's leading environment groups, exemplifies the way many eco-activist organizations in the region adopt spiritual language, emphasizing values such as care, honour, justice and restoration.)

Sustainable Northwest: Our Mission
Sustainable Northwest partners with communities and enterprises to achieve economic, ecological and community vitality and resilience.

Our Vision and Values
Sustainable Northwest envisions an economy and society in the Pacific Northwest where people, communities and businesses refuse to sacrifice the good of the land for the good of the people, or the good of the people for the good of the land — finding a new path which honors both. We are committed to a human community working together — able to think beyond itself to embrace the entire biological community and from one generation to many. We believe the following:
   – people are an indivisible part of the ecosystems they inhabit;
   – economic and environmental health are interdependent;
   – communities have the energy and creativity to develop innovative, lasting solutions to complex environmental, economic and social challenges;
   – effective ecosystem stewardship is adaptive, place-based and founded on evolving scientific and practical knowledge;
   – connections between rural and urban communities and collaboration between diverse interests and individuals are integral to local and regional sustainability;
   – A sustainable society is one that persists and thrives. It provides a high quality of life for all of its inhabitants without harming the integrity and productivity of the natural systems and resources upon which all life depends. Humans' needs and desires are met within the limits of what nature can provide. People are a part of nature and depend on its capacity to provide food, water, energy, fibre and life-support services such as the pollination of crops and creation of soils. . . . Sustainability means achieving satisfying lives for all within the means of nature — now and in the future. Sustainability is not just about

the environment. A sustainable society must be just and equi-
table, and provide opportunities for each member of the community to reach his/her potential.

CHAPTER 2

cᴖ

Mapping Spirituality and Values in the Elusive Utopia

ANDREW GRENVILLE

*A map of the world that does not include Utopia
is not worth even glancing at, for it leaves out the one
country at which Humanity is always landing.*

— OSCAR WILDE, *The Soul of Man under Socialism* (1895)

THIS BOOK IS ABOUT Cascadia, the elusive utopia. It is about what is, and was and could be. The Cascadia we deal with in the book is here, but not yet. It is now and it is tomorrow.

"For we know in part, and we prophesy in part," the Apostle Paul wrote (I Corinthians 13:9, KJV). He was not writing about Cascadia, but what he was saying about the Kingdom of God applies to Cascadia, as it does to all elusive utopias.

Paul knew that trying to divine the shape of a utopia was difficult. "For now we see through a glass, darkly. . ." he continued (I Corinthians 13:12, KJV). As we try to locate the landmarks of Cascadia, we have to wonder if the faint outlines we discern in the murk are real, or shadows twisted into the shapes of our dreams and fears?

To this book on the elusive utopia, I add a shadowy and incomplete social/spiritual map of Cascadia — seen through a glass, darkly — with design work by my long time colleague and friend Carolyn Clegg-Brown. (See Social/Spiritual Map of Cascadia.) In doing so, I have tried to focus on what "we know, in part."

Drawing on survey research conducted by myself and colleagues, I have sketched out some of the social and spiritual contours of Cascadia. Far from being a definitive record of all the contours of Cascadian public opinion, this map has more unknown zones — where no surveyor has ever trod — than it does sharply defined contours. But that is all right. The blank spaces give us more room to peer into shadowy glens and try to glimpse the elusive utopia we hope for.

WHY A MAP?

Cascadia is, after all, a place of the heart as much as it is a specific landscape. No one really agrees what its physical borders are. Is it a bioregion? Is it a repressed nation defined by state and provincial borders that strains to free itself from the smothering clutches of the imperialist US of A and Canada? Are its borders defined by the tectonic plates of the Cascadia Subduction Zone, or the spawning grounds of the enigmatic Pacific Northwest Tree Octopus?

To ask these geographic questions is, of course, to miss the point: Cascadia is "as much a state of mind as a geographic place," according to the Cascadia Institute's David McCloskey, a professor of sociology at Seattle University. Indeed, the surveys I am drawing on were analyzed expressly to tap into Cascadian's mindsets. So, why a map?

Cascadia is unique in that its landscape casts a shadow — often quite literally — over everything Cascadians do. Across much of the rest of Canada and the US, the landscape is subjugated by urban sprawl. You do not have to drive through too many kilometers of clogged freeways, big box stores and fast food alleys in Ontario, Texas or New Jersey to know you could be anywhere. Much of the

FREEDOM-LOVING CASCADIAN VALUES. Andrew Grenville's tailored polling reveals Cascadians tend to be less trusting of religion and more tolerant of marijuana (see above) and homosexual relationships than others across the continent. Even though Cascadians' individualism could harm their chances of building strong communities, Grenville believes that their live-and-let-live attitude, optimism and self-responsibility could create a culture that serves as a beacon to the planet.

CASCADIA: A MAP
OF THE SOCIAL AND
SPIRITUAL LANDSCAPE

In this map of Cascadia,
the region's social and
spiritual qualities are
imagined as mountains
and valleys, hills and dales.

Mountains denote a tendency
for Cascadians to be "more" of
something, while valleys indicate
"less." So Mount Do-Right indicates
that Cascadians put more trust in
people to do what is right. Likewise,
the Valley of Biblical Scepticism
reveals that fewer Cascadians
believe the Bible is the inspired
word of God — compared to
others in North America. Hills
and dales indicates the same
types of greater/lesser
differences, only of a more
modest degree.

ANDREW GRENVILLE'S MAP OF
CASCADIANS' SPIRITUALITY AND VALUES

land in and around cities and towns seems blasted into submission and, just for good measure, covered with pothole-splattered asphalt. But in Cascadia, the landscape is ever present, even in most urban centers. The mountains of Cascadia mock our hubris, and the oceans continually remind us of the depths of infinity. So representing mindsets as physical features on a map seems a fitting tribute to Cascadia, a utopia where the land inspires and defines the people who live there.

A MAP OF THE SOCIAL AND SPIRITUAL LANDSCAPE OF CASCADIA

In this map of Cascadia, the region's social and spiritual distinctives are imagined as mountains and valleys, hills and dales.

Mountains denote a tendency for Cascadians to be "more" of something, while valleys indicate "less," compared to others in North America. So Mount Do-Right indicates that Cascadians put more trust in people to do what is right. Likewise, the Valley of Biblical Scepticism reveals that fewer Cascadians believe the Bible is the inspired Word of God. Hills and dales indicate the same types of greater or lesser differences, only of a more modest degree. To keep the landscape a little more varied, I have also used lakes and ponds in some places, as water-filled valleys and dales, to represent lower levels.

In conveying the data in what is intended to be a visually interesting and metaphorical manner, I have made some positive statements into negatives and vice versa — to balance the landscape. So for the more data-driven among you, I apologize if some of the poetic license I have used distracts you. My hope is that the mapping of this information delivers you up to the heights of epiphany, rather than down to the depths of confusion.

This map of Cascadia covers five main themes or "ranges": the Range of Faith, the Human Nature Range, the Marijuana Mountains, the Porous Border Range and the Peaks of Personal Responsibility.

RANGE OF FAITH

The Range of Faith dominates the heart of Cascadia. It is filled with summits of privatized belief and shadowy valleys of scepticism.

Mount Religious Distrust looms at the north edge of the Range of Faith. It reminds us that Cascadians are more likely to have "not very much" trust or absolutely "none at all" in organized religion, with 50 percent versus 33 percent in the "Rest of North America" (RoNA).

The nearby mossy-green slippery slopes of the *Valley of Biblical Scepticism* reflect the fact that Cascadians are less likely to agree that "the Bible is the inspired Word of God" (69 percent Cascadians versus 82 percent, RoNA). Rising up beside the valley is *Private Faith Hill*. Cascadians are more likely to strongly agree that "You don't need to go to church in order to be a good Christian" (53 percent versus 44 percent, RoNA). In its shadow is *Salvation Valley*. People in the rest of North America are more likely to believe that "through the life, death and resurrection of Jesus I have forgiveness of my sins" (83 percent agree versus 69 percent Cascadians, RoNA).

Towering alongside is the *Mount of Non-Attendance*. Cascadians are more likely to never attend church or go just once a year or so (51 percent versus 29 percent, RoNA). Stretching out from the mountainside is the *Valley of Megiddo*. Cascadians are less likely to believe that "the world will end in the battle of Armageddon between Jesus and the Antichrist" (29 percent versus 43 percent, RoNA). The *Prayer Pond* dots upper levels of the valley (24 percent Cascadians never pray, versus 9 percent RoNA) while the deep water *Lac Religious Relevance* fills out the plain (35 percent say that religion is not important to daily life, versus 21 percent RoNA).

MARIJUANA MOUNTAINS

The high cloudy peaks of the Marijuana Mountains are west of the Range of Faith and closer to the coast — a land where the *Cannabis sativa* plant flowers abundantly in sheltered and sun-dappled valleys of acceptance.

Puffer's Peak is the highest summit of the Marijuana Mountains.

It points to the fact that Cascadians are more likely to smoke marijuana. In British Columbia, 16 percent of those fifteen years of age and older had used cannabis in the past year, compared to a Canadian average of one in eight (12 percent). The US numbers are not directly comparable, but the pattern is the same: a higher percentage of Cascadians smoke marijuana than people elsewhere in North America. In Oregon 8 percent of those age twelve and greater have smoked marijuana in the past month. In Washington State the rate is 7 percent, versus an American national average of 6 percent.

The *Mount of Decriminalisation*'s blunted summit denotes that Cascadians are more likely to agree that Canadian government "legislation that would not legalize marijuana but would make possession of small quantifies not a criminal offence" is "a sound idea" (57 percent in B.C. versus 51 percent Canadian average, and 45 percent Oregon/Washington versus 36 percent US average).

HUMAN NATURE RANGE

At the northern end of Cascadia lie the sunny peaks of the *Human Nature Range*, a region of trust, hope and tolerance.

Do-Right Mountain dominates this region, a gentle giant that reminds us of the fact Cascadians are more likely to agree that "people can generally be trusted to do what is right" (73 percent versus 58 percent, RoNA). Rising alongside, to the northwest, is *Trust Hill*. Fewer Cascadians agree that "when I put my trust in people they usually disappointment me" (27 percent versus 36 percent RoNA). Thrusting up to the south is the third peak of the region: *Gay Mount*. Three quarters of Cascadians (75 percent) agree that "Homosexuals should have the same rights as other American/ Canadians" versus 63 percent, RoNA.

POROUS BORDER RANGE

Two thirds of the way down the coast, the pinnacles of the *Porous Border Range* shine as beacons of neighbourly trust. This north-south-oriented range reveals that Cascadians are interested in erasing existing national borders.

A series of items about national and continental priorities, asked as part of a study for the Woodrow Wilson International Center for Scholars, depicted here as the *Peak of Cross-Border Transit*, revealed that Cascadians placed greater priority on the free cross-border transit of people and goods, are more in favour of "creating a North American identity card for both Americans and Canadians that could be used for border transit" and reducing trade irritants. *Lac Security* denotes that Cascadians also placed less emphasis than other North Americans on cross-border security and the need to "tighten it."

RANGE OF PERSONAL RESPONSIBILITY

A sense of independence and personal engagement is revealed by the strapping summits of the southern *Range of Personal Responsibility*.

The *Peak of Political Empowerment* towers over the southern-most reaches of the region. A greater sense of do-it-yourself (DIY) politics is exposed by the fact Cascadians are more likely to disagree that "voting is the only way people like me can have a say about how the government runs things" (54 percent disagree versus 37 percent, RONA). Standing next to it is *Charity Hill*. Cascadians are more likely to report making charitable donations (61 percent versus 52 percent, RONA). In between lies the *Economic Disparity Dale*. Cascadians' belief in the rewards of DIY makes them less likely to agree strongly that "the gap between rich and poor in this country is a significant problem" (44 percent Cascadia versus 55 percent, RONA).

MILE HIGH VIEW

If we zoom back a bit from this map, what does the big picture reveal about Cascadia? Firstly, we see that Cascadians are definitely different from the others with whom they share this continent. In a number of fundamental and interrelated ways, Cascadia can be considered to have a distinct culture.

Secondly, I believe the pieces of the puzzle fit together to describe a people who tend to be more individualistic, with a do-it-myself mentality. Cascadians are, for example, less trusting of religious organizations, and place higher value on their own personal religious or spiritual beliefs. Cascadians think that they can make a difference in politics — outside of voting. They are also less concerned by people who are different, like marijuana users and gays and lesbians, and they are more trusting of people in general. This suggests something of an "I'm okay, you're okay" way of thinking.

Driven by their faith in the individual, Cascadians also expect their fellow travellers to be involved and to share in doing the right thing. They will lend a hand if need be, but you are expected to carry your own weight eventually. If New Hampshire's licence plate motto is "Live Free or Die," Cascadia's might be "Live and Let Live."

"WE KNOW IN PART, AND WE PROPHESY IN PART"

What do we really know? Is this data-driven analysis really useful? As any good contrarian knows, all data is suspect and nothing lies quite as well as a statistic. So do these statistics lie?

While we were at the conference that spawned this book, sad news came of the fate of an undergraduate statistics student who had ventured out into the Cascade Mountains on an adventurous cross-country walking tour. He could not swim, so he carefully checked the average depth of each mountain stream and river he had to cross on his trek. He figured that if he knew the average depth of each river, he could correctly choose which ones he could ford and which ones he would have to cross on a bridge.

Sadly, he drowned while crossing a river high in the mountains that was one meter, or just a little more than a yard, deep on average. His fate was sealed when he boldly tried to wade across a river that was wide and shallow in the main, but very deep and swift-moving in the center. His fatal assumption was that the average depth told him it was shallow enough to wade across. His middling grasp of statistics killed him. If we are not to suffer this same fate, what must we learn from this tragic tale?

We too looked at averages, with a focus on differences between groups: Cascadians versus other North Americans. It is therefore important to note that we are looking at tendencies and not absolutes. While Cascadians tend to be less religious, for example, it does not mean that all Cascadians are not religious. It simply means they are — compared to other North Americans — less religious, *on average*. Indeed, this book has much to say about the religiosity of Cascadians and even makes a convincing claim for a unique Cascadian brand of spirituality. Obviously averages do not tell the whole story.

SO WHAT IS TRUE?

The story I've told about the shape of Cascadia is true, based on the evidence I have at hand. Cascadians tend to lean one way. But does that mean they are all the same? Absolutely not. Cascadians are not a homogenous group. They are individualists.

On one hand, you could say that this (or any) analysis of Cascadian tendencies is a sham; it papers over the cracks between a wildly diverse set of constituencies that share little or nothing. You might ask the question: how do you understand an individualistic society by studying a group's tendencies? It is a good question.

On the other hand, you have to acknowledge that Cascadians are distinct from the others with whom they share this continent. In many ways, Cascadians are more similar to each other (despite their differences) than they are to the others.

So we know about Cascadians, in part. We see through a glass, darkly. Regardless of how smoky or wavy the glass is, the outline of one fundamental finding is clear: Cascadians tend to have an individualistic "live and let live" mentality. This "live and let live" mindset has a number of implications, some good and some bad. It has a profound impact on how the future of Cascadia will unfold. So let us consider some possible futures.

THE DYSTOPIA

An individualistic and diverse society can move toward a co-operative and collaborative model, or it can spiral down into mistrust, withdrawal and the death of community. The difficulty is that a multi-polar society has more potential for conflicts between groups and individuals and few or no large forces able to provide a sense of community that can work toward building and maintaining peace.

If people who live in an area do not have a common vision, they will not agree on what to do as a society. If no one agrees, decision making is paralyzed. When that happens, nothing gets done: people blame each other and tensions become more deeply entrenched. There are too many societies tragically and gruesomely consuming themselves from the inside out to belabour the point about how wrong it can all go. But can Cascadia go there?

I can, disturbingly, foresee a future where Cascadia fractures into a thousand jagged shards. There is an incredible rift between the seemingly limitless riches of West Vancouver and the horrible poverty and despair of downtown Vancouver's Hastings and Main area. What if that rift is just the beginning of a fault line that smashes Cascadian society? Or, in the face of an infrastructure-destroying, region-wide Earthquake, I wonder if there would be any Cascadian social glue that can hold together a third-generation logger and a Hong Kong jet-set international? And how does a "live and let live" ethos help maintain community when the economy is not booming and the stress of highly leveraged, high density living gets too great?

Cascadia can crack. And if it does, it will not be pretty.

THE UTOPIA

Cascadia can, alternately, help save the Earth. In a rapidly globalizing world, with no dominant society and a bewildering diversity of cultures and perspectives, Cascadia's utopian co-operative and tolerant "live and let live" model could serve as a beacon for the world to follow.

A utopian Cascadia would be one where the society's vision transcends borders, finds a sustainable balance between man and nature, respects differences between peoples, and reaches out a helping hand to those in need. That is a vision the world needs. And the seeds of it are all there, in Cascadia.

In the international world ahead, societies that can look beyond their own borders and have easy exchanges with other nations and regions are the ones that will flourish. Cascadians, with their north/south fluidity, can lead the way here — if they maintain and intensify a borderless mentality.

Cascadians, with their natural resource orientation, have not always been friends of the Earth. But sometimes a society can learn its most profound lessons from its mistakes. Hopefully, the current swell of eco-consciousness grows to become a gigantic wave that sweeps Cascadia clean, so that a sustainable balance of man in nature can be found and maintained.

The Cascadian willingness to take personal responsibility and the DIY mentality we observed are also essential underpinnings of any utopia. If everyone waits for someone else to build a society, nothing will ever happen. But if everyone contributes, it is amazing what can be accomplished.

Cascadians' willingness to allow for differences between people, to give space to the outsider and the different, is laudable. The world is now so porous, soon everyone will be everywhere. And willingness to accept differences will be a key to success for all societies.

I believe that it is these last two items — a sense of personal responsibility and a willingness to embrace the different — that will be the fulcrum upon which Cascadia's future will balance.

The DIY instinct can go horribly wrong when it is not tempered by the compassionate embrace of those who are different. The survivalist groups found deep in the woods of Cascadia are a toxic home-grown example of individualism gone wrong. Willingness to accept others, without engaging with them, is likewise equally ineffectual. Acceptance without compassion and communication is just indifference — which is hardly a virtue.

Cascadians must combine their sense of personal responsibility with a consciousness of the needs of others. If they do that, Cascadians can lead the world to the elusive utopia we all seek.

AFTERWORD: ABOUT THE RESEARCH

Some people like to pore over baseball statistics, while others devour car specs. And some want details on how the research was done. All are geeky pursuits. But that is okay. In a Cascadian utopia there is room for everyone.

Most public opinion surveys are conducted within national boundaries. In preparing this analysis, I wanted to be true to the Cascadian ideal, which meant that I wanted to examine only data which would allow me to have representation from Cascadians on both sides of the Canada/US divide. There are, unfortunately, not many studies that are North American in scope, and even fewer that provide adequate samples for Cascadia. We are handicapped, in part, by the fact that the US samples typically include just a handful of interviews in Oregon and Washington State, because they represent a relatively small proportion of the overall US population.

To create this map I mainly drew on two studies: *God and Society in North America* and *God and Society Revisited*. The original *God and Society* study, funded by the Pew Charitable Trusts, was a telephone survey conducted in the autumn of 1996 with a random sample of 6,023 people: 3,000 Canadians and 3,023 Americans. The second study was conducted in the spring of 2006 with a sample of 1,582 people: 814 in Canada and 768 in the US. The original study was more in-depth and much of the data shown here is drawn from that study. While the 1996 data is relatively old, the fact that the items tracked from 1996 to 2006 showed no significant change indicates the 1996 data is still representative of people's values.

CHAPTER 3

✎

Memory, Novelty
and Possibility
in This Place

PATRICIA O'CONNELL KILLEN

ON SEPTEMBER 4, 1906, Arthur Van Ackere, a Belgian immigrant farmer recently arrived in Oregon's Tualatin Valley, wrote to his brother-in-law, Emil Duyck, who was working as a coachman in Rock Island, Illinois, "The Belgians around here don't get along too well." Three decades of letters among this extended immigrant family contain repeated comment on how, in Oregon, Belgians do not co-operate with each other as they did in Illinois and Iowa, the intermediate stops for most who finally settled in the Pacific Northwest at the turn of the twentieth century (Duyck correspondence collection in the possession of the author). While none of the letter writers offers an explanation for why, the persistence of the theme and repeated comparison with the Belgian community in the Midwest suggest that the issues involved more than clashing personalities. Something happened to the Belgians in this new place. What happened to them occurred in other immigrant ethnic communities and among other in-migrants to the region who referred to themselves simply as "Americans" or "Canadians" as well.

What happened to these immigrants continues to occur. People who enter Cascadia experience a loosening of connection to social institutions that may be experienced as exhilarating, frightening, or both. At the same time, they experience a natural geography of scale and grandeur. What results in Cascadia, where social and geographic landscapes are intertwined, is a rethinking of identity and community.

The features of the geographic landscape may be relatively fixed, but the reactions of people to them and the relationships of people with them are not. The past experiences that in-migrants bring with them to the region, their dreams and aspirations, the physical space within which they reside, the climate and the socially constructed institutions of family, economy, politics, religion and culture intertwine to shape the contours of reality in this place and how they react to it. Reaction, re-affirmation and innovation in identity and social relationships are equally viable options, precisely because of the relative social fluidity, impulse toward individualism, and natural beauty of the place (Killen and Silk). What people bring to the region and what they experience here are the constraints of actually possible futures for Cascadia.

This chapter explores the constraints and promise of Cascadia's future through the lens of its religious environment. British Columbia, Washington and Oregon share a distinctive religious configuration and sensibility that present challenges and opportunities to the project imagined in and for Cascadia. They significantly influence people's access to cultural wisdom traditions. They shape the context within and strategies by which concerned citizens and communities can harness the passion, identity and commitment of individuals, and hence create social capital. They influence the degree to which individuals in the region feel claimed by the needs of beings beyond themselves, and hence their capacity to create and maintain sturdy, sustainable communities.

To put the central issue of the dream of Cascadia quite simply: Can and does this place, in which so many experience themselves to be free from the past, from tradition, and from constraining ties, inspire a vision compelling enough to viably reweave the bonds of humans with each other and with the "more-than-human" (the natural world) for a twenty-first century, global people?[1]

CASCADIA'S RELIGIOUS CONFIGURATION

To be sure, Arthur Van Ackere and his family, along with other European, Canadian and US immigrants to Cascadia, helped to organize or joined already-existing churches. But theirs was the choice of the minority. It took until 1970 for the religiously involved population of Oregon and Washington to reach the percentage of the United States in 1890. By 2000 the gap between the nation and the region in institutional religious involvement was greater than it had been in 1970. In Cascadia most people are outside the doors of church, synagogue, temple and mosque (68 percent for Washington and Oregon and at least 60 percent for British Columbia), and always have been (Killen and Silk, 28; Statistics Canada, 2001: 9, 16). As a result, religion as a factor in individual and social identity and as an agent of social control has never been as strong in Cascadia as in other parts of the US and Canada. This is a key dimension of the distinctive religious configuration of the region that Douglas Todd notes in his introduction. Religion's presence in private and public life in Cascadia is complex, elusive and often difficult to discern.

Today, the population falls broadly into three categories religiously: "Adherents," "Identifiers" and "Nones." "Adherents" refers to the institutionally religiously active, the minority of the population. "Identifiers" and "Nones" make up the majority of the population, those outside the doors. While all three categories are found elsewhere in Canada and the US, the proportion of each is different in Cascadia.

Most striking is the significant number of adults who, when asked, "What is your religion, if any?" give the answer "None." A quarter of adults in Oregon and Washington and 35 percent of adults in British Columbians no longer identify with a religious heritage or family.[2] Institutionally disconnected, Nones are not spiritually disinterested. Instead, they constitute a limit case, individuals who no longer organize their lives according to role and institution in the way that most humans have done from the early modern period to the present. "Nones" exemplify one path to the composition of the human self and human groups in a postmodern context (Killen and Silk, 41, 139–167; Statistics Canada, 2003).

Identifiers claim a religious heritage, for example, Catholic, Lutheran, or Jewish, but do not participate in religious institutions on anything like a regular basis (understood minimally as monthly participation). They make up about 38 percent of Washingtonians and Oregonians and about 21 percent of British Columbians (Killen and Silk, 40; Clark and Schellenberg, 3–4).

What identification with a heritage without institutional religious participation means to these people is not clear. It may signify the residue of eroded connection to family or ethnic community. It may be a point on the path to becoming Nones. Another possibility, though less likely, is that Identifiers are waiting to find the faith community that fits them. Whatever the meaning, Identifiers exemplify an abandonment of institutional connection that is prevalent in the region. That disconnection may well signal the fate, in the wake of late industrial capitalism, of all denominations descended from Reformation bodies that presumed the need for co-operation between a church and established political power to ensure the welfare of the wider community.

British Columbia has fewer Identifiers than the US states. This may be the result of differences in the way data on religious identification and participation are collected in the two places, or to the different status of social institutions generally in Canada and the United States. Research shows British Columbians moving in significant numbers from the Identifier category, identifying but not attending services, to the None category between 1995 and 2004 (Clark and Schellenberg, 3).

Understanding the meaning and motivation of Identifiers is significant for thinking through the future of Cascadia. We do not know what influence, if any, religious heritage has on these individuals when they make decisions on public issues. We do not know if they vote in numbers equal to, greater than, or less than those of the religiously active. We do know that, given their numbers, they make up a swing constituency. Any institutional- or movement-based initiatives or visions for the region must gain traction with Identifiers to be successful. How Identifiers think about the environment, sustainability, housing, health care, and other issues, matters (Killen and Silk, 4).

Identifiers seem to exemplify a deep-seated element in the religious and larger cultural sensibility of the region: a quality of tentativeness, a desire to keep options open, and to be looking for the next best opportunity. This tendency is illustrated by a story from a history of Methodism in Washington State. A woman attended services at a large Methodist church in Seattle one Sunday and signed a visitor card. The pastor called at her home and discovered that she was rather elderly. When the pastor asked her why she had not been to church before, she responded that she had been a Methodist in Ohio but considered herself a "temporary resident" of Seattle. She had been in the city 35 years (Howell, 159–160).

While Nones and Identifiers stand out in the Pacific Northwest, and together comprise the majority of the population, Cascadia is hardly devoid of institutional religion. In 2000, Adherents, those people who cross the transom of church, synagogue, temple, mosque or gurdwara often enough for optimistic religious bureaucrats to count them, made up about 37 percent of the population of Oregon and Washington. Regular (at least monthly) attendance at religious services in Washington and Oregon is closer to 25 percent. In British Columbia, adherents make up about 40 percent of the population, but those who attend services at least monthly only make up 27 percent of the population (Clark, 25; Killen and Silk, 28–31).

In Washington, Oregon and British Columbia, the single largest religious body is the Roman Catholics. In neither of the US states nor British Columbia is the active Catholic population even half the size of the Nones. In Oregon and Washington the next largest denomination is Latter-day Saints. If one combines all types of Lutherans they rival the Latter-day Saints in size at about 3 percent of the population. In British Columbia the second largest religious body is the liberal United Church of Canada with 9.4 percent of the B.C. population, but with a much lower rate of attendance than Latter-Day Saints.

In Oregon and Washington, the minority of the population that makes up the Adherent pie — those inside the doors of religious institutions — is fractured and fractious. The top five groups capture only about 60 percent of the church-going population, while in other regions of the US the top five capture 75 to 85 percent. In British Columbia, the situation is less fractious in terms of religious bodies whose roots lie in Europe. British Columbia, however, has larger numbers of followers of Asian religions than do the states of the Pacific Northwest (Killen and Silk, 31–33; Statistics Canada, 2003). In addition, British Columbia, Washington and Oregon have higher concentrations of Native American or First Nation peoples whose indigenous religious beliefs and practices are complex. They are given attention in the chapters by Jean Barman, Mike Carr and Eli Enns.

While religious communities have always struggled as mere minorities on the public stage of the region, they have nevertheless found ways to play important roles in Cascadia. One part of their role has been pragmatic. In the 1860s even Protestants helped to pay for the hospital and orphanage run by the Sisters of Providence, who also built Catholic schools in Oregon and Washington. (The Catholic church that provided the institutions was until the 1880s a predominantly French Canadian one.) In British Columbia, Catholic priests and sisters, and dedicated Anglican and Methodist clergy and laity, also built schools, hospitals and orphanages when settlement moved beyond Hudson's Bay Company forts and factories.

Priests, ministers, vowed female religious (sisters) and lay missionaries, and the churches and social services they provided, functioned as symbols and forces of "civilization" during Cascadia's settlement period. Catholic priests first came to what was then called the Oregon Territory (the Columbia District of the Hudson's Bay Company), with the permission of the Hudson's Bay Company, at the request of voyageurs who had mustered out of the Company and wanted to regularize their marriages to Native American women and have the sacraments available as they reached old age (Schoenberg, 17, 20–22, 25).

Institutionally religiously active people played significant roles in temperance, anti-prostitution, anti-gambling and anti-political corruption movements in Cascadia during the nineteenth and early twentieth centuries. In the mid- and later twentieth centuries religiously active citizens and the religious institutions they represented have been vocal in the region in support of open housing, civil rights, restitution to First Nations, low-income housing, social welfare, global peace and environmental protection.

Because of the minority status of religious institutions in the region, religiously motivated social and political movements have succeeded in Cascadia through pragmatic religious co-operation. In Washington State in 1924 a Ku Klux Klan initiative that would have outlawed parochial schools was defeated through the work of an ecumenical coalition of successful businessmen who described the initiative as bad for the image, and therefore the business, of the state. The region's history is full of pragmatic religious co-operation, and a willingness to subsume religious language to the language of the common good (Killen, "The Geography of a Minority Religion").

The other role of religious institutions has been symbolic. In Cascadia, as in previous frontier regions, the existence of religious institutions and the presence of religious functionaries signalled the arrival of civilization. That symbol appealed to some and concerned others. It still does. Symbols, however, are received with ambivalence. In 1855, the first Catholic bishop in the western Washington diocese of Nisqually, Alexandre Magliore Blanchet, complained in respectful tones to Marcel Bernier that he had failed to provide the priest stationed at the Cowlitz mission with "meat" as well as bread, which had been their original agreement (Archives of the Archdiocese of Seattle, A2: 269–270).

Despite some influence in shaping Cascadia, religious institutions and functionaries have, however, remained minority players in the region in both their pragmatic and symbolic roles. As a result, they have not wielded the social control in this region that they have had, and continue to have, in other regions of the United States and Canada.

RELIGIOUS ENVIRONMENT AND RELIGIOUS SENSIBILITY

Because the institutionally religiously active have always been a minority in Cascadia and because those who are institutionally religiously active are divided among many groups, the most significant defining feature of the region's religious environment is this — Cascadia has never had a dominant religious reference group. Historically no group has ever gained the political, religious or cultural traction to be "the" established religion in Oregon and Washington. In British Columbia neither the Catholic, Anglican nor United Church of Canada denominations succeeded in overcoming the disinterest in institutional religion of most people in the province (Burkinshaw).

In New England, the dominant cultural story is still the Puritan story, even though Jews and Catholics outnumber the descendants of Puritans. In Quebec, the dominant story remains a Catholic story despite the mass exodus of Quebec Catholics from institutional religious participation. In the West the dominant narrative is the West itself. Against this narrative, more staid storylines, like those of religious institutions, pale (Szasz). Cascadia is a particular version of the West. This is a place conceived as a land of infinite opportunity that has also been and continues to be, in the words of Bruce Barcott, "a catch-basin of washed up westering dreams" (Barcott, xviii).

The absence of a dominant religious reference group structures individual and institutional religious sensibility in Cascadia. It transforms religious identification and belonging into lifelong projects. At the same time, it creates a social space in which both abandoning institutional religion and innovating within or inventing religious forms become real possibilities. As an example of innovation, Seattle was the site of the first television show built around a priest, rabbi and Protestant minister discussing religious and social issues, ranging from open housing legislation to whether Jews were responsible for the death of Jesus or whether Christmas should be celebrated in public schools. The television program, called The Challenge, ran throughout the 1960s. Catholic priest William Treacy and Rabbi Raphael Levine became fast friends and together founded Camp Brotherhood for the purpose of advancing interfaith understanding and world peace (Killen, "The Geography of a Minority Religion").

The absence of a dominant religious reference group and the never-ending task of constructing religious meaning, identification and belonging, lead to a religiousness in the region that is quite fluid. Individuals pursue spiritual quests largely unfettered by religious institutions. Publicly, religion is present like magma under the volcanoes. It is invisible, erupts explosively, and then hardens. During the past twenty years in Oregon, Washington and B.C., the magma has been closer to the surface, visible in the heated debate around issues such as same-sex marriage and the environment (Killen and Silk, 169–179).

The lack of a dominant religious reference group makes Cascadia an open religious environment. With few people in church, many different kinds of religious groups present, and those outside the doors serving as the largest population, the region is left open to many interpretations and possibilities religiously. Cascadia is both indifferent to or inviting to religion, an obstacle or opportunity, a refuge or revelation. It is all of these and any of these and all at the same time.

Oregon, Washington and British Columbia have a highly elastic religious reality. Boundaries and identifies are fluid, movements coalesce, and then dissolve. Religious identity and commitment and their consequences are complex and contradictory. The lack of a dominant religious reference group, the fascination with nature, a disconnection from social institutions and disregard for the past — all of these add up to a situation in which innovation and preservation are equally of concern (Killen and Silk, 10–14).

Two growing centers of religious gravity have emerged in the Pacific Northwest. One is the alliance of secular, humanist, biocentric, and religiously moderate and liberal individuals and groups who share an environmental spirituality. The Catholic bishops' "pastoral letter" on the Columbia River, a collaborative project of the bishops of Oregon, Washington and British Columbia (2001) and projects such as the Seattle-based Earth Ministry, designed to help people in the pews understand the importance of stewardship of nature, are examples of the first.

The other is a more theologically literal, socially conservative, entrepreneurial, evangelical Christian group. The latter preaches a gospel in which supernatural beings are palpably real and actively intervening in human lives. At the same time, the evangelical entrepreneurs employ highly sophisticated communication technology. Most organize their congregations and other assemblies on a "flat," networking basis, not unlike high-tech companies. The evangelical entrepreneurial congregations often attract in-migrants to the region and are effective to the extent that they can re-broker attachments for these in-migrants.[3] In Washington State there is a concerted effort on the part of evangelical entrepreneurs to become the dominant reference group by defining the culture in broadly southern evangelical and Pentecostal terms. In reaction to this concerted effort, young, "twenty-something" atheists have organized in Seattle to support separation of church and state (Killen and Silk, 84–85; Pasquale).

British Columbia provides a contrast on this point. While British Columbia has a larger population of Nones than do Washington and Oregon, it has a smaller, though assertive, population of evangelicals, with significant real institutional presence through Regent College and Trinity Western University. Although Canadian evangelicals are generally considered more moderate than American evangelicals, pollster (and book contributor) Andrew Grenville has suggested they are becoming more of a coherent political force, credited with playing a key role in helping elect Conservative Party leader Stephen Harper (an evangelical) as Canadian prime minister in 2006 (albeit as head of a minority government). Still, across Canada, evangelicals remain largely a religious subculture, with Roman Catholics, United Church of Canada, Anglicans, Lutherans and other world faiths playing a larger, although typically subdued, role in national public life.

British Columbia is an open religious environment in a slightly different way from the US's version. Canadians' appropriation of multiculturalism as a central national value and practice contributes to the province's population being open to the world faiths and to the no-faith options of newer immigrants and other Canadians. This is especially so when coupled with the number of British Columbians who claim no religion. Religion is perhaps more fluid and less fractious in British Columbia than in the US Pacific Northwest. However, the growth of Nones and evangelical Christians in the Vancouver area in the face of the decline of historic churches of the magisterial Reformation may signal a polarizing development that will influence British Columbia and perhaps Canada more broadly.

A second persistent characteristic of the region's religious environment is that religious institutions in Oregon and Washington lack numerical depth. Religious leaders are aware that their operations exist at the will of the participants. Church planters (ministers with the specific work of beginning new congregations) from the southern United States are sometimes surprised when they come into the region, because local evangelical pastors are not willing to co-operate eagerly in establishing new congregations. Because of the thinness of the churchgoing population in the region, certain styles of being public that work in the southern US or the Midwest are not effective in the Pacific Northwest. In British Columbia, a history of greater church and state co-operation may compensate for demographic thinness to some degree (Noll).

If defining features of the postmodern are the lack of a dominant, overarching narrative and the impulse for the individual increasingly to become the center of all experience, the arbiter of truth and the creator of meaning, this region long has been, and remains, postmodern in a way much of the rest of the US may only now be heading. British Columbia is not only postmodern but global. Because of massive in-migration, from Asia especially, British Columbia, or at least Vancouver, is more cosmopolitan than either Seattle or Portland.

There are real differences between the US states and British Columbia in how people respond to the lack of a dominant religious reference group and the relative fragility of churches and other social institutions. In Oregon and Washington this combination generates a space within which the apocalyptic impulse that rinses through US culture can develop unrestrained. Both those within and beyond the doors of religious institutions in these states tend to construe events, especially events and actions related to natural resources and individual freedoms, in dichotomous terms, frequently as a battle between good and evil forces. The region lacks a sturdy, moderate middle of the sort that contributor Mark Silk and I believe might be found in the Upper Midwest. In the US part of Cascadia, innovation in ideas and practice — and obsession with keeping ideas and practice clear, consistent, and unchanging — are equally present.

British Columbia retains to some extent a more positive view of social institutions. This is because of Canada's different historical trajectory from the US in working out the relationship between religious and political institutions. Nones in British Columbia as well as Identifiers and Adherents are less likely than in the US to innovate and experiment in direct opposition to existing social institutions. Hence, British Columbia may have better resources for a vision of sustainable communities in Cascadia, a vision which is more realistic about and less hostile to the role of social institutions (Noll, 245–273).

Any consideration of the religious environment in Cascadia has to take account of the space and grandeur of this place. Here nature dwarfs the human. The environment is alternately a place that overwhelms and destroys people, a place of refuge, and a place of revelation. The space and grandeur of this place decenters humans and so requires a rethinking of the meaning of the human person.

Histories and literatures of the region reveal the extent to which many found their spiritual needs met by the beauty and magnificence of the environment itself. As Caroline C. Leighton wrote in her journal in 1868, from Astoria, Oregon, "We reached here Saturday night. Sunday morning, hearing a silver triangle played in the streets, we looked out for tambourines and dancing-girls, but saw none, and were presently told it was the call to church. We were quite tempted to go and hear what the service would be, but the sound of the breakers on the bar enchained us to stop and listen to them" (Leighton, 83).

Institutional religious bureaucrats looked at the region differently, and generally as an obstacle. All regional denominational histories of the Pacific Northwest, be they Catholic, Methodist, Latter-day Saint or Seventh-day Adventist share a common narrative thread: the pastor is either bigger than life, or he leaves broken. In these histories the grandeur of the region is integral to the West itself, and only an heroic figure can face it down.

Institutional religious leaders have also blamed the environment of Cascadia for making laity "indifferent" to religious worship and responsibility. In the 1850s Fr. James Croake rode a circuit from Portland, Oregon, south to Jacksonville, west to the Pacific, up the coast, and inland back to Portland. He wrote to Archbishop Francis Norbert Blanchet: "It takes so long to find the Catholics. And when you find them you have to follow them. And you have to follow them long enough to make them interested" (O'Hara, 167).

In the 1880s the Anglican bishop of British Columbia, George Hillis, wrote to his superiors in London of the "constitutional religious apathy" that marked "the people of the whole Pacific slope" (Burkinshaw, 4). In 1898 the pastor of St. Leo Parish in his annual report to the Diocese of Nisqually wrote, where the form asked for "number of people," it was "impossible to keep track. They come and they go. They are all headed to the mines" (Archives, Archdiocese of Seattle, Parishes). In the 1980s, historian Jeffrey Burns referred to the work of building the Catholic Church on the Pacific Coast of the US as the task of inspiring an "indifferent people to devotion" (Dolan, 15).

What these writers were noticing was a phenomenon that continues — religious life followed and still follows economic life and individual aspiration in Cascadia. From the time of early Euro-American settlement this has made it difficult for religious institutions that understand part of their community's role as care for the common good to advance projects of caring for the wider community as part of religious/moral obligation. If regionally and globally we are moving from an industrial economy to a knowledge economy, the meaning of that shift for the common good, especially with regard to sustainability over the long term, is an intimate part of the larger discussion of Cascadia's promise.

In Cascadia, people's capacity to experience religious and moral obligation is influenced profoundly by the way that mobility affects their religious sensibility. People move to Cascadia. Most of the growth in population in British Columbia, Oregon and Washington is by in-migration. Between 1970 and 2000, the population of Oregon and Washington increased 70 percent, with most of the growth occurring in Washington State. The national increase was about 38 percent. The percentage of the total population inside the doors of religious institutions remained steady in the middle of the 30 percent range. It took incredible effort for institutional religion simply to tread water.

British Columbia also saw very significant growth during this period, with much higher in-migration from east and south Asia than in the US. In British Columbia the pull away from conventional religious institutions also was strong during this same thirty-year period. Something about Cascadia draws many people away from institutional religious participation.

In Cascadia it becomes a lifelong project for most people simply to maintain a religious identity and sense of belonging. With social reinforcement to be institutionally religious largely absent, the preoccupation that shapes much of individual and institutional religious life is to make religion real. Hence an ambition of some pastors in Puget Sound is to build a sanctuary that dwarfs Mount Rainier (an impossibility). The more successful strategy for making religion real in Cascadia is to build something from the ground up, to begin a new project. The region is rife with small, grassroots organizations, foundations and alliances.

Even more conventional religious institutions tend to do things their own way. For example, the number of Reform Jewish congregations is growing in the Pacific Northwest. Recently a national leader in the Reform movement noted how the Pacific Northwest congregations were doing "being Jewish congregations" in a different style. Whether Jewish congregation or Catholic parish, institutionally religiously active people in the region want to develop their own ways of doing things, and this in respect to finding financial support, picking leadership, and educating their children in the faith tradition. In Cascadia, people make religion real to themselves by creating something new. When the project no longer is new, many people move to something else.

Spiritual seeking is the pull in the Pacific Northwest. The glue of deep social bonds and long-term commitment is more difficult to come by. But the latter is crucial to the people of Cascadia if they are to fulfill the dream of this place. Both traditional institutions and institutionally averse individuals and groups face the question of how, in Cascadia, creativity and commitment combine. The answer to that question, especially as conceived with regard to the environment and sustainable human communities, will reveal much about the future of Cascadia and the world.

The Pacific Northwest's open religious environment makes it a fertile context for creativity. Novel approaches to welcoming people into congregations and providing religious education and social services were developed in the Pacific Northwest and then adopted in the rest of the US. For example, the North American Forum, which promotes the Rite of Christian Initiation for Adults (the major way that adult converts have entered the Catholic Church over the past twenty-five years), was organized by a priest from the Archdiocese of Seattle. A plethora of grassroots organizations, foundations and think tanks are leading the way into a global, sustainable future. Some are explicitly focused on the environment, such as EcoTrust in Portland, Oregon, or on research to support sustainability, such as Sightline Institute in Seattle, or on developing an emergent spirituality and ethic for a new global commons, such as the Whidbey Institute in Clinton, Washington. Others develop from innovations in conventional religious communities and address a wider array of issues, such as Seattle's Earth Ministry or the two giant charities founded in Cascadia, Mercy Corps and World Vision. Organizations that appeal to individual commitment such as Jesuit Volunteer Corps, also do well in the region.

But an open religious environment that supports seeking, an unconditional and continual search, is also a context within which people can become lost. There is a fine distinction between creative seeking on one hand and personal alienation and inability to make commitment on the other. For some in Cascadia, albeit a minority, the need to belong, to have clarity and visible social boundaries leads to significant commitment to traditional faith and ethnic communities. These communities have played a much larger role in the region, especially with regard to social welfare, than numbers would seem to warrant. For others the need for boundaries leads to innovations that are, quite simply, aberrant. The same factors that contribute to Cascadia's embrace of the environment and global futures contribute to the growth of survivalist and Christian Identity movements, which are located in significant numbers along the I-5 corridor from Everett to Medford.

POSSIBILITY AND PITFALL FOR CASCADIA'S PROMISE

The features that make Cascadia a place of such possibility can also work against a vision of a sustainable future for the human and the more-than-human. Potential pitfalls of the Pacific Northwest's religious configuration, environment and sensibility stand out in three areas.

First, in the very ways that Cascadia frees individuals and weakens constraints upon them, and so opens up space for creativity, it also erodes their memory. Memory, especially deep memory, is the story within which one lives, the story that inspires the imagination, weaves together mind and heart, elaborates the connections among the physical, social and natural body. For most of human history, religious and other cultural wisdom traditions carried that decidedly human-centered memory.

Eroded memory deprives people of the resources of their tradition, which is a community's corporate wisdom communicated beyond a single lifespan that, to borrow from theologian Edward Farley, "assists a people in the ordering of life, the interpretation of situations, and even in creative responses to the new" (Farley, 29). Historically, and this is part of the appeal of First Nations cultures to many, a community's memory provides accumulated "insight into the way things are, into what we human beings are up against, into the perils and promises of life" (Farley, 31). The danger of becoming a memory-less and "traditionless" society is, as Farley suggests, the "dispersal of consciousness, and perhaps a new kind of human being . . . one whose consciousness is incapable of empathetic response to the claims of other living beings" (Farley, 38). Farley argues that traditions, especially religious traditions, have been through human history integral to the creation of sustainable communities. From this perspective, eroded memory, evidenced in a decided lack of interest on the part of most institutional religiously active people with the history and theology of their traditions, puts the promise of Cascadia at risk.

The possibility, perhaps even the task of Cascadia, is the creation of a biocentric memory, that is, a memory that puts all living things and the Earth itself in the center, a memory in which humans understand themselves intimately and totally as part of some larger web of life. The challenge for Cascadia is to create a biocentric memory in a region in which the traditional social carriers of memory — church, education, social service agencies, ethnic and family networks — are relatively weak or weakening.

Can a biocentric memory emerge in a region in which memory is assaulted by so much that people experience and bring with them into the region? How do physical and psychic mobility, a desire to forget painful and failed pasts, separation from family or place and preoccupation with economic and personal possibilities play into this project? What do the more compelling myths of the West, and sensitivity to an expansive and grand environment, capable equally of inspiring and destroying human beings, mean for the project of creating a biocentric memory?

Douglas Coupland, Vancouver raised, and perhaps the quintessential Generation X author, exemplifies something of the effort to create a biocentric memory in his *Life After God*, a novel set in British Columbia. The novel ends with a scene that, though set in nature, is profoundly liturgical, a statement that God is in and encountered through nature. The protagonist strips naked and walks into a clear pool under a waterfall. The water roars "Like a voice that knows only one message, one truth-never-ending, like the clapping of hands and the cheers of the citizens upon the coronation of the king, the crowds of the inauguration, cheering for hope and for that one voice that will speak to them" (Coupland, 357–358). Submerged in the pool he continues to "hear the roar of water, the roar of clapping hands" (Coupland, 360). Nature's hands of water and the protagonist's own hands merge into one. The protagonist experiences his body and soul being washed clean. In that process he is also able to acknowledge his secret: "I need God — that I am sick and can no longer make it alone. I need God to help me give, because I no longer seem to be capable of giving; to help me be kind, as I no longer seem capable of kindness; to help me love, as I seem beyond being able to love" (Coupland, 359). Coupland collapses the human and the natural, and, in the process, imagines a different way of being in the world with both nature and other humans.

If eroded memory is the first potential pitfall, then the second is the way in which Cascadia invites a flight from commitment precisely as it invites the possibility to do something entirely new. The tension between flight from commitment and a desire to create a new order generates ambiguity and ambivalence in individuals. Even those who choose to be religious breathe this ambivalent Cascadian air. To create a new thing that is more than private or ephemeral requires shared social meaning and durable relationships. These are difficult to maintain in a fragile social fabric. Further, because in the absence of social reinforcement being religious takes repeated attention and is the work of an entire life, individuals must keep choosing. They tend to be attracted by what is new. In the Pacific Northwest newness is often equated with significance, and so long-term commitment is difficult to maintain.

Cascadia may well be the "canary in the mine," with regard not only to environmental sustainability and the creation of a global human community, but also as an experiment about the consciousness and conscience of humanity. Douglas Coupland's closing scene in *Life After God* is a description of losing human memory and going into nature through immersion in a clear, cold pool under a waterfall to emerge with a new human/more-than-human memory. He talks about nature as a sanctuary. His language about nature in that final scene of the novel echoes the language of community that begins the Ignatian practice of the "Contemplation to

Learn to Love like God." I have no idea if Coupland knows about Ignatian spirituality. But I do want to suggest that the ending of his novel hints at a significant dimension of the promise of Cascadia, and one that is crucial to sustainable human and more-than-human communities, namely a different kind of consciousness, a consciousness that is memory-less in one way, but in another way, provides a new memory by relocating the human and, perhaps, moving us more fully toward the deepest meaning of ancient faiths.

Another writer, David James Duncan, whom many consider the resident theologian of Cascadia, reflects a similar project in his own work. As Duncan puts it in one essay, "We need God in order to love and steward Creation. We need Creation to true our love for God. We also need Creation to better love one another" (Duncan, 20). Both of these authors are writing about what we might call the Cascadian wager — that a novel relationship with nature, one with heightened sensitivity and sensibility to the human in nature and as part of nature, is crucial to the emergence of new, sustainable social communities.

Finally, the question for Cascadia is whether in this place humans will find a way to experience themselves to be claimed by each other and by the larger-than-human in a way so compelling that they will "grow up," that is, learn to endure frustration, negotiate conflict and get to the other side of disillusionment with a capacity to hope. In other words, can the possibilities for sustainable community become sufficiently compelling that the institutionally averse will feel so powerfully claimed by living beings other than themselves that they are capable of sacrifice? Pollster Andrew Grenville provides original survey data in Chapter 2 of this book that shows there exists a higher emphasis on personal responsibility and a lower concern about the gap between rich and poor in Cascadia when compared to the rest of Canada and the United States. Similarly, it is harder for the poor to obtain adequate food in Washington and Oregon compared to other states with lower income levels but higher levels of institutional religious participation. These two pieces of data suggest that the capacity of the people of Cascadia to feel claimed by the needs of others is much more than a rhetorical question.

The question of Cascadia is, as Mark Silk notes in his chapter, whether we are seeing in the dream of a new society in this place an extension of self-deceptive individualism or the emergence of a new kind of claiming of the human by the larger, geo-biosphere. If we are seeing an extension of self-deceptive individualism, then the descendants of Arthur Van Ackere and all the rest who call Cascadia home will continue to "not get along so well" with each other as do those residing in regions with society organized around more demographically robust and durable traditional social institutions. Nor will they be able effectively to steward the environment. If we are seeing a new kind of claiming of the human by the larger, geo-biosphere, then Cascadia is the "nurse log" for a new understanding of human maturity, a new anthropology, a new way of conceiving community, a new practice of social life. That might be its greatest possible gift for the future.

Part Two

✑

CASCADIAN HISTORY

GEOGRAPHY SHAPES SPIRITUALITY IN CASCADIA. Many people in Cascadia, also known as the Pacific Northwest, find sacredness in the wild, wet and imposing landscape, which dwarfs humans and their accomplishments and can evoke a sense of humility, awe and gratitude. This is Long Beach on Vancouver Island, British Columbia. (Photo Credit: Marilyn McEwen)

SECULAR BUT SPIRITUAL. The people of the Pacific Northwest are among the least likely on the continent to be active in an institutional religion. Mark Shibley calls them "secular but spiritual." They believe that a walk in nature can be a transcendent experience. Sallie McFague says that's not a bad thing, but she calls on Cascadians to go deeper and envision nature as the source and ground of everything that is. (Photo Credit: Richard Lam, *Vancouver Sun*)

EXPERIENCING THE SACRED. Spiritual practices in
Cascadia are often unstructured, private and experiential.
More than most places in North American they are shaped
by Asian philosophy, focused on health, and reflect a do-it-your-
self-attitude. Many feel spiritual when they experience oneness
with nature, in effect practising a form of Earth reverence.
(Photo Credit: Glenn Baglo, *Vancouver Sun*)

NATURE INSPIRATION. Even organized religion in Cascadia is strongly influenced by the natural world. The architecture of this Benedictine monastery in Mission, B.C., echoes a forest canopy of trees and leaves. Although institutional religion is less dominant in Cascadia than elsewhere in North America, Christians and others have been at the forefront of efforts to protect the region's forests, rivers and wildlife, which they consider God's Creation. (Photo Credit: Stuart Davis, *Vancouver Sun*)

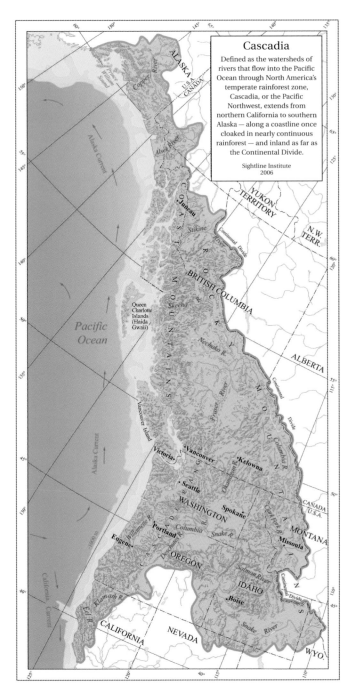

Cascadia

Defined as the watersheds of
rivers that flow into the Pacific
Ocean through North America's
temperate rainforest zone,
Cascadia, or the Pacific
Northwest, extends from
northern California to southern
Alaska — along a coastline once
cloaked in nearly continuous
rainforest — and inland as far as
the Continental Divide.

Sightline Institute
2006

CASCADIA BIOREGIONAL MAP. Cascadia is a distinct bioregion of northwestern
rainforest, towering mountains and tumbling rivers that flow into the Pacific
Ocean west of the Continental Divide. (Although the Cascadian bioregion includes
Idaho and tips of Alaska and California, this book focuses on the most populous
jurisdictions in Cascadia: B.C., Washington and Oregon.)

THE ORIGINS OF "CASCADIA." Multnomah Falls in northern Oregon is one of the highest year-round waterfalls in North America. The term "Cascadia" came from the early Scottish botanist David Douglas, who was inspired by the "cascading" waterfalls connected to the mighty Columbia River. As well as becoming a synonym for the Pacific Northwest, the name has been applied to the Cascade Mountain Range, the Cascadia earthquake zone and the Cascade Volcanic Arc. (Photo Credit: Mike Norton)

THE LAND CALLS FOR ECO-ACTIVISM. Oregon's spectacular beaches were in the early twentieth century protected from private ownership by Governor Oswald Davis, a Canadian-raised politician who felt a religious duty to preserve the oceanfront for the common people. His bold act was a precursor of the spiritually shaped Cascadian eco-activism that led to the founding of Greenpeace in the Pacific Northwest in 1971 and continues to reverberate today. This is Heceta Lighthouse at dusk.

A SENSE OF PLACE. Many Cascadian thinkers, writers, ecologists and artists believe that nurturing a "sense of place," a rootedness in the fertile land, will lead to the region's inhabitants developing a distinct culture and spirituality — which may serve as a model for the planet. In his prose poem, George Bowering suggests there is something in the Cascadian woods that is overpowering, which "you need all the time." (Photo Credit: Stuart Davis, *Vancouver Sun*)

CHAPTER 4

✍

Cascadia Once
upon a Time

JEAN BARMAN

THE EMPHASIS IN the Cascadian movement on the coherence of the Pacific Northwest has deep historical roots.[1] The international boundary was imposed on a single region rather than confirming separate regions already in existence. Attention to Cascadia once upon a time helps us to appreciate how deeply embedded are the similarities that energize its proponents (Sparke, Smith).

The term Cascadia originates with the Cascade Mountains paralleling the Pacific Ocean about 160 to 240 kilometers, or 100 to 150 miles, inland. The volcanic range runs from northern California through Oregon and Washington into southern British Columbia. The highest point is Mount Rainier at 4,392 meters, or 14,410 feet, with other well-known peaks being Mount Hood in Oregon, and Mount St. Helens and Mount Baker in southern and northern Washington.

Cascadia has numerous spatial definitions, each taking the Pacific Ocean as the western boundary.[2] Those who envisage Cascadia as a bioregion sometimes limit themselves to the area around the Georgia Basin and Puget Sound. Others with a principally environmental interest use the Cascades or the continental divide in the Rocky Mountains, from which waters wash into the Pacific or Atlantic oceans, as the eastern boundary. By the larger measure, Cascadia takes in all of Washington, most of Oregon, Idaho, and British Columbia, and parts of California, Montana, Wyoming, Nevada, the Yukon and Alaska.[3] A socio-economic or political perspective might encompass wealthy Alberta, as does a regular news section beginning in 2007 in the *Vancouver Sun* newspaper. Where a distinctive lifestyle is emphasized, the focus can be urban, extending along the Canadian Highway 99/American I-5 corridor. Vancouver, Seattle, and possibly Portland receive most attention.[4] Yet another perspective contends that actual boundaries may not much matter, given Cascadia is "not a state, but a state of mind . . . a fluid, evolutionary, and quite plastic notion capable of morphing into different shapes and sizes according to the particular needs of particular 'practical' visions" (Sparke, 7). Many equate Cascadia for practical purposes, much as I do here, with Oregon, Washington, and British Columbia (Beebe). By this measure, Cascadia and the Pacific Northwest are effectively synonymous.[5]

The border that from 1846 divided Cascadia along the 49th parallel has troubled our understanding of the region. Almost all subsequent accounts have been written from a national perspective. Writers limit themselves to their side of the border, be it the United States or Canada, as if the line on paper determines how people relate to their settings.[6] The minority of writers going beyond a single nation have mostly done so within a cross-border or borderlands frame of reference.[7] They take the boundary as a given and focus on how it can be mitigated as opposed to conceiving of the Pacific Northwest region as a single entity.

We obtain another perspective on Cascadia by glimpsing four

historical moments. The first is indigenous peoples prior to contact, the second the first century of contact, marked by a single Cascadian economy. The third glimpse is of the layering of nation on region, and the fourth the lingering hope for the next quarter of a century that a single nation might still emerge.

INDIGENOUS PEOPLE PRIOR TO CONTACT

Indigenous peoples living in the Pacific Northwest prior to contact shared important attributes. Although originating after the fact, sources of information are so consistent and so coherent as to be persuasive. Indigenous peoples' common goal was to live in harmony with nature. Two means for doing so were their relationship to the land and their spirituality.

Kinship and other groupings possessed exclusive rights to natural resources and particular geographical areas, and in this sense indigenous peoples owned the land. Ethnographer Wilson Duff explained about British Columbia:

> The patterns of ownership and utilization which they imposed upon the lands and waters were different from those recognized by our system of law, but were nonetheless clearly defined and mutually respected. . . . Except for barren and inaccessible areas, which are not utilized even today, every part of the Province was formerly within the owned and recognized territory of one or other of the Indian tribes. (Duff, 8)

Concepts of spirituality were shared across the Pacific Northwest and also more generally. Indigenous peoples gave precedence to the group over the individual, to an ethic of sharing, and to a set of spiritual values which did not distinguish between the sacred and the profane. Supernatural beings pervaded the natural environment, and both animate and inanimate beings possessed spirits, whose power could either confer blessings or bring disaster. All aspects of life, from rites of passage to everyday activity, encompassed an element of ritual and respect.

The indigenous peoples who called the Pacific Northwest home were, at the same time, among the world's most distinctive in making use of their environments. By the time of the first contacts with outsiders in the mid-eighteenth century, they had adapted so effectively over such a long time period that more cultures and languages may have existed there than in any other part of North America.

Differences in settings made cultures more complex along the coast than in the interior, whose harsh environments put the emphasis on survival. Interior peoples had to remain flexible, material possessions often being more of a hindrance than a help. While interior ways of life were similar in many respects to those of indigenous peoples across much of North America, cultures along the Pacific Ocean and the major rivers emptying into it were extremely complex. While summers were given over to fishing and food gathering, the abundance of natural resources meant that rainy winters could be passed indoors engaged in ceremonial activities, artistic creation and socializing. Coastal peoples developed sophisticated social organizations based on inherited rank, accumulated wealth and intricate patterns of sanctioned and prohibited behaviour. Coastal cultures in the Pacific Northwest were in many ways more developed than in any other part of the continent north of Mexico.

Most of the numerous languages that were spoken belonged to language families that knew no borders, indicating, according to specialists, "considerable communication between neighbouring groups" (Silver and Miller, 341). The largest family of languages, being distinguished by few vowels and complex consonant clusters, extends from southern British Columbia through most of Washington and into northern Oregon and Idaho and western Montana. At contact, the Salish or Salishan language family consisted of twenty-three separate languages and within them upwards to seventy-five mutually intelligible dialects. Linguists believe that Salishan speakers initially settled along the mouth of the Fraser River and adjacent waterways, and developed their distinctive ways of speaking as they expanded over time along the Georgia Basin to the north and Puget Sound to the south (Thompson, 692-765). At the other extreme is the Kutenai language, spoken in extreme eastern British Columbia and south into Montana and Idaho, which is not part of a family, indicating cultural isolation through time.

The variety of languages did not prevent ongoing communication. Complex trading relations existed, leading to surprisingly varied local economies. Through interpreters and middle men, such items as mountain goat skins were exchanged for abalone shells, lichen dyes for dried seaweed. It has been estimated that over fifty kinds of trade goods and twenty separate trade routes were in use by 1750 by just the ten thousand Tsimshian living near present-day Prince Rupert along the British Columbian coast (Harris, plates 13–14). Rivalry over control of goods and routes sometimes erupted into conflict and open warfare.

The journals of the first outsiders to cross the Pacific Northwest by land make an important point attesting to indigenous peoples' familiarity with the region far more generally than their own small piece of it. Alexander Mackenzie, the first to do so, recounted how a local man "depicted the lands of three other tribes, in succession, who spoke different languages." Indigenous people assured him that "the way is so often travelled by them that their path is visible throughout the whole journey" and, indeed, Mackenzie was able to follow well-marked trails as he made his way to the coast (Lamb, *Mackenzie*, 314, 319–320, 322). Fifteen years later Simon Fraser would note in his journal:

> I have been for a long period among the Rocky Mountains, but have never seen anything equal to this country. . . . We had to pass where no human being should venture. Yet in those places there is a regular footpath impressed, or rather indented by frequent travelling upon the very rocks. (Lamb, *Fraser*, 96)

Indigenous people in the Pacific Northwest present a double face. Distinctive settings within the region and the distinctive ways of speaking that developed within them separated indigenous people from each other. They were at the same time joined by lines of communication and by a common outlook in the two central realms of the land and spirituality.

CASCADIA ONCE UPON A TIME

The near century between the first intrusions by outsiders in the mid-eighteenth century and the imposition of an international boundary in 1846 may come closest to Cascadia as envisaged by its present-day supporters. The basis of Cascadia once upon a time was economic rather than political.

Cascadia was able to exist for so long as a single entity because no nation cared enough to take control of this distant corner of North America. Even though four countries — Russia, Spain, Britain and the United States — explored the Pacific Northwest's coastline, none claimed exclusive sovereignty over the land mass lying behind it. Russian territorial expansion reached the Pacific Ocean by the early seventeenth century, but today's Alaska was as much as Russia comfortably needed. The Spanish, based in Mexico, made several trips up the coast as far as northern British Columbia during the 1770s but thereafter, except for a brief occupation of Nootka Sound on the west coast of Vancouver Island, limited their colonizing activities to California. While ships from Britain repeatedly ventured along the coast, Britain did not take control either.

Much the same occurred with the young United States, whose ships controlled a coastal fur trade in sea otter pelts, at its height in the early nineteenth century. In the course of this trade, American Robert Gray came upon the mouth of the mighty Columbia River in 1792, being followed by Meriwether Lewis and William Clark's dash across the continent in 1804–1806 and business magnate John Jacob Astor's establishment of a fur trade post on the mouth of the Columbia forming the border between present-day Oregon and Washington in 1811.

About the same time as American interests were moving onto

land, the North West Company out of the British colonial metropolis of Montreal dispatched a trio of partners — Alexander Mackenzie, Simon Fraser and David Thompson — to search out water routes permitting furs acquired east of the continental divide to be taken to market via the Pacific Ocean, and also to establish trading posts. The War of 1812 between Britain and the United States rebounded on the region, but not to the extent that one country or the other was determined to exercise sovereignty. Rather, they agreed in 1818 that the Pacific Northwest would be jointly occupied.

The Hudson's Bay Company (HBC), a private fur trade enterprise based in London, gained economic control of the Pacific Northwest on absorbing the North West Company, which had earlier assumed Astor's claims. For a quarter of a century, from 1821 to 1846, the HBC ran Cascadia as a private fief. The center of operations was Fort Vancouver located near present-day Portland, not far from the older post of Astoria. From there a series of trading posts extended along the coast from northern California to Alaska and inland across the region. In addition to water routes, a brigade trail linked interior to coastal posts.

Not only the HBC's economic reach but the career paths of employees testify to Cascadia as a discrete entity. The handful in charge of the fur trade were English or Scottish, ordinary workers a mix of Orkneymen, French Canadians and indigenous Hawaiians. A typical post contained two or three officers and a dozen to fifteen employees who, in exchange for their hard work, received accommodation, a weekly allowance of basic foodstuffs composed principally of potatoes and salmon or meat, and an annual wage against which they charged such items as clothing and tobacco at the company store. Men virtually never transferred back to fur-trade jobs across the continental divide once they began employment in the Pacific Northwest, and most began their fur-trade careers there. While some returned home at the end of their initial contract, usually of three years' duration, many others remained in the region, eventually settling down in Oregon's Willamette Valley, Fort Victoria on

Vancouver Island, or near their last place of employment. Through the links forged while in the fur trade and with most of them taking indigenous wives, they encouraged a sense of the Pacific Northwest as a single region.

Cascadia once upon a time was an economic enterprise with lifestyle consequences. The Hudson's Bay Company was out for profit, and profit pure and simple. It was not, and had no interest in becoming, a leading edge for political pursuits. It is precisely for this reason that the HBC years make such an important point about the Pacific Northwest. The region was economically coherent and, as indigenous peoples had earlier demonstrated, manageable by water and land across long distances.

NATION LAYERED ON REGION

The layering of nation on region was a slow process. To the extent that Russia, Spain, Britain and the United States initially shared a common goal for the Pacific Northwest, it was to ensure no other nation exercised exclusive sovereignty, but not to do so themselves. Their principal political and economic interests were elsewhere in the world.

Then the United States changed its mind. Virtually from its declaration of independence from Britain in 1776, the United States was ambitious to acquire more territory. The treaty of 1783 with Britain set the new nation's western boundary at the Mississippi River. Two decades later, just as President Thomas Jefferson was dispatching Lewis and Clark across the continent, the United States purchased the Louisiana Territory from France, which doubled its land mass. The War of 1812 dashed hopes that Britain's remaining North American colonies to the north could be absorbed, but did nothing to stifle westward ambitions. The Monroe Doctrine promulgated in 1823 warned outsiders not even to think of colonizing North America, for it was manifest that the United States was destined to have charge of the continent from sea to sea. One prong of manifest destiny looked to California, which would be acquired by force from Spain in 1848, the other to the Pacific Northwest where the Hudson's Bay Company had charge.

This Cascadian vision was not new. As early as 1813 the president responsible for the Lewis and Clark expedition had characterized Astor's post as "the germ of a great, free and independent empire on that side of our continent" (Merk, 596). Thomas Jefferson foresaw a Republic of the Pacific, and others were determined to realize his vision. The 1818 convention following the War of 1812 set a boundary between Britain and the United States at the 49th parallel east of the continental divide, and it seemed only a matter of time before it would be extended west to the Pacific Ocean.

In the interim, Americans took charge on the ground. The earliest settlers to arrive in what became known as the Oregon Territory, essentially the area lying south of the Columbia River and the origin of whose name is obscure, survived largely through Hudson's Bay Company largesse. That reality in no way eased the strong antipathy toward all things British harking back to the struggle for independence from the former mother country, still raw in living memory. The HBC was emblematic of the yoke that the United States had overthrown. One officer explained how "Britishers were looked upon as intruders, without a particle of right to be there" (Shepard, 173). An early settler from the United States recalled sixty years later "having considerable prejudice as an American citizen, against the Hudson's Bay Company and its influences here." Time had not softened his views. "I consider the company the vilest of the vile."[8]

As numbers of American settlers grew during the 1830s, the United States became increasingly possessive. In 1838 a bill was introduced in the Senate calling for military occupation of land west of the Rockies north as far as the Russian boundary at 54° 40'. Three years later an American naval expedition visited the Pacific coast, supposedly for the purposes of scientific exploration but in reality to gather intelligence. Its report gave a detailed description of Hudson's Bay posts, including their defences, and urged military action to secure the entire area between California and Alaska for the United States. One of the 150 arrivals the next year held a commission signed by the US secretary of war appointing him subagent of Indian affairs west of the Rockies; on that basis he confidently assured his fellow settlers that the American government intended to put them under its protection.

A year later, in 1843, the Hudson's Bay Company tacitly acquiesced — hardly surprising, given its interest in the region was wholly economic. In anticipation of an international boundary being set, not as had initially been anticipated along the Columbia River but at the 49th parallel, the company moved its Pacific Northwest headquarters north to a new post of Fort Victoria on Vancouver Island. The same year the US Senate declared the Oregon Territory to be American territory. By then Americans were gearing up for a presidential election in which the Democratic Party looked to manifest destiny for its inspiration. Campaigning on the slogan "54° 40' or Fight!" its candidate James Polk swept into office.

The Treaty of Washington followed in 1846. From the perspective of Britain, with its vast empire stretching across the world, the Pacific Northwest counted for little. The principal concern was to maintain American goodwill at a time when relations with its European neighbours were strained, and the two countries agreed to extend the existing international boundary at 49° westward, with a jog around Vancouver Island, which Britain retained in its entirety. Two years later the area lying south of the Columbia River was given official status as the Oregon Territory.

TWO NATIONS, NOT ONE

The possibility that nation and region could be coterminous did not cease with the establishment of the international boundary in 1846. Without the presence of the Hudson's Bay Company, Britain might well have acquiesced to the most extreme of the American demands. In retrospect it is amazing that the border did not extend to 54° 40' — with the United States acquiring all of Cascadia — than that the division went along 49°. British interest remained minimal, and it would take a quarter-century for the compromise to become irreversible.

Once the international boundary was set, Britain again disengaged. The territory it retained was handed over to the Hudson's Bay Company to administer. The partial exception was Vancouver Island, which was in 1849 made a British colony under HBC oversight. Newcomer settlement remained sparse. At the time of the first census, taken in 1855, Victoria contained about 200 non-indigenous inhabitants. Another 500 lived elsewhere on Vancouver Island, handfuls at the various HBC posts north of the 49th parallel. In sharp contrast, by 1850 the Oregon Territory was home to 13,000 newcomers.

The major event which first threatened to overwhelm and then ensured the survival of a British presence in the Pacific Northwest was a gold rush erupting on the mainland north of the 49th parallel in the spring of 1858. Most of the upwards to 30,000 men who arrived in the hopes of getting rich quick came north from California, whose gold rush, now a decade old, was losing its luster. Their presence seemed to confirm that the United States was still destined to control the entire Pacific coast stretching north from Mexico to Russian America, the future Alaska. Since the Oregon Territory's official creation in 1848, the same year that the United States took charge of California, Americans had moved north of the Columbia. The governor of the new Washington Territory, established in 1853 and named for the first American president, pursued an aggressive settlement policy. Military forts were established at strategic points, and indigenous people unwilling to surrender their land were brutally suppressed.

The situation appeared to be going America's way. Newly arrived miners began passing resolutions that were able to become the pretext to assert sovereignty. The United States rushed a special commissioner to the gold diggings to protect its citizens from supposed harsh treatment by the Hudson's Bay Company. His report to Congress declared it only a matter of time before both Vancouver Island and the mainland came under American control. Indeed, he considered that outcome so certain that no special effort need be made in that direction, unless of course the government wanted to use evidence of HBC harassment as a pretext for intervention.

Britain was forced to act. A bill was introduced into the House of Commons to create a mainland colony, comprising that part of the HBC's fur trade monopoly lying west of the continental divide. Royal consent for the new British colony of British Columbia followed in August 1858. The first choice of name, New Caledonia, which was the Hudson Bay Company's name for its large interior fiefdom, had to be abandoned on learning it had already been given to some French islands in the Pacific Ocean. The second choice of Columbia, in honour of the river, was able to be confused with a region of South America with a variant spelling. In the event, Queen Victoria made the decision by tacking "British" on to Columbia.

The initiative did not stem American interest. Early the next year, 1859, the head of a small detachment of engineers dispatched from England to the mainland colony predicted that it "will be an American Country before long, if not neutralized by the presence of many Englishmen coming out at once" (Ireland, 97–103, 106). The worst fears were soon seemingly confirmed. The international boundary ran through the middle of the channel separating Vancouver Island from the mainland, but no one knew precisely where it was. A fracas on San Juan Island adjacent to Victoria gave the military commander of the Oregon and Washington territories the opportunity he sought. General William Harney reported to the commander-in-chief of the US army:

> The population of British Columbia is largely American and foreigners; comparatively few persons from the British Isles emigrate to this region. The English cannot colonize successfully so near our people; they are too exacting. This, with the pressing necessities of our commerce on this coast, will induce them to yield, eventually, Vancouver's Island to our government. It is as important to the Pacific States as Cuba is to those on the Atlantic. (Richardson, 55)

While the confrontation was soon referred to arbitration, it signalled that Cascadia was still up for grabs.

The subsequent, and final, moment when a single Cascadia might have emerged came in the next decade. By 1866 the gold rush had largely run its course, and Britain for reasons of economy merged its two Cascadian possessions into a single colony of British Columbia. As conditions worsened, there seemed to be three options: continuation as a British colony, annexation to the United States and union with the new Dominion of Canada, which was being formed out of today's Ontario, Quebec and part of the Maritimes. Britain had no more love for its remote possession than it ever had, and union with Canada seemed impossible given the huge intervening distance. That left annexation to the United States. While most early miners had departed, the minority who remained were reinforced by Southern refugees escaping the Civil War. The American consul in Victoria reported enthusiastically that "the people of Vancouver Island, and of British Columbia, are almost unanimous in their desire for annexation to the United States" (Shi, 222).

The timing was propitious. On March 20, 1867, just one day after the Britain confirmed the new Canadian Confederation, the United States purchased Alaska from Russia. Not only was manifest destiny reawakened, but British Columbia was now flanked on two sides by the United States. American Secretary of State William Seward was convinced that "our population is destined to roll its restless waves to the icy barriers of the north."[9] Indeed, among explanations advanced for the sale was Russian inability to maintain Alaska in the face of "the feverish activity and enterprising spirit of Americans."[10]

British Columbians were well aware of the implications, one leading figure later recalling how Americans "boasted they had sandwiched B. Columbia and could eat her up at any time!!!" (Smith, ed., 243). A newspaper characterized the colony's British connection as a "fast sinking ship," whereas the United States was a "gallant new craft, good and strong, close alongside, inviting us to safety and success" (*British Columbian*, May 18, 1867).

Britain itself may have been momentarily tempted to cede its remote possession to the United States. At the time of the Alaska sale, Britain was negotiating with the United States over reparations for having permitted the South to build warships on British territory during the recently concluded Civil War. The US secretary of state proposed to take British Columbia as suitable settlement, but the British demurred on the grounds that the Royal Navy would be deprived of its Pacific base located just outside of Victoria. American claims were eventually submitted to international arbitration.

The American initiative was not yet thwarted. The railroad, one of the most significant practical consequences of the Industrial Revolution, reached the west coast in May 1869, linking San Francisco, British Columbia's gateway to the world, to the eastern United States. The Americans were, moreover, planning a second, more northerly, transcontinental line running just south of the border. The future seemed to belong to the United States.

In August 1869, Secretary of State Seward made a personal reconnaissance to Victoria, where he declared publicly that the Pacific Northwest's common interests would be best served by Oregon, Washington, Alaska and British Columbia joining together into what would have become a version of Cascadia. Back home Seward reported confidently that British Columbians were getting up petitions addressed to Congress in favour of annexation. In the end, two petitions were dispatched, containing 104 signatures. Most of the signatories were Victoria merchants who had come north from California during the gold rush, suggesting that economic stagnation may have played as large a role as pro-American sentiment. While the petitions were mentioned in the American Congress, no further action ensued and the surge abated.

Most importantly, Britain stepped into the breach. Once Confederation became a reality, it concluded that the best course lay in joining its distant possession to the Dominion of Canada as quickly as possible. Britain assisted the new Dominion, over which it exercised close oversight, to buy out the rights of the Hudson's Bay

Company to the immense intervening land mass that lay between British Columbia and Ontario. If still caught between the Americans on the north and south, British Columbia was by 1870 bounded on the east by Canadian territory. Negotiation of terms for British Columbia joining Canada got underway.

The longing by some contemporaries for another option was such that one of the most vocal advocates of British Columbia remaining a British possession toyed briefly with a declaration of independence much as the most fervent advocates of Cascadia do today:

> What do you say to a large English Kingdom here west of the Rocky Mountains. . . . If they despise us at home . . . [can] we be the worse off as an entirely separate Country? . . . All the armies in the World cd not get into the Country if we defended the only passes. . . . I can readily imagine a great future. (Elliot, 68)

For most of the pro-British faction, however, their republican neighbour posed a greater threat than did a parliamentary Dominion loyal to the queen. British Columbia was still a fragile entity, its non-indigenous population in 1870 just over ten thousand, a tenth that of neighbouring Washington and Oregon. Expressions such as "when we get Vancouver's Island" and "when British Columbia belongs to us" remained commonplace south of the border, leading many to believe that only Confederation would prevent the colony from eventually falling into the hands of the Americans (Lady Franklin, 116, 145). In the event, British Columbia was cajoled into Confederation by the promise of a transcontinental rail line and other goodies. The consequence was to ensure that Cascadia would be permanently divided between two nations.

⚘

Attention to Cascadia's history underlines how long-lived is realization of the region's communalities. Indigenous peoples were both joined and divided by spatial and natural attributes. The first outsiders treated the coastline as a single entity, as did the land-based fur trade, with considerable success. The idiosyncrasies of international politics eventually divided the region in half. Even then, for a quarter-century thereafter, the alternative of a single nation continued to exercise appeal.

The international boundary was a political imposition that has, all too often, been allowed to intrude on aspects of everyday lives where it need not do so. The emphasis in much of the writing on the Pacific Northwest on borderlands and on cross-border and trans-border issues takes the border as a given, rather than thinking bravely about what might be. Business scholars Michael A. Goldberg and Maurice D. Levi are among those who do so:

> The historical accidents that shaped the division of the Hudson's Bay Company's Oregon Territory [by the Treaty of Washington in 1846] and that resulted in the purchase of Alaska [in 1867 by the United States from Russia], detached the "Lower Forty-Eight" by a sovereign state in between, have no bearing on the economic realities of the region, which has become known as Cascadia. The national and state borders that cross the land between the Arctic Ocean and Oregon's southern border are simply political artifacts. (Goldberg and Levi, 99)

Political scientist Patrick J. Smith argued in 2002, in reference to Cascadia: "The phenomenon of new, emerging global regions that are simultaneously subnational, bi(or multi)national and international, challenges traditional 'nation-state-centric' notions of territory" (Smith, 114).

Proponents of Cascadia want to focus on the geographical, ecological, economic, spiritual and lifestyle similarities that unite the Pacific Northwest despite an international boundary dividing Oregon and Washington from British Columbia. Cascadia once upon a time was a potent force, just as it has the potential to become again.

CHAPTER 5

⌘

Cascadian Civil Religion from a North American Perspective

MARK SILK

PERMIT ME TO BEGIN with a little personal testimony. I am neither a birthright Cascadian nor a migrant to the region. Until the summer of 2006, my knowledge of the place, apart from a few quick trips to Seattle, came exclusively from the written word. As editor of a series of volumes on religion in the public life of each of eight regions of the United States, I had learned something about what we Americans call the Pacific Northwest and its distinctive ethos. I was aware that "the environment" was a concept with more moral throw-weight there than elsewhere — that it was not merely one among many public policy rubrics but the pre-eminent cause and *casus belli* of the region's socio-economic life.

Yet book learning, as Bernard of Clairvaux pointed out back in the twelfth century, only takes one so far. A couple of weeks travelling in and around Puget Sound may not have done for me what the trip to Damascus did for St. Paul, but it did have considerable force. It was not just the encounter with the massive trees of the Olympic Peninsula, including the huge "bones" flung hither and yon where the rivers meet the Pacific, that knocked me into another state of consciousness. Equally, I experienced desecration more powerfully than I ever had before at the sight of the swaths of clear-cut land, the twisted roots and stumps rising up out of the ground like victims of some hideous massacre. Was I ready to take the pledge? To get up off the anxious bench and make my way down the sawdust trail to acknowledge the gospel of biodiversity? Well, perhaps not quite. But I learned something about how the physical landscape has shaped the culture of Cascadia. That's not nothing.

Here, my aim is to put Cascadia's distinctive spirituality into a larger context, in an attempt both to consider whether this elusive utopia has something to offer by way of a model for North America and to make a few points about the meaning of a civil religion that is not only regional but (whether Cascadians like it or not) binational. Our Religion by Region project was designed to get at how religion relates to the public culture — including the politics and public policies — of each of the regions we studied. In the United States, there has been an increasing readiness to recognize the continuing significance of region: witness the ubiquity of the red-and-blue maps of the 2000 and 2004 presidential elections.

While I am wary of exaggerating the case, I do think that, more than anything else, what accounts for regional differences in America today are religious differences, both in terms of the sectarian layout and the extent of religious affiliation. How these religious differences make themselves felt in public life has to do with many factors — historical, geographic, cultural and economic. But however one weighs the factors, any attempt to discern the character of each region must take religion into account. Let me offer a few examples focusing on how religion shapes political culture.

NEW ENGLAND: By way of settling the bitter conflict between Irish Catholics and Yankees in the nineteenth century, there came to be a tacit agreement to keep religion out of electoral politics. When a politician running for national office like Vermont's Howard Dean or Massachusetts' John Kerry says he is uncomfortable speaking about religion on the stump because he is from New England, people in the rest of the country tend to hear this as a statement that religion does not mean much to them. In fact, what they are saying is precisely the case: New England politicians do not do religion on the stump. The recent exception to this rule is Connecticut Senator Joe Lieberman. An Orthodox Jew, Lieberman talked about religion like a Southern evangelical in campaigning around the country for the vice-presidency in 2000. Yet Lieberman has never campaigned that way when running for office in Connecticut. It is simply not done. Running for the presidency in 1960, John F. Kennedy denied that religion would influence his conduct in office, not only because he was a Roman Catholic who needed to reassure Protestants that he would not be taking orders from the pope. He was also articulating a point of view characteristic of his region.

MIDDLE ATLANTIC: This region, powerfully shaped by continuing immigration, follows something of a European model, in which religion becomes a powerful marker of communal identity — defining people by tribes: Irish and Italians (Catholic), Jews (ethnic as well as religious), African Americans (Protestants), WASPS, and so on. This was the vision articulated by Will Herberg in his highly influential book *Protestant Catholic Jew* (1955), which contended that ethnicity was being subsumed into the religious plurality of a "triple melting pot." Only in the Middle Atlantic — really, only in New York City — could you make a demographically plausible claim that the country was divisible in this way. It was an image of the country seen, *à la* the famous *New Yorker* cover, from the vantage of Manhattan.

MIDWEST: The vast Midwest is where the US comes together. It is a place with the largest political deviations — from deep red states like Kansas and Nebraska to the deep-blue state of Illinois to the swingiest of swing states — Ohio, Michigan, Wisconsin, and Iowa. Although it is far from the most religiously diverse region, it is the region where the country's main religious players all have strong hands to play. It owes much of its public character to Methodism, the evangelical-turned-mainline Protestant tradition that emphasizes personal spiritual discipline (like the more conservative evangelical denominations) and social reform (like the liberal mainline denominations). The ideal of community matters a lot in this region. In 2006, Keith Ellison, who converted to Islam as a nineteen-year-old in his native Detroit, won in the fifth district of Minnesota (Minneapolis and St. Paul) with the help of Muslims among a coalition of liberal anti-war voters. "We were able to bring in Muslims, Christians, Jews, Buddhists," he said after the election. "We brought in everybody."

PACIFIC: This region is dominated by California, though it also includes Hawaii and Nevada (most of whose population lives within ten miles of the California border). Here we point to a style of spiritual individualism that is in some ways the antithesis of the Middle Atlantic ethos. Take the case of Madonna's highly publicized involvement with Kabbalah, the Jewish mystical tradition. In the Middle Atlantic states, the question often posed was, "Has Madonna converted to Judaism?" In other words, has she changed tribes? In California, that was not considered relevant. Madonna's involvement in Kabbalah — and her adoption of the name Esther — was simply understood as part of her (current) spiritual practice.

SOUTHERN CROSSROADS: This region, comprising Louisiana, Arkansas, Missouri, Texas and Oklahoma (what historians call "the Old Southwest") has a remarkable history of contentiousness. We called the subtitle of the volume "Showdown States," and the ethos of the region involves conflict over religion as well as just about anything else. It is also the region that has been the crucible of Pentecostalism — which is descended from Methodism and retains a good deal of that tradition's readiness to remake the world according to its own lights. Meanwhile, Crossroads Baptists were heavily influenced by Landmarkism, which was based on the idiosyncratic view that the Baptists were not Protestants but rather represented a strain of Christianity that stretched directly back to John the Baptist. In place of traditional Baptist adherence to strict separation of church and state, Landmarkism substituted a hyper-patriotic Christian republicanism that saw America representing a godly society that would be a light unto the nations. Can there be any doubt that the presidency of George W. Bush is an expression of Crossroads religiosity?

∽

Rather than go through the other regions — the Mountain West along with that part of the South east of the Mississippi (we call it just "the South"), let me briefly indicate one of the ways the regional characteristics I have outlined have affected American culture as a whole, and that is the evolving national approach to religious pluralism since World War II, including questions relating to separation of church and state.

After the war, the country bought into the Middle Atlantic model of separate religious communities as a way of creating a united front against a common "atheistic" foe during the Cold War. Then New England had its day, during the brief Kennedy-era high watermark of religious separationism, emblemized by Supreme Court decisions on school prayer and Bible reading. This was succeeded, from the late sixties into the 1980s, by a Pacific version of spiritual individualism — if you will, the US conceived as the nation of spiritual seekers studied by sociologist Wade Clark Roof. And since the rise of the Christian Right, we have increasingly been afflicted with the

influence of what might be called Crossroads ecumenical fundamentalism: evangelicals, traditionalist Catholics and Orthodox
Jews allied against the forces of secularism, liberalism, relativism
and, one must say, militant Islam. I'm not suggesting here that one
region's style dominates the thinking of all Americans, but rather
that a given style comes to the fore nationally *from some place* —
often but not always thanks to particular political figures like Jack
Kennedy or George W. Bush.

To what extent do these regional beliefs and attitudes deserve to
be conceptualized into something more concrete — an ethos or
even a civil religion? In the case of the South (however precisely
defined), separate national identity during the Civil War and the
memory of it created what can unquestionably be considered a
civil religion of the Lost Cause, about which the co-editor of our
South volume, Charles Reagan Wilson, has written eloquently. Yet
there is no reason to expect that all should be equally distinctive
and pronounced. From where I sit, Cascadia does seem to have
something like its own civil religion. But before saying why, let me
take a moment to define the term. According to the Italian historian
Emilio Gentile, civil religion is

> the conceptual category that contains the forms of sacralization of a
> political system that guarantee a plurality of ideas, free competition
> in the exercise of power, and the ability of the governed to dismiss
> their governments through peaceful and constitutional methods.
> Civil religion therefore respects individual freedom, coexists with
> other ideologies, and does not impose obligatory and unconditional
> support for its commandments. (Gentile, xv)

The problem with such a definition, when applied to a region —
especially a binational region — is that in such a case there is no
obvious *political system* that is being sacralized. The American
South *once* had a political system: "The South will rise again" is an
irredentist national slogan if ever there was one. One can also, or
could once, in the United States, identify the civil religion of a given
state. In my own state of Connecticut, a civil religion was devised in

the nineteenth century around the story of the Charter Oak — a tree in Hartford where, in 1687, the leaders of the Connecticut colony hid their 1662 charter to protest incorporation into a single New England colonial entity. (If you look at the 1999 Connecticut quarter, you'll find the Charter Oak splendidly engraved on the reverse.) The most that can be said about Cascadia in this regard is that, from time to time, its devotees have entertained hopes of its becoming a single political system. Its civil religion exists by way of theological expectation, a millenarian hope on the part of the citizens of a New Cascadian Jerusalem.

But if there is a Cascadian civil religion in *this* world rather than the world to come, what exactly *is* being sacralized? Presumably it is the land of Cascadia itself. America has a history of doing this sort of thing. A twentieth-century evocation may be found in Robert Frost's World War II–era poem "The Gift Outright," which begins, "The land was ours before we were the land's." What was required was that we Americans make ourselves independent of England.

> Something we were withholding made us weak
> Until we found out that it was ourselves
> We were withholding from our land of living,
> And forthwith found salvation in surrender.

The revolutionary act was thus surrender to the land — a sort of collective hitting of the sawdust trail to accept America as our personal Lord and Saviour. Canadians, of course, never made such a surrender, least of all in *British* Columbia. For this and other reasons, they have been seen as civil religiously challenged — for example by Andrew Kim in a 1993 article, "The Absence of Pan-Canadian Civil Religion" (Kim, 257–275). Regionalism, biculturalism, English sovereignty — these have made it difficult for Canada to create the kind of civil religious paraphernalia and mentality that can be found in most other Western nation states. That might be a good thing from the standpoint of Cascadian identity, for to the extent that national civil religions trump those of subordinate political units, there has never been, on the Canadian side of the border, the kind of barrier to regional particularity that was to be found on the American side — up to a point.

For in fact, Cascadian history reveals a good deal of melding of the two national realities. Here, for example, is how Brebner characterizes what happened when thousands of American gold rushers flooded into British Columbia in the late 1850s: "American institutions were accepted, but British sovereignty was maintained and all men treated equally." On the civil religious front, "Nobody bothered about the frequent displays of the American flag or the Californian custom of wearing a revolver on one hip and a bowie knife on the other, for both practices died a natural death" (Brebner, 177–178).

So much for Yankee obstreperousness. It is telling that ecological realities — the thirst for mineral wealth and the great watershed of the Columbia — created this intermingling of national cultures in the first place. Without lingering on the importance of the environment in the region, let me simply state *ex cathedra* that if there is a Cascadian civil religion, then it centers on beliefs and practices relating to ecological activism, concern and belief. That is the sacred umbrella that hangs over the denizens of the place — though to be sure, there are recusants (as civil religion *à la* Gentile permits), be they clear-cutters and strip-miners or evangelical Protestants. That this civil religion extends beyond environmental issues narrowly defined can be seen, as our Pacific Northwest volume makes clear, in the language that was used to rationalize physician-assisted suicide in Oregon. It is language that talks about the practice in terms of natural processes, not technological efficiency (Killen and Silk).

If Cascadia has so robust a civil religion, what are the prospects that it might, like other regional civil religions, extend its geographical influence? Here, it seems to me, we should take Stephen Colbert's apothegm, "Oregon is California's Canada," more seriously than he perhaps intended. I understand that British Columbians feel distant and alien from the rest of Canada, especially from that part of Canada that is closest to them. But without putting too fine a point on it, and from my possibly too-distant American perspective, the Cascadian thing is more Canadian in character than it is American. The centrality of natural resources to the history and existential reality of the region is more Canadian than American. The region's connection to the larger Pacific Rim is more Canadian than American. The weakness of institutional religion in the region is more Canadian than American. And the public posture of the region seems more Canadian than American. Take the 2004 election, in which a plurality of Northwest voters — 31 percent, more than twice the national average and far more than any other American region — named Iraq as the issue that mattered most to them when they cast their vote for president. In opposing the war, as well as in other ways, Oregonians and Washingtonians seem more Canadian than American. Where else in America would we find a bumper sticker reading "US out of . . ." this place?

Still, in the US, there are a few signs that the region may be becoming less of an outlier. Religious "Nones" have been on the rise — from 7 to 14 percent of the population between 1990 and 2001. As of 2006, Americans appeared to have turned decisively against the Bush administration's Iraqi venture. No small thanks to Al Gore, global warming seems to have crept into the American national consciousness, with even Republican governors like Schwarzenegger of California and Crist of Florida undertaking to make up for the failure of the Bush administration to acknowledge that something must be done. On the other hand, binationalism seems utterly alien to the current American mood, as witnessed by the revival of nativism in the form of opposition to comprehensive immigration legislation. In short, straws in the wind there may be, but the idea that America will any time soon embrace the ethos of Cascadia still needs to be kept in the usual category of Cascadian utopianism.

What does seem likely, from the vantage of the 2008 presidential election campaign, is that the sway of the Southern Crossroads is coming to an end. What is next for America? In the regional sweepstakes, my money is on the Midwest: a region that sets a high stock

on religion but is not unpleasant about it; that privileges communi-
ty-building over showdowns; that manages to be at once inclusive
and very American. But that is a story for another day.

CHAPTER 6

⚮

Secular Utopias Versus Religious Credos — One Cascadia or More?

PHILIP RESNICK

IN HIS *PHILOSOPHY OF HISTORY*, Hegel writes: "America is a country of the future. . . . It is a country of hope for all who loathe the storehouse of history contained in the Old Europe" (Mate, 101). The contributors to this volume on *Cascadia: The Elusive Utopia* may want to bear Hegel's prophecy in mind as we grapple with the subject we have set ourselves.

Before the coming of the Europeans in the aftermath of Columbus's voyages and those of subsequent explorers, North America was homeland to aboriginal peoples with their own nature-derived religious and spiritual credos. It was the European settlers — be they Spanish, Portuguese, French, British or Dutch — who brought Christianity in its Catholic and Protestant versions to the New World.

There was a strongly religious motivation, along with the search for gold and silver, to the Spanish conquest of Mexico and of South America. The conversion of the natives and their treatment by their colonizers loomed large in debates such as the famous one that pitted Bartolomé de las Casas against Gines Sepulveda in 1550–1551.[1] There was a religious motivation as well to the colonization of New France and to the role played by the Jesuit missions. In the case of New England and other British colonies, there was less concern with the conversion of the natives than with the attempt to realize dreams of a new Jerusalem unrealized back home. The language of John Winthrop's "city on the hill" speaks to the underlying ethos of Puritans and Quakers setting out for the new world, much as does John Edwards' call for a "Great Awakening" in the early eighteenth century (Hollinger and Capper). This in turn could give life to the American civic credo in the centuries that followed the American Revolution and the founding of the United States. In Conrad Cherry's words: "The history of the American civil religion is a history of the conviction that the American people are God's New Israel, his newly chosen people. The belief that America has been elected by God for a special destiny in the world has been the focus of American sacred ceremonies, the inaugural addresses of our presidents, the sacred scriptures of the civil religion. It has been so pervasive a motif in the national life that the word 'belief' does not really capture the dynamic role that it has played for the American people, for it passed into the 'realm of motivational myths'" (Cherry, 129).

As settlement moved westwards, so did the underlying religious institutions cultivated on the Atlantic Seaboard. Sects proliferated, with new ones being forged out of the wilderness, such as Seventh-day Adventists and Mormons. Immigrants also brought their religious institutions with them, as they came to the New World, from Mennonites to Doukhobors, from Lutherans to Pentecostals. There was a regional reality to the religious map of North America, with more established religions, such as Episcopalian, Anglican and

Catholic in the East and a greater fluidity of sects in the West.

Another element was at work in the settling of North America — the notion of new beginnings, of a promised land, of manifest destiny. This could take economic, political or cultural forms, finding inspiration in the geography, geology and natural habitat of the New World. The utopian sense of beginning the world anew was present in the original American colonies of settlement, but even more so in the Midwest and West. One thinks of Frederick Jackson Turner's frontier thesis of 1893,[2] and of the lore of the west, from cowboys and Indians to vast plains and West Coast Eldorados, in both American and Canadian popular culture.

At the political level, populism found a home in the middle and western parts of North America. Farmer-based movements of the turn of the twentieth century took root there, as did anti-monopoly sentiment, and the pressure for new forms of grassroots democracy like the initiative or recall. These gained strong support in states like Oregon or California, much less bound to older, establishment patterns of politics than states in the east. In Canada, too, support for grassroots democracy proved a good deal stronger in Western Canada than in the East. One thinks of political parties and movements like the United Farmers of Alberta, Social Credit, the CCF, and the Reform Party of Canada. The same pattern holds true down to today, with the recent example of the Citizens' Assembly on Electoral Reform established in B.C. in 2003–2004 with two delegates, one male one female, chosen at random from each of the province's seventy-nine ridings to deliberate on alternatives to the first-past-the-post electoral system. It is the public at large through a referendum as in 2005 (and again in 2009) that will determine the fate of the Assembly's proposed single transferable ballot reform.

The West was also the birthplace of radical trade unionism — the International Workers of the World, the One Big Union, the Winnipeg General Strike and Seattle General Strikes of 1919. So radical was Washington State's political tradition that it led Jim Farley, the Democratic National Chairman in the 1930s, to coin his famous quip about "the forty-seven states and the Soviet of Washington." The Socialist Party of Canada found a home in B.C. in the early twentieth century, electing members to the provincial legislature. Its adherents were labelled "Impossiblists" by their opponents, denoting their extreme opposition to capitalism as an economic system. Subsequently, the CCF and the NDP acquired deep roots in B.C., and the province was the scene of a general strike in the public sector in the autumn of 1983 at a time of polarized conflict between a Social Credit provincial government committed to neo-conservative reforms and trade unions and social activists organized in the Solidarity Movement (Magnusson et al).

The political reality of the Pacific Northwest today, as in the past, is of culturally divided polities. In the contemporary period this translates into smaller centers in the interior with strongly religious and conservative outlooks, and metropolitan centers on the coast such as Vancouver, Seattle and Portland with more secular and liberal values. This is reflected in voting patterns in recent decades with smaller town, suburban and rural areas in B.C., Washington, and Oregon voting for Alliance, Reform, the Conservatives or the Republicans as the case may be, and the urban coast equally strongly, voting Liberal, NDP or for the Democratic Party. It makes sense, at one level, to talk about two B.C.'s, two Washingtons and two Oregons, rather than one — though the divisions do not run quite as neatly along territorial divides as the metaphor might suggest.

The inhabitants of the Pacific Northwest's coastal cities are open to radical ideas about the environment — Greenpeace was a Vancouver creation — about lifestyle, sexual choice and new spiritual beliefs. The big cities have become multicultural, Pacific Rim cities, staking out their own place as secondary centers of importance in a global world. Their hinterlands seem far away — when it comes to values, even more than in spatial terms.

The inhabitants of non-coastal areas hue more closely to traditional beliefs. Religion matters more to them, as do conservative family values. Nor are they comfortable with radical versions of environmentalism, with aboriginal rights, with gun control, or with the cosmopolitan turn that globalization may bring.

For all the talk about Cascadia in this volume, it is worth pointing out that in the State of Washington it is common to evoke the Cascade Curtain that divides eastern Washington from the coast. "The East-West divide of the Cascade Curtain has long been Washington's homegrown version of the red state–blue state divide that is the current darling of the national punditry. The East looks to the West, and sees arrogant urban liberals; the West thinks of its neighbours to the East as dim-witted rural conservatives. From time to time, a handful of legislators and citizens seriously propose splitting the state in two" (de Place). So it is a shade ironic to advance the term Cascadia as a term connoting cross-border regional unity, when it is so often a term underlining intra-state division just south of the 49th parallel!

Nonetheless, the term Cascadia has been around since the early 1990s, as one way of describing a geographically driven version of regionalism. For its leading promoters "[Cascadia] is a shared notion, and one in active evolution. We're still inventing ourselves as a regional culture. Cascadia is a recognition of emerging realities, a way of celebrating commonality with diversity. . . . Cascadia is not a State, but a state of mind. But a state of mind can have important practical consequences" (Schell and Chapman, 7).

The Pacific Northwest does, for certain purposes, constitute a distinct region of North America, located on the Pacific Coast, with a rainforest climate. At first, British Columbia, Washington and Oregon were overwhelmingly resource-based economies, with lumber, salmon, coal and hard-rock mining dominating; by the time of World War II, they had developed a significant manufacturing sector, and in recent decades, they have evolved into high-tech and service-oriented economies as well. Boeing, Microsoft, Starbucks and Nike come to mind.

At the cultural level, there seem to be certain themes that cross the border: a Pacific Rim orientation, for example, with a fusion of populations, cuisine and culture; an environmental orientation; a liberal set of social values, at least on the coast; a more experimental attitude to religious and spiritual beliefs; a very North American-type belief in the future, rather than in the past. Here I am in closer agreement with many of the contributors to this volume regarding the spiritual basis of a Cascadian mentality, if not quite a civic religion!

For it is nature — the coastal mountains and Douglas firs, for example — that provide a common denominator for many who live in this geographical region. It provides a sense of regional identity when setting B.C. off from the rest of Canada or the Pacific Northwest states from the rest of the Union. And it helps impart an understanding of its inhabitants' place in the larger physical world and of their responsibility for the preservation of its ecosystem into the future. In some ways, the Pacific Northwest/Cascadia is the most utopian of North America's regions, the one where a belief in new beginnings and remaking the world afresh is most firmly embedded. This is reinforced by the fact that so many of its inhabitants have come here from elsewhere — be it from other parts of Canada or the US, or be it from abroad.

Can one, however, speak of the Pacific Northwest as a civilizational constellation, with a distinct merger of European, indigenous and Asian streams? At times, some have seen the region as the last hope of Western civilization, praising it for its excellent public schools, its open political system and its competent politicians.[3] Others have looked to the region as a potential bridge between Asia Pacific and North America. Others would emphasize the urban liveability of the region's cities, when compared to cities elsewhere in North America or beyond. Still others would define the region as showing a penchant for the experimental, for a casting off of familiar bonds and ties.

It is this future-orientedness that I would highlight in distinguishing Cascadia/the Pacific Northwest from most every other region of North America. But this can easily have its own downside. Let me cite from an interview with Douglas Coupland, author of *Generation X* and most recently *JPod:*

> The past? I don't want to see the past. I want to see the future. I need to see 100 years into the future. I get very jealous of the future, because I know I'm not going to be around. The future — what, of this view, will there be? Will it all be charred stumps? Or more of the same but, say, no trees? Or more trees but something else new, for good, or to worry about? What's it going to be? Time is going so fucking fast. After 40, it's just . . . hell, I'm not going to see it, see that future, and that angers me. Frankly, it angers me.[4]

There is a good deal of narcissism and spleen to Coupland's perorations, but what concretely do they signify? A heightened sense of self, on a continent where individualism already runs rampant? Potty-mouthiness as an expression of one's primordial self? A sudden realization that we too are mortal, each generation no more immune from the depredations of time than all those that have come before or that will follow?

One looks in vain for intonations regarding the wisdom of the past — secular or religious — from writers such as Coupland. It is as though the metaphysical dimensions of human existence have given way to a high-tech or science fiction world where *carpe diem* reigns. And it can leave us spiritually impoverished as a result, so that even the sight of soaring Douglas firs and snow-capped mountains can fail us in the breach. Certainly, there is no Cascadian public philosophy here that can even begin to match the futuristic claims sometimes made for the region when it comes to ecology, economics or technology.

Where the past often overwhelms the present in much of Asia, the Middle East or Europe, where it is a major ongoing presence in Eastern Canada (the Maritimes and Ontario with their Loyalist heritage, Quebec with its motto *je me souviens*), where one finds it on the American eastern seaboard, from New England to the Deep South — it progressively weakens as one moves westwards on the continent. Too much present- and future-mindedness, too little history: Is that the fate of being a Cascadian? Is it an identity the inhabitants of this region would be comfortable to adopt? So here is one good reason to be cautious about embarking on a vessel named Cascadia.

But there are others. As I have already pointed out, there is no unanimity of views within each of the region's constituent units. For example, a full 35 percent of British Columbians, according to the 2001 census, claimed that they had no religious affiliation, by far the highest percentage in Canada. But significant numbers in places like the Fraser Valley or the Okanagan had evangelical leanings, reflected in voting patterns both at the provincial and federal levels. These British Columbians would feel far greater affinity with their evangelical, or religious fundamentalist, counterparts in non-coastal Washington and Oregon than with the denizens of Seattle, Portland or Eugene. Would their Cascadia be the same as that of their urban counterparts? Hardly.

Then there is the political reality that binds B.C. to Canada and Washington and Oregon to the US. The histories of our two countries are not identical; nor are our political institutions; nor is the role that each of us plays in the world. True, we are both in North America, and despite differences on a range of issues over time, we have managed to cohabit in peace and relative harmony. And there is NAFTA, an agreement that for certain purposes speaks to a larger continental identity. But there is little political will to forge a single North American community, not only where the US and Mexico are concerned (note the impassioned debate about Mexican immigration now sweeping the US), but also where the US and Canada are concerned (for example, accusations from the American right that Canada is a haven for terrorists seeking entry into the US, or deep-rooted Canadian opposition to the Bush administration's war in Iraq). What is true at the national level is also true at the regional one. The Cascadia lobby, despite occasional attempts in the past, has never really gotten off the ground. Vancouver and Seattle are as often in competition with one another — for example, as gateways to the Pacific — as in alignment. B.C.'s and the Pacific Northwest's softwood lumber industries do not see eye to eye when it comes to tariffs on Canadian exports to the US. The region's tourist industries seek their own particular advantage when it comes to cruise ship marketing or most anything else.

What we are left with is a sense of place that for certain purposes generates a sense of a common physical reality — the Coastal Mountains, the Gulf and Juan de Fuca islands, the Pacific — and of a plasticity and openness characteristic of newly settled societies. And those societies have room both for utopian experimentation and secular liberal values, side by side with more traditional and religiously conservative values.

I began by invoking Hegel and his vision of America as history's ultimate hope. Let me conclude by invoking the leading German philosopher of our day, Jürgen Habermas. In January 2004, in a notable exchange with Cardinal Ratzinger, now Pope Benedict XVI, Habermas, a secularist much like myself, stressed the need for the liberal state "to treat with care all cultural sources on which the normative consciousness and solidarity of citizens draws. . . . In sacred writings and religious traditions, intuitions of sin and redemption, of deliverance from a life experienced as unholy, have been articulated, subtly spelt out and kept alive through interpretation over millennia. . . ."[5]

We need some of that same openness to dialogue across the religious-secular divide here in Cascadia, or across the liberal-conservative one, so that the two Cascadias become less estranged from one another. We need a greater openness to the accumulated wisdom of the past, despite our physical distance both from Europe and from Asia, and our civilizational distance from aboriginal cultures. Cascadia may be a distinct region of North America, but its inhabitants are no less marked by the metaphysical riddles of existence than the inhabitants of civilizations that have come before.

This is why we will need to do better than simply invoking Cascadia as a mantra for an alternative west-coast lifestyle. We may become more sensitive ecologically than our predecessors, as well we should. We may, with time, learn to live with less, because the Earth cannot sustain the kind of ecological footprint we and our fellow humans, especially — though not exclusively — in the Western world, currently require. We may develop deeper cultural and spiritual formulations for the kind of existence we seek to map out for ourselves in this particular corner of the continent and of the planet. But we also need to cultivate modesty, rather than hubris, in our endeavour, something that religion in its more ecumenical guise and a due reverence for nature can help instill. Let us attempt to imagine new beginnings, knowing at the same time that B.C. and the Pacific Northwest may not be the harbingers of secular — or religious fundamentalist — utopias here on Earth.

Part Three

✍

CASCADIAN NATURE

CREATING UTOPIA. Cascadia, which many consider an experimental "last frontier," has long drawn idealists bent on creating utopian communities. Prominent Indian yogi Bhagwan Shree Rajneesh drew thousands of well-off North Americans to his free-love-promoting commune in northern Oregon during the 1980s. It fell apart largely because of the Bhagwan's self-absorption and controversial love of Rolls-Royces.

RADICAL COMMUNITIES. The pacifist Sons of Freedom Doukhobors escaped persecution in Russia and moved to the mountains of B.C. Radically anti-materialist, some in the 1960s stripped off their clothes and burned down the buildings of Doukhobors they believed too worldly. While some alternative communities in Cascadia are considered flaky, others have matured and flourished.
(Photo Credit: George Diack, *Vancouver Sun*)

ECKHART TOLLE IN THE MOMENT. The religiously unattached
people of Cascadia are often lured to new forms of "non-exclusive"
spirituality. After glowing praise from Oprah Winfrey, Vancouver
spiritual teacher Eckhart Tolle has sold millions of copies of his books,
The Power of Now and *A New Earth*. Tolle teaches that the self is
sacred and seekers can attain enlightenment by living in the moment.
(Photo Credit: Steve Bosch, *Vancouver Sun*)

CASCADIAN GURUS. Oregon's Neale Donald Walsh (see above), author of the best-selling *Conversations with God*, teaches that social change will occur once humans raise their consciousness. Walsh does not offer a political strategy. The contentious documentary linking science and religion — *What the Bleep Do We Know!?* — was made by filmmakers who follow the noted Washington State psychic channeler, J.Z. Knight.

ABORIGINAL SPIRITUALITY. For thousands of years the indigenous people of what is now called Cascadia did not conceive of invisible borders on maps. They shared traditions that made no distinction between the sacred and profane, explain Jean Barman, Mike Carr and Eli Bliss Enns. These Bella Coola dancers, wearing "Crooked Raven Masks of Heaven," reflected in 1886 how aboriginals experienced kinship with the land and spiritual power in all things. (Photo Credit: City of Vancouver Archives, Number P30)

CAPTAIN VANCOUVER. Two cities in Cascadia are named after
the English ship captain who charted this spectacular coastline
of the Pacific Ocean in the 1790s. Marvelling at the region's
magnificence, Vancouver and other explorers, such as
David Thompson, opened up the Pacific Northwest for
economic and religious outsiders who almost
overwhelmed indigenous cultures.

"THE REPUBLIC OF THE PACIFIC." US President Thomas Jefferson dispatched Meriwether Lewis and William Clark to the region in 1804 to establish "The Republic of the Pacific," which the president thought should include what is now B.C. In one of the first dreams of a freestanding Cascadia, Jefferson idealized the idyllic new nation as "a great free and independent empire."

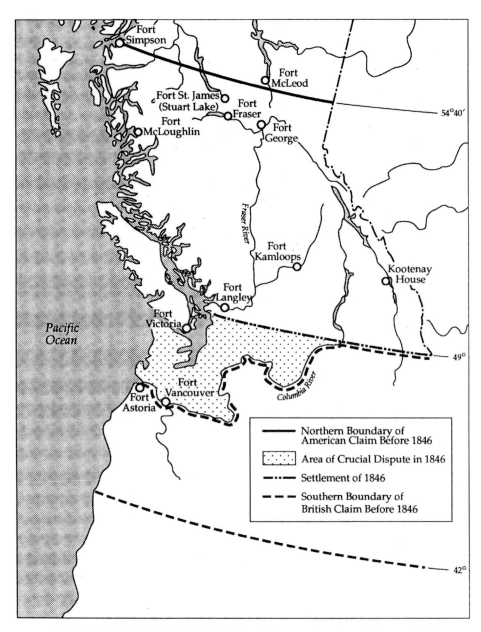

EARLY CONFLICT OVER BORDERS. The US came close to gaining control of British Columbia in the mid-1800s, writes Jean Barman. Instead, the international border that was delicately negotiated in 1846 has prevailed. For good and ill, the border has politically divided a vast region that many say has a surprising degree of historical, geographic, economic, cultural and spiritual cohesion. (Courtesy of Jean Barman)

CHAPTER 7

༄

Geography, Spirituality and Social Change in Cascadia: A Bioregional Perspective

MIKE CARR

LONG BEFORE I CAME to this part of the planet, which some call Cascadia, I was attracted by the promise of mountains meeting the ocean. The beauty of this place that is now my home, the lower Fraser Basin where the Northern Cascades meet up with the Coastal Mountains, is breathtaking. I arrived here over twenty-five years ago at the beginning of summer. For three months I roamed the many spectacular beaches of the delta which hosts the city of Vancouver, British Columbia, drinking in this truly magical place with all my senses.

A few years later, I met David McCloskey, bioregional mapper, poet and professor in the Department of Sociology at Seattle University at the third Continental Congress of the North American Bioregional movement in 1988. David McCloskey has probably wandered over more territory in Cascadia than anyone. His maps and many slides, which he has presented at various bioregional gatherings, including the Third Cascadia Bioregional Congress I attended in 1991, testify to the incredible natural diversity and beauty of Cascadia. When I visited McCloskey in Seattle about a year later, we had quite some time to discuss his vision of Cascadia. Cascadia as a bioregion is connected by a number of key characteristics.

The name Cascadia refers to the fact that the series of large river basins west of McCloskey's eastern boundary, the continental divide (marked by the Rocky Mountain Range), all drain into the North Pacific Ocean. Cascadia is made up of the complex jigsaw puzzle of these waters flowing down their respective watersheds to the sea: from the Copper and Alsek rivers in the far north, to the Klamath, Snake, Salmon and Eel rivers in the far south. Other major watersheds include the Stikine, the Skeena, the Fraser, the Columbia and the Willamette. Cascadia is a mix of biomes from coastal temperate rainforests (the largest in the world), dry interior plateaus and desert lands, all amidst a series of mountain ranges from the Rockies in the east to the Coast Mountains and the Cascade Mountains on the Pacific side. The coastal rainforests range from the subpolar and the perhumid rainforests in the north to the seasonal rainforests ranging approximately from the northern end of Vancouver Island to northern California, where they join coastal redwood forests. In the interior of Cascadia there are cold winter deserts and mixed mountain systems. Below all this lies the Cascadia tectonic plate and the continental shelf under the Pacific Ocean, the Cascadia Shelf.

The coastal rainforests of Cascadia are shaped by the cycling of water between the land and the sea. The forests influence the abundance and distribution of coastal sea life, and, in return, species such as the salmon bring forest-nourishing marine nutrients back into the forests of Cascadia where they are further distributed by the bears and eagles that eat the salmon. The forests and the ocean also shaped the indigenous peoples up and down the coast for millennia. The wet coastal influence penetrates far into the interior as the rain-laden weather systems hit interior mountain ranges, dropping still-significant rainfalls. Consequently, certain interior valleys such as the Slocan Valley in B.C. also support many coastal tree and plant species adapted to the wet temperate pattern. The salmon too penetrate deep into the interior waters of eastern Cascadia. Salmon were (and still are in many cases, especially in British Columbia) the major food supply of many of the indigenous peoples of Cascadia, both on the coast and in the interior. Many indigenous peoples regarded the salmon as people, and due respect was paid to the salmon people through First Salmon ceremonies.

Cascadia is a land of cedars, firs, hemlocks, spruce and pine; sage and bunchgrass; eagles and ravens; bears, coyotes and cougars; orcas, seals, sea lions, dolphins and humpback whales. The rugged relief of the far north creates a steep climate gradient that confines the forest to a narrow coastal strip which marks the northern tip of Cascadia. To the south, the many long fjords of south-eastern Alaska and the central B.C. coast penetrate far inland expanding the width of the coastal forest zone as the rainforest follows the fjords inland. Most of all perhaps, Cascadia is a land of falling waters, of huge rivers emptying into the Pacific. These cascading waters gave Cascadia its name, as McCloskey explained to me on that bright sunny afternoon in Seattle so many years ago. Still, even today Cascadia is a land nourished and held together by the sacred salmon cycle.

In this chapter, I now present my understanding of bioregional Earth-centered spirituality, then discuss why I think bioregional spirituality has a deeply geographical dimension and illustrate my case with examples from Cascadia, both native and non-native. Finally, I make the case that, for a truly sustainable Cascadia, our society needs a new story, a new Earth-centered root metaphor for humanity that replaces the dominant and failing capitalist growth story.

However, before beginning my task, and because the bioregional movement and bioregional social, cultural and political thought may be unfamiliar to readers, I begin with a brief orienting introduction to bioregionalism.

In "Bioregionalism and Civil Society: Democratic Challenges to Corporate Globalism" (2004), I argue that bioregionalism as a place-specific cultural, social and community-based economic movement within civil society presents a challenging alternative model to an unsustainable corporate world order. Industrial consumer capitalism's root metaphor — unending economic growth and material expansion — can only prescribe even more growth as "the" solution to both global economic and political injustice and growing ecological breakdown. Indeed, the very process of capitalist growth that is the root cause of our unsustainable global "ecological footprint" (Wackernagle and Rees) is viewed by the neoliberal captains of finance, industry and advertising as the solution to all our problems. On the contrary, if humankind is really to work out viable sustainable solutions to unfettered industrial/consumer growth, we will have to deeply examine our entire modern way of life, especially in the consumer heartlands of capitalism such as Cascadia.

A bioregional perspective on lasting social change (or rather, social transformation) calls on us all to abandon our prevailing globalist root metaphor — the capitalist myth (or story) of perpetual economic and industrial growth and consumption. A key foundation of this myth is the modernist construct of "economic man" (*homo economicus*). Economic man, Duncan MacPherson's infinite maximizer of utilities (1973), is a central pillar of and model for consumer humanity upon which growth-oriented capitalism rests. The cultural core of economic man is the modern middle-class image of the acquisitive and selfish individual disconnected from community. Instead of community as the basic social unit, private accumulation by the atomized, isolated individual becomes the chief measure of success in a society based on unlimited consumption (Carr 2004, 33–36).

Bioregionalism provides an alternative economic and cultural model to that of corporate globalism and economic man. Grounded in civil society, the bioregional movement is inspired by and organized around the concept of sustainable local communities and eco-villages, networked in broader scale "regional," or bioregional economic and political configurations that could become economically self-reliant entities, producing all or most of their own basic necessities of life, rather than producing primarily for the world market as neoliberalism prescribes.

Bioregionalists were among the first to initiate community visions, proposals and projects for green or ecological cities in the early 1980s (Berg, Carr 196–220; Todd and Todd; Todd and Tukel). Since then, the worldwide eco-village movement has moved from 500 eco-villages globally in 1989 to over 15,000 by 2002 (Carr 2004, 288). The bioregional movement itself is a melding of a broad spectrum of social and ecological perspectives and peoples, all well represented in Cascadia. The movement includes environmentalists, greens (whose eco-reverent world view often goes beyond conservation to include spiritual and non-violent philosophies), social ecologists, deep ecologists, eco-feminists, libertarian leftists, ecologically inspired Christians and Jews, green Buddhists, neo-Pagans, New-Agers and a range of indigenous peoples.

In fact, a great part of the inspiration for the genesis of the bioregional movement lies in our growing knowledge of the bioregional dimensions of indigenous peoples' ways of life. In British Columbia, if not Cascadia, probably the greatest number of people actually living a bioregional way of life are certain First Nations people who are practising — to the best of their abilities and means in very difficult circumstances — their own traditional ways of living in and with the land. Most, if not all, indigenous peoples on the Fraser River still fish in the same fishing spots on the river they have used for many centuries.

The concept of a bioregion is obviously central to bioregional philosophy. In discussing this concept, I integrate my own understanding of bioregional Earth spirituality and examples of its geographical basis. One of the very earliest definitions of a bioregion refers to both "a terrain of consciousness and a geographical terrain, to a place and the ideas that have developed about how to live in that place" (Berg and Dasmann, 218). This is a dialectical concept. Bioregions are unique life places with their own soils and land forms, watersheds and climate, native plants and animals, and other distinct natural characteristics.

However, for those in the bioregional movement, the concept of a bioregion moves beyond mere descriptive geography into the realm of the cultural and the phenomenological. This dimension includes what Peter Berg, one of the founders of bioregionalism, has called a "distinct resonance among living things" and the ecological relations which influence them. Jim Dodge, another very early bioregionalist, includes "spirit presences" or "psyche-turning power-presences" in his definition of bioregion (Andruss, 7). Here we move from natural science ecology into the domain of what some call sacred ecology. Indeed, for bioregionalists, the concept of "community" includes the non-human micro-organism communities that live literally inside us and on our skins as well as around us and without which we could not survive. Thus, bioregionalists do not make a hard and fast separation of human spirituality from ecological, or Earth spirituality. Bioregional educator Frank Traina, influenced by both Thomas Berry (also a bioregional thinker who attended the first North American Bioregional Congress in 1984) and by Gregory Bateson, speaks of the ecological "self" as an interpenetration of beings — not just separate entities in the "web of life," but as merging beings extending into each other, as open boundaries, as flows and inclusivity. This relational concept of the self bespeaks a very different concept of the human being from that of atomized economic man.

In an Earth-centered paradigm, separateness is an illusion. Our entire existence in nature is a process of metabolic exchanges — we literally live in our places and bioregions, not on them. Bioregionalists recognize that we are thoroughly interdependent with the other species and life systems of our planetary biosphere. Moreover, as human animals we have the capacity and the power to perceive, to experience directly something of this fluid interdependent dimension of ecological relations. It is a profoundly sacred ecological experience actually to feel this awesome life force, to experience directly this "metapattern which connects," as Gregory Bateson has described it.

I say "life force," but how is this life force perceived? Dolores LaChapelle has described our human connection with the sacred as a felt sense of being part of the whole of life and realizing it. LaChapelle further asserts that it is possible to begin to live in a sacred manner even within modern industrial/consumer growth society by "setting up ritual structures where we can feel nature moving deep within us in response to the patterns of all of nature without." LaChapelle came to understand that in traditional indigenous cultures, the people are aware that sacred reality *is* the reality — it is always accessible to them, it is always ongoing and they go in and out of it to do specific tasks, but it is always there and easily entered. By contrast, in our modern culture the "out of the sacred" state is the only state we consider as real, and the occasional times modern humans experience "the sacred" is considered occult or weird, or supernatural (LaChapelle, 128).

For First Nations, on the contrary, bonding with the land has been the norm. Okanagan First Nations educator, author, artist and Director of the En'owkin Centre in British Columbia, Jeannette Armstrong was raised by traditional elders. Armstrong has expressed the profound levels of bonding with the land that are possible in traditional Okanagan culture: "When we say the traditional Okanagan word for ourselves, we are actually saying 'the ones who dream the land and the land together.' That is our original identity. Before anything else we are the living, dreaming Earth pieces" (1999). As an Okanagan person, Armstrong avers that "our most essential responsibility is to bond our whole individual and communal selves to the land. Many of our ceremonies have been constructed for this. We join with the larger self and the land, and rejoice in all that we are" (1999). For Armstrong, this ecological bonding is essential for practising bioregional economies.

While this is a traditionally informed view, some might object that today traditional views are exceptional, even marginal to current indigenous peoples whose languages are endangered and who have been harmed by colonialism. While it is true that indigenous peoples today face many serious social problems, including potential language loss, there is a truly amazing recognition by many such people that spiritual connections to the land still exist in indigenous cultures. This was testified to over and over, all across Canada, during the process of the Royal Commission on Aboriginal Peoples (1996). I myself have witnessed a great variety of expressions of this spiritual cultural connection to "the land" at meetings, conferences, ceremonies, social events and protests over many years, from a wide range of Native people from different social backgrounds. The indigenous relationship with local ecologies was an early influence on the development of bioregional thought in the US.

As I have already pointed out, the bioregional movement has diverse roots, informed by a variety of movements and traditions. The bioregional movement is also very accepting of religious diversity, to the point where one may ask: What are the common features of bioregional spirituality? From my observations of bioregional congresses and gatherings, discussions and interviews with a wide range of bioregionalists, as well as extensive literature reviews, it is clear that bioregional spirituality entails a belief in the sacredness of all species and all their ecological relations. Bioregional spirituality is an Earth-centered spirituality much akin to the ancient "community of beings" kinship ethic of indigenous communal societies. Cascadian Native American thinker Dennis Martinez has pointed out that indigenous peoples' spirituality is centered on their relationships to all species and to the land. Their lives are reflected in what we can think of today as kinship ecologies. The well-known ceremonial phrase "all my relations" refers to the fact that all living things on Earth were regarded as kin to the humans. Indigenous kinship ecologies thus reflected a practice of general reciprocity with all kin, not merely or exclusively human kin (Martinez).

For bioregionalists (as for traditional indigenous peoples) Earth spirituality, or ecological kinship, is experienced and understood as intimacy with local life-forms and topography. For Native cultures, their language and origin stories are thoroughly informed by the land, indeed, inseparable in meaning from the land. As bioregional philosopher David Abram has commented: "The local Earth is for oral cultures the very matrix of discursive meaning; to force them from their native ecology is to render them speechless — or to render their speech meaningless — to dislodge them from the very ground of coherence." (Abram, 178)

In northern Cascadia, Gitxsan map team member Russell Collier put it this way:

> When we record names and information about a place, we are also recording the experience about that place in the description. Our language is well suited for describing geographical things. It's oriented that way. In fact, it is very difficult to talk about the land without talking about your relationship to it, simply for that reason. When we talk about things or places or actions in Gitxsanimx, our language is more pictorial than English; it's a lot more pictorial and less abstract than English; it's a lot more like painting a picture with words — how tired you get before you reach a certain spot, where the sun is in relation to your back. The name of a boundary rock and how it makes you feel when you stand before it. When you're talking about a geographical location in our language, you are talking about the encoded, built-up experience of that location, all of which reinforces the basic relationship to it. (B.C. Environmental Network, 41)

Origin stories of the people of Cascadia express both the sacredness of the Earth and the oneness of all life forms. Among the Kwakwaka'wakw people, the concept of "*oweetna-kula*, living as one with the land and sea" expresses the essential unity of people and place (Percival in B.C. Environmental Network, 48). Local story cycles support this perspective by establishing a direct mythic relationship between the tree and human realms, mediated by the spirit power known as *nawalak* that is resident in the cedar trees and accessible through winter ceremonials or spirit questing. In a traditional Hesquiat story (neighbours of the Kwakwaka'wakw), three young women tricked by Raven into fleeing up a mountain were long ago transformed into yellow cedar trees and so melded the ancient bonds of tree and human (Alice Paul as told to Nancy Turner, in B.C. Environmental Network 1998, p. 48).

Origin stories of the Coast Salish Sto:lo people in Cascadia express a range of interspecies kinship values and beliefs. One origin story of the Sto:lo explains "how Xexa:ls (the Transformers), three sons and one daughter of black bear and red-headed woodpecker, came to 'make the world right' for people of the present age," thus giving birth to the Sto:lo people. Other Sto:lo stories provide explanations for the intimate kinship between certain species (for example, sturgeon, sockeye salmon and mountain goats) and various Sto:lo communities. Other stories provide information on the origins and character of animal and plant resources (Carlson, 185–186).

These stories also have shared meanings with all Coast Salish peoples. As anthropologist Wayne Suttles explains,

> The Transformers came through the world, transforming monsters and other myth-age beings into rocks and animals, and setting things in order for peoples of the present age. These stories usually tell how a community's founder came to find his winter village or summer camp, where the Transformer (sometimes singular) gave him technical or ritual knowledge whereby he was empowered to establish special relationships with local species. One example is the ancestor of the Katzie people who married a sockeye salmon woman and was taught how to perform the rite that ensures the return of her people, the summer run of sockeye salmon. (Suttles, 466)

Xa:ytem, the large boulder near Mission, B.C., is one of the transformer rocks. The story told by Sto:lo elder Bertha Peters is that three *si:ya:m* (chiefs) were supposed to teach their people writing, but they did not, so they were turned into stone. Sto:lo spiritual leaders explain that the *Shxweli*, or life force, of the three *si:ya:m* continues to exist within the boulder (Carlson, 187).

For the traditional Nimkish (a Kwakwaka'wakw people), the Nimpkish river was once a human being who became a river because he wanted to flow forever. The village at the mouth of the river was founded by Salmon and Thunderbird. Kwakwaka'wakw writer Haile Bruce recounts that:

> Amongst the Kwawaka'wakw, wooden Boxes of Treasures contain certain songs, dances, crests, coppers and other valuable objects that represent the relationships that locate individuals and families within Kwakwaka'wakw society and their connections, obligations and rights to certain territories. . . . Through our Oral Traditions we know that the river or the mountain is our ancestor, and that beneath our waters, spirits live. When our creation or transformation stories speak of how a mountain or river came into being, they are doing more than simply providing an interesting story. They tell of our relationship to that mountain, or that river, and our responsibilities to them. There can be no continuity of culture unless there is continuity of our relationship and jurisdiction over the land. It is precisely because the river is our ancestor that we have an obligation to protect and guard the spirits that live within the waters from pollution, logging, mining, hydroelectric development and all other activities which do not respect the sacred nature of the river. (Walkem and Bruce, 347–348)

So, here we see very clearly expressed the linkage between Earth spirituality, geography and social, ecological and political responsibility and obligation. In Kwakwaka'wakw understanding, the ecological sacredness of the river is that it is experienced as an ancestor to the people. And with that profoundly experienced phenomenon comes the obligation to respect and defend the river. Such a profound social ethic is built on these sacred foundations.

In Canada, the potlatch was outlawed from 1884 to 1951. The Kwakwaka'wakw were among the strongest resisters to that law. Today, they have a rebuilt Big House in Alert Bay, B.C., in which they practise their traditional ceremonies. There is also a museum, the U'Mista Cultural Centre, which houses an impressive collection of carved masks used in potlatch ceremonies. These masks were recovered after serious efforts by the Kwakwaka'wakw to repatriate them. They were stolen in the 1921 potlatch raid organized by the Indian Agent William Halliday. The U'Mista Cultural Centre opened in 1980. The Centre also houses other cultural exhibits and from the gift shop sells jewelry, carvings, silkscreen prints and other craft items by Kwakwaka'wakw artists and crafters. The Centre also shows two films, produced by the Centre about the potlatch prohibition and cultural survival. There is also a serious effort (which needs more support) to keep the Kwakwala language alive. The Namgis at Alert Bay are planning a series of cultural regeneration and sustainable natural resource management projects under their own land use plan.

To the north of the Kwakwaka'wakw, the Heiltsuk people are also working to maintain both their traditions and their natural resources under their land use plan. Chief Ross Wilson has said that "our elders taught us that our land is sacred. Through *Gvi'ilas* (the traditional way or customary laws) and *7axvi* (power derived from connection to and ownership of the land), we are gaining control of our land and our resources" (Heiltsuk Land Use Plan Executive Summary). Under the Heiltsuk Land Use Plan, the rights of the Heiltsuk to hunt, fish, trap and continue activities for social, cultural, commercial, ceremonial and sustenance purposes are not limited by the establishment of any land use designations. Two broad designations govern this plan: Heiltsuk Natural and Cultural Areas (mainly left in natural or "wilderness" condition) and Ecosystem-based Management Areas.

The Tsleil-Waututh Nation (TWN) in North Vancouver, B.C., a mountainside suburb of Metro Vancouver, have been practising bioregional mapping for about a decade. The TWN are a very urban nation. Supported by their chief Lea George, their map team stresses the importance of developing a community vision. Through bioregional mapping methods, including a series of interviews with elders and hunters, they have generated a powerful tool to bring the community together around a vision for the land that can work in an urban region. Through building that common vision and building community capacity, they have been able to go out to the larger world and make partnerships and protocol agreements with other First Nations, government agencies, private businesses and NGOs such as EcoTrust. They have a project in riparian habitat enhancement. Another, with the University of British Columbia Faculty of Forestry, is looking at ways to produce timber for traditional dugout canoes. They are also conducting forest inventory updates for better data to be able to calculate a sustainable allowable annual cut. With the District of North Vancouver, the TWN is undertaking a co-management plan of Whey-au-Wichen (or Cates Park), which is beginning to erode at the shoreline. Over two years ago, along with B.C. Parks, they reintroduced a small herd of twenty-one elk into the Indian River watershed. As the Tsleil-Waututh take on these projects they also work on developing their own internal capacity by sharing in the work and having young people "shadow" with a trained expert. The TWN Takaya Tours operates educational tours of Tsleil-Waututh territory in traditional canoes as well as plant walks focusing on the many uses the people made of local flora. Most importantly, the TWN is developing a holistic vision of where they want to go from here, integrating a mix of social, cultural, economic and environmental values.

In the bioregional movement, the sense of obligation to place emerging from the experience of place has been expressed very directly by Peter Berg:

> Wherever you live, the place where you live is alive and you are part of the life of that place. No matter how short a time you've been there, or whether or not you're going to be leaving it and going to another place, it will always be that situation throughout your life. The place that you end up being in is alive and you are part of that life. Now what is your obligation and your sense of responsibility for the sustenance and support that these places give you and how do you go about acting on it? (Carr, 73)

Embedded in Berg's notion here is a deep sense of reciprocity with place. Developing a philosophy and practice around place is the foundation of bioregionalism. Bioregional intentional communities are created and built sharing this profound social ethic, and dedicating their lives to putting it in practice.

The practice of learning to live in place is called reinhabitation: "It means understanding activities and evolving social behaviour that will enrich the life of that place, restore its life-supporting systems and establish an ecologically and socially sustainable pattern of existence within it" (Berg, 218). Bioregionalists have developed, borrowed and adapted a whole range of tools for building communities of place, watershed councils, congresses and what Berg calls "seed groups" (affinity groups of nearby watershed neighbours), including consensus process, sharing circles, story, ritual and ceremony, undoing "isms" workshops and talking circles, bioregional and community mapping, ecological restoration, permaculture design, and bioregional education methods such as all-species days (Carr, 101–158). All this is to help put the experience of place and the practice of reinhabitation into peoples' consciousness and practice. Then, neighbourhood by neighbourhood, place by place, bioregion by bioregion, a social ethic of deep interconnection, interdependence and reciprocity can become a socially shared norm. This is the lifelong and difficult process of building a democratic and sustainable civil society.

This reflection brings me to my concluding remarks and policy recommendations for a sustainable Cascadia. Planners are trained to make policy recommendations, but as a bioregionalist and community activist, I have difficulty making recommendations to governments, agencies and institutions that will not implement them under the current corporate globalizing system. A sustainable bioregional Cascadia is not possible under the prevailing political economic regime. Instead, I argue that a true, democratic, ecologically sustainable Cascadia can only come about through a revolutionary transformation at the base, in civil society. This includes transforming ourselves by consuming much, much less — as the voluntary simplicity movement recommends. In urban Cascadia, it also means building solidarity and understanding in our neighbour-hoods so we can reclaim the privatization of space, turning auto-mobile-dominated spaces into real public places. That's what an organization called City Repair is doing with much success in Port-land, Oregon, where all ninety-five neighbourhood associations are now in the process of transforming and democratizing civic gover-nance in that city, neighbourhood by neighbourhood (City Repair Project). This quiet revolution includes the transformation of our culture of fear and possessive individualism into a culture of Earth-loving, co-operative, community-oriented and actively democratic peoples who value the richness of growing social and ecological re-lations over materialistic consumer narcissism. It is only from the base of a much more actively democratic civil society that we can truly begin to influence effectively state and corporate structures so as to transform them into decentralized and democratic institutions.

In short, as the cosmologist Thomas Berry has argued, we need a new story (1988). Cascadia, to be viable and sustainable, needs a new story, a story inspired and informed by indigenous wisdom and bioregional sensibilities, including what Mark Lakeman, founder and spark of City Repair, calls "the spirit of the village." To give this new story integrity, he says we need to remember that "water is sacred, so is the air. The Earth is sacred and when two people love NO MATTER HOW — that is sacred. When a community stands up and has a vision for itself that is sacred." These communities, Lake-man pleads, "need you now to come together once again in a place where time and space are not for sale — where these communities await you in a place you've never left, the tree of life" (Lakeman, presentation in Asheville, NC, 2003).

When a certain democratic momentum has been built up in civil society, when relationships of community at the base in civil society become strong, when new norms of co-operation are born or re-claimed, when civic responsibility becomes a daily practice, when our human spirituality becomes life affirming and inclusive of all species, then the communities, the eco-villages and their networks can truly and effectively begin to democratize state and corporate structures. Real lasting and effective policy change can only flow from this new, lived story.

CHAPTER 8

✐

Sustainability and
Spirituality in Cascadia

PETER DRURY

THE PACIFIC NORTHWEST is my home. I find renewal, connection, inspiration and courage in its mountains, waterways, forests, salmon, eagles, barnacles and moss. My parents, grandparents and great-grandparents have cherished the Northwest in much the same way. And my two young daughters are only beginning to forge a relationship with this remarkable place.

Any modern textbook would describe the Pacific Northwest as being divided by borders both international and intra-national: Canada from the United States, and Oregon by states on three sides: Washington, Idaho and California. However, these boundaries are actually relatively recent and functionally contrived. Were the nature-scape to speak for itself, it would articulate a natural unity defined by the water flowing out of the Cascades to nourish a bio-regional ecosystem: Cascadia. Long united by similar indigenous cultures, Cascadia was once briefly a single political unit — the Oregon Territory — and was shared by several nations.

Were Cascadia to be viewed without reference to the borders we have come to accept as given, one would see today a region hosting more than fifteen million people alongside abundant (yet diminished and threatened) wildlife. Were it to be an independent nation, Cascadia, in terms of population, would be counted among the world's sixty largest countries. Of these countries, its economy would rank fifteenth in size, generating over $450 billion annually in goods and services.

For the sake of cultural coherence and practicality, this book on Cascadia focuses mostly on the political jurisdictions of B.C., Washington and Oregon. But, as a bioregion Cascadia stretches somewhat farther, including much of Idaho and the lower part of Alaska. As a bioregion, Cascadia is larger than France, Germany, the United Kingdom, Italy, Switzerland and Belgium — *combined*. Cascadia boasts the largest rainforest outside the Tropics, with stunning mountain ranges and woodlands holding the heaviest accumulation of living matter ever found anywhere on the planet.

Cascadia retains a larger share of its ecosystems intact than any other part of the industrial world. It helped set the conservation agenda for the continent by way of the first bottle bills and urban growth management laws in the 1970s, trend-setting energy conservation and curbside recycling efforts in the 1980s, old-growth forest protection in the 1990s, and the first endangered species listings to affect major cities. Cascadia has traditions of innovation in the public and private sectors, a well-educated populace, and a reputation for a commitment to the environment and quality of life that continues to draw migrants even when unemployment rises.

Thanks to a robust economy and the rapidly advancing technologies of our time, we Cascadians have the opportunity to align our lifestyles with our landscape, not only for ourselves but also as a global proving ground. The following provocative statement from Northwest author Alan Durning has often been cited: "This is the greenest part of the wealthiest civilization ever to inhabit the Earth. If we cannot reconcile our way of life with this bountiful place, it probably can't be done. But if we can, we may set an example for the world."

CHARACTER OF A PLACE

One could attempt to describe the state of the Northwest by summarizing a singular nightly news broadcast in any one of its cities on a randomly selected day of the year. But this would be misleading, like attempting to describe the whole of a person by pointing to several isolated actions on a single day. The deeper qualities of people — such as resilience, hope, integrity, wisdom, endurance or love — are less quickly observable than favourite foods, family size, driving habits, choice of toothpaste, or even religious identification. The character of a person is best known through *patterns* of actions, rather than the actions themselves. So too is the character of a place known by observing its patterns through varied seasons across many years.

It is difficult to know what is *really* going on in a given place, at a given time. In an age of fast food, fast cars and fast computers, the news we hear comes fast as well: quick stories and brief headlines accentuate the sensational, favour the tragic, and typically pass over the slow and enduring. Subjects like regional health, child poverty rates, and wildlife or climate change, frequently play second fiddle to the activities of the celebrity-in-crisis *du jour* or the odd behaviour of someone, somewhere.

Were the average person curious to learn how the abundance of Northwest wildlife compares today to times in its past, for example, could they find the answer before losing patience with the search? If they sought to understand the root causes of child poverty, would they know where to begin? Cascadia's homegrown think-tank on a sustainable future, Sightline Institute, has committed itself to "measure what matters" in order to highlight the "slow news" in Cascadia. Sightline equips leaders with the data they need to work for a way of life that can last. Through focused analysis of seven key trends shaping the Northwest — energy, population, health, wildlife, economy, pollution and sprawl — Sightline continually compares Cascadia's performance in each of these areas relative to the best case scenario worldwide (for example, Germany regarding energy or Japan regarding health). By way of overview, Sightline Institute reported the following observations in 2007:

Wildlife

Cascadia's wildlife exists, on average, in 18 percent of its historic abundance. Orca, wolves, salmon, sage-grouse and caribou — which serve as reasonable proxy indicators for Northwest wildlife at large — each abide at one-fifth their abundance in history. (See Table: *Selected Populations of Northwest Wildlife*).

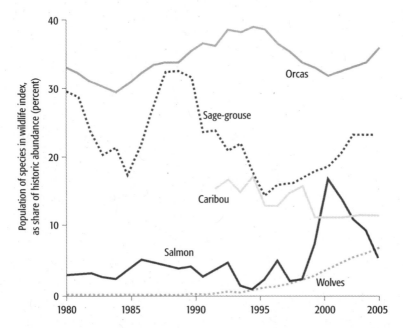

Selected Populations of Northwest Wildlife — Courtesy of Sightline Institute

Economy

For the past number of years, the Cascadian economy was doubling while the Dow Jones Industrial Average soared (although this has not continued into 2008). Did the quality of life of Cascadians similarly improve? No. For nearly a generation, Cascadian median income has actually remained flat.

Health

The health of Northwesterners, on average, is excellent. And British Columbians lead the pack. However, as will be noted below, North-westerners face serious threats to health due to both pollution (body burden of toxic chemicals) and the sprawling design of many com-munities (which plays a substantial role in both rapidly escalating obesity and traffic fatalities).

Population

The Northwest is among the world's leading regions when it comes to managing population. Birth rates for teen mothers have been on a rapid decline since 1970.

Pollution PBDEs

(toxic flame retardants) are attested in Northwesterners at levels higher than most of the world.

Energy

Cascadian energy efficiency, as well as total consumption, is among the worst in the world, nearly twice that of Germany, per capita. Al-though gasoline use has notably decreased, per capita, electricity use has sharply increased.

Sprawl

Cascadia's automobile-dependent community infrastructures are strongly correlated with obesity (rapidly increasing in the Northwest) and car-crashes (the leading cause of death for Cascadians under the age of forty-five).

Lest the picture of Cascadia appear now to be painted in colours far too dim, it is important to note that Northwesterners are on the leading edge of emerging models of business and organizations, which are increasingly sustainable in design. Bellingham, Washing-ton State, boasts the largest "Chamber of Commerce" style associa-tion of sustainably driven businesses and entrepreneurs. Sustainable

Connections is an international leader in fostering a comprehensive network of businesses that define goals according to the triple bottom line: lasting growth relative to profit, people and planet. Not at all disconnected, Bellingham was the first municipality in the United States to commit to 100 percent clean energy for its public utilities. And Earth Ministry — an organization that brings Christians of all denominations together to play a leadership role in planetary concerns — was birthed in Cascadia and has been influential around the world. Given the pronounced divides within and between religious bodies in recent years, Earth Ministry's successes are particularly laudable.

Other signs of hope abound. A recent effort to unravel decades of wise land use planning ("smart growth") in Northwestern states was handed a gigantic setback. After Oregon's disastrous Measure 37 was passed in 2004, in 2006 wealthy East Coast "property rights" advocates bankrolled efforts to pass bad-neighbour laws, efforts which were cleverly concealed to appear as if they were local Northwest uprisings. These initiatives would have rolled back democratic, community-based zoning and land-use planning. Although the initiative passed in Arizona, it failed to win in a single Cascadian state. One year later, Oregon voters modified and overturned the lion's share of the original Measure 37. And, all the while, Vancouver, B.C., has been the world leader in building complete, compact communities which support vital local economies, effective transit, reductions in carbon emissions and stronger neighbourhoods.

The 2010 Olympic Games will feature, we're promised — for the first time in the history of the games — a rigorous dedication to sustainability. The eyes of the world will be focused on British Columbia, and the opportunity to inspire sustainable futures should be unparalleled.

Other successes are notable as well, including strong new commitments to reduce carbon emissions throughout the governing bodies within Cascadia. When the US federal government would not affirm the Kyoto Protocol, it was the City of Seattle that launched a commitment by municipalities to affirm the standards of Kyoto regardless of the position of the federal government. The conservation movement is as strong as ever in Cascadia, and numerous organizations and individuals are working tirelessly to preserve millions of acres of unspoiled wilderness.

It is, indeed, fitting to ask whether Cascadians are in fact actively engaged in pursuit of the elusive Utopia. Certainly there is a deep drive here to enjoy beauty, preserve it and pass it along to future generations.

THE GREATEST CHALLENGES

Although roundly impressive successes are routinely being demonstrated in Cascadia, there are nonetheless several major problems. Sightline Institute's Cascadia Scorecard highlights three arenas in which Cascadia is in great trouble: wildlife, sprawl and energy — and the greatest of these is energy.

Cascadians presently consume nearly twice the amount of energy, per capita, as their counterparts in Germany, and this stuck-in-high-gear habit emits carbon, threatens security, and sends $17 billion out of the Northwest economy each year.

Sprawl might seem a curious thing to measure, but it is inextricably linked to energy consumption. Additionally, considering that the leading cause of death for Cascadians under the age of forty-five is, in fact, automobile accidents, a car-maximizing approach to community design becomes worthy of review. Car crashes also lead to approximately one hundred thousand injuries each year in Cascadia, a number greater than sell-out attendance at two Mariners baseball games (in Safeco Field which holds 47,000 fans).

It is easy to be swept up in the grandeur of Cascadia, seduced into ignoring the trouble that is brewing below the surface. The Northwest is beautiful, yet at risk. Current matters of land use and water policy, transportation planning, climate pricing, environmental clean up and economic security all play critical roles in the push for sustainability. And our attention simply must be shifted to matters of energy, sprawl and wildlife.

SPIRITUALITY AND ETHICS IN CASCADIA'S FUTURE

Given this backdrop to the present state of Cascadia, I wish now to speak of spirituality and ethics. By spirituality I mean a personal quest for transformative meaning, a quest which embodies hunger for insight, connection, healing, impact or hope — a landscape of the heart. And by ethics I mean integrity of right action in relation to a given community context — a compass of right and wrong.

Given that the three arenas of poorest Cascadian performance vis-à-vis sustainability concern energy, wildlife and sprawl, they seem a fitting place to focus. I ask three questions, not through a narrow lens of policy and politics, but rather through a wide-angle lens of spirituality, ethics and deeply held personal values. The questions are these:

- How should we fuel our work and pleasure?
- How may we live in harmony with nature's bounty?
- How shall we best design the places where we live, work and play?

They may not sound like *spiritual* questions at first blush. But I am given to wonder: Can any serious spiritual seeker, living in this time and place, not ask them? What would it mean to continue along a spiritual path, here in Cascadia, while living out poor stewardship? What do Cascadians fundamentally believe when it comes to the best sources of energy, the valuing of wildlife, and the building of places for life and labour?

In the twenty-first century, Cascadians who are spiritual seekers must strive to reconcile their heart and their home, their way of life and their natural heritage. It would be pointless for individuals to grow spiritually in their own time at the expense of compromising their children's future. Of the vast diversity of spiritual traditions practised in Cascadia — whether conservative or progressive — I do not know of any that instructs its adherents willfully to compromise the future of their children in service of short-lived prosperity today. As the facts of global climate change gain broader public acceptance, people living spiritually principled lives will increasingly ponder their relationship with global warming and the future of the planet.

Let us look at this matter more concretely. An example of an intersection between sustainability and spirituality might be as close as our feet: walking. Across nearly all spiritual traditions — and throughout many lands — walking plays a central role in spiritual practices, texts, disciplines and customs. Contemplative walking, while perhaps a spiritual exercise for a Zen Buddhist or a Roman Catholic, can both nurture one's inner life and reduce one's carbon footprint while simultaneously honouring nature (creation).

Interestingly, the relationship between walking and community design ("walkability") is of tremendous significance as an indicator of sustainable community planning. It ties into reducing driving to increase the benefits which accrue from density (for example, physical exercise, personal health, economic vitality, congruence with transit planning and preservation of urban growth boundaries). To illustrate the difference between a neighbourhood that has been planned for walking and a neighborhood planned for automobiles, consider the contrast between the following two maps.

Each map shows a one-mile (1.6 kilometer) walk from home (marked as a star in the middle of the map) in a Northwest residential neighbourhood. In the urban neighbourhood (see map #1) designed for pedestrians, walking is encouraged along a grid format, which provides easy access to open spaces, business districts, transit and neighbours, together with the sense that you can "get somewhere" on a walk. However, in the curving, twisting streets of the suburban neighbourhood (see map #2), which is ultimately designed for automobiles, walking is discouraged, thereby erasing incentives for healthy behaviour, reducing driving and friendly neighbourly relations. You can walk for a mile and "get nowhere." Walkability is a

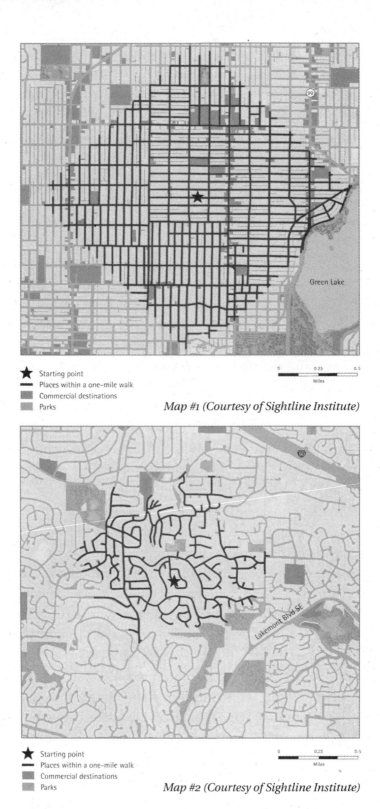

★ Starting point
— Places within a one-mile walk
■ Commercial destinations
■ Parks

Map #1 (Courtesy of Sightline Institute)

★ Starting point
— Places within a one-mile walk
■ Commercial destinations
■ Parks

Map #2 (Courtesy of Sightline Institute)

simple, yet critical, element of a sustainable future. A spiritual practice and a sustainable practice can be one and the same.

A second example of the intersection between sustainability and spirituality derives from ancient Judaism. Consider the idea and practice of Sabbath observance. If people across Cascadia were to assume a once-weekly personal prohibition from igniting energy sources, our bioregion would become measurably healthier in many ways. A reduction of one-seventh (14 percent) in energy use would be a great place to begin! It is not necessary for Cascadians to share any dogma or doctrine (which they would not, in any case), but a shared practice of refraining from energy use once each seven days would have a large positive benefit for the region.

A third example of the intersection between sustainability and spirituality might be self-examination relative to consumerism and simplicity. It is from within our world of excessive consumerism that Richard Louv has recently coined the term, "nature deficit disorder," the ready understanding of which exemplifies its relevance. In his 2005 book, *Last Child in the Woods*, Louv examines the massive cultural, educational and psychological shift that has transpired because so many children are not exposed to the great outdoors — much less taking delight in them — as they were one and two generations ago. Can Cascadians afford to raise children with nature deficit disorder? Is this a concern with policy, with spirituality, with education, with community, or with recreation? The answer is probably: all of the above.

Although Cascadians are notable for their identification as "Nones" when it comes to institutional religious adherence, they are certainly not divorced from the very human quest for transformative meaning, nor from daily judgments of right and wrong. It is precisely these spiritual and ethical drives to which I would appeal.

As Cascadians go about their work, their leisure, they simply must consider the character of their place, the patterns in which they participate, and the trends shaping the future. It is *not* true that we can meet our personal needs only by adversely affecting our children and grandchildren. Instead, it is true that a healthy regional life today will help birth a healthy regional life tomorrow.

A STORY

A few years ago I took a walk through one of Cascadia's iconic urban centers — the Pike Place Market in Seattle — a walk I expected to be a routine stroll for groceries. I had no idea that it might present me with lasting spiritual and ethical lessons and opportunities. And yet now, some years later, it is a poignant experience of which I hope one day to tell my children.

The longest continually running farmer's market in the country, Pike Place Market is a major tourist attraction, an economic hub, a community center and a refreshing experience of vigorous community in the midst of metropolis. It is famed for its fresh produce, beautiful artisan crafts and the way its fish vendors make a show of skillfully throwing salmon, cod and halibut through the air, to the delight of camera-snapping visitors.

As I approached the market, I passed several people who were either homeless or close to it. As I often do, I felt conflicted about how to respond to requests for spare change. Even though I have a well-reasoned ethical formula for not giving out cash (instead, I support organizations that help people in such crises), I knew that if I answered someone's plea for cash with — "Sorry. You'll be pleased to know that I just made a tax-deductible contribution to an organization which helps" — I would be met with a blank stare, at best.

As I entered the market I juggled competing emotional states of guilt, regret and compassion. Most of all, I felt helpless to make a difference. I soon, however, became distracted by a wealth of artisan crafts: candles, hand-knit sweaters, wood carvings and paintings. As I continued, I smelled fresh baking cinnamon rolls and watched vendors arranging handsome produce in decisive rows. Flower arrangements were being assembled and filled the market stalls with purples, reds and yellows.

I made a few purchases along the way — seafood, produce and dried fruit — and then suddenly was interrupted by a large man who jumped out in front of me, near a produce stand, looked me straight in the eye, and said, "All these for a dollar!" He was holding about fifteen bananas.

As my shock slowly subsided, I realized that he was offering me bananas that were bruised but still quite edible. I felt like telling him, "I don't need fifteen bananas!" But I also appreciated he was offering me an amazing deal! I smiled as I handed him a dollar. I then walked off with a big bag while visions of banana bread danced in my head.

As I walked along, I continued to encounter people begging for change. Almost instinctively I looked at them face to face, smiled, and offered them each a banana!

I stopped for my ritual cup of coffee, and then continued along my way with bags of seafood, vegetables and bananas. As people continued to ask for spare change, I handed out bananas. The feelings of guilt slipped away. They were replaced by joy. And when I ultimately arrived home and set my groceries on the counter, I discovered that I had two bananas left — *exactly what I needed* — no more, no less.

I could not escape the overwhelming hold that this realization placed on me: that I was moved from despair to hope, and that when I lived in right relation to those around me, I had exactly what I needed. I'll not split hairs over whether this was a story of sustainability or spirituality, but I will remember it forever.

CHAPTER 9

༄

Toward a New Cascadian Civil Religion of Nature

SALLIE MCFAGUE

I AM A CASCADIAN. I support the "civil religion" of Cascadia as described by Douglas Todd: finding God by taking a walk in the forest. I do this every morning in Metro Vancouver's Jericho Park. I also published a book a few years ago entitled *Super, Natural Christians*. I stole the title from the B.C. tourist logo: "super, natural British Columbia." That comma makes all the difference: it claims that Christians are not supernatural (belonging to another world), but *super, natural* (in love with this world and its flourishing).

But is it enough to love nature and take walks in the woods? Increasingly, human beings in all parts of the world are living in cities. What is the relation of the city to nature? To be sure, the best cities, like Vancouver, welcome nature into the city with such wonders as Stanley Park as well as many pocket parks throughout the city, which are precious oases for rest and recreation. But there is a deeper and more pervasive meaning to "nature": nature as the source and ground of everything that is. Cities are made from nature; one could say they are "second nature," made of transformations of energy from "first nature." All human building and transformations are but changes *within* nature, for there is nothing "outside nature." This deeper meaning of nature — nature as the source of energy that sustains all life and all change — is the nature we city dwellers tend to forget. We slip into simplistic, dualistic thinking when we think that nature in our cities involves only the trees, gardens and beaches — and that we create the rest.

For example, what about electricity? This summer I read an article in the *Globe and Mail* that claimed there is no province in Canada where consumers actually see the true cost of the electricity that is the lifeblood of our cities (*Globe and Mail*, July, 2006). We neither know the cost nor pay the cost. Yet, as we quickly realize when electricity is cut off in a city, all life stops: cities are dark and dead without electricity — no light, no heat, no refrigeration, no cooked food, no air conditioning, no theatre productions, no symphony performances, no computers, no TV, no video games, no electric toothbrushes! Our reliance on nature — on energy — is the bottom line; it is what life is all about. As the biggest consumers of energy and the biggest deniers of excessive use, city dwellers need to wake up. Beneath the trees, parks and beaches of our cities is the deeper meaning of nature as source of life and its flourishing. Yet, increasingly, we human beings are literally changing "the face of nature." Two illustrations are cities and global warming. Some geographers now speak of the city as "re-placing nature," and daily we read in the newspapers how climate change is moving toward a tipping point of irreversible temperature increases (Soja).

Do we need a new Cascadian "civil religion," one that helps us city dwellers become aware of our daily, hourly, dependence on first nature? Nature is not just there for walks in the forest; it is the source of our very existence — a fact that is becoming increasingly clear as millions of city dwellers attempt to eat, breathe, work and play in our crowded cities. Within the complex relationship of city and nature that faces us in the twenty-first century, how can we, in the words of Douglas Todd, promote "creative social change in a way that protects liberty, respects human dignity and advances the common weal"? (Todd)

NATURE ENCOMPASSES THE CITY

While the city in many ways has replaced nature — both concretely as the habitat of most human beings and as our own construction — nonetheless, the bottom line is that we are totally and minute-to-minute dependent on nature and its services. Nature in the first sense — the all-encompassing source or ground of all there is — and more specifically our own planet Earth with its particular constitution of elements suitable for living things is the *sine qua non*. No matter how much we transform "first nature" into cityscapes and other myriad interpretations, it is not infinitely malleable. Our gradual transformation of first nature, from when we lived as hunter-gatherers, into second nature — the twenty-first century city — now faces us with the deterioration and destruction of everything we hold dear. The human ability to distance ourselves from first nature, both by changing it and by objectifying it, is causing a deep forgetfulness to overtake us.

This forgetfulness is epitomized in the city dweller's relationship to food. Our ability to distance ourselves from first nature is nowhere more evident than in our ignorance and denial of our total dependence on the Earth with every mouthful we eat. As Michael Pollan puts it in his book tracing "the natural history of four meals" back to their roots: "All flesh is grass." The Scriptural text takes on new meaning when we consider that even a Twinkie or a Big Mac "begins with a particular plant growing in a specific patch of soil . . . somewhere on Earth" (Pollan, 17). Our flesh (and the flesh that we eat) can be traced back to the grass that feeds us. "At either end of any food chain you find a biological system — a patch of soil, a human body — and the health of one is converted — literally — to the health of the other" (Pollan, 9). And yet we city dwellers have forgotten this all-important piece of information: the inexorable, undeniable link between our health and the health of the planet. The physicality of the connection needs to be underscored: it is from body to body. "Daily, our eating turns nature into culture, transforming *the body of the world into our bodies and minds*" (emphasis added) (Pollan, 10). It is impossible to make our absolute dependence on first nature any clearer. We need to relearn the importance of this most basic of all transformations. "For we would [then] no longer need any reminder that however we choose to feed ourselves, we eat by the grace of nature, not industry, and what we're eating is never anything more or less than *the body of the world*" (emphasis added) (Pollan, 411).

But urban dwellers seldom see this. The city is the prime example of both our greatest accomplishment and our greatest danger. Jerusalem, the city of desire and delight, is fast emerging as Babylon, the city of excessive luxury in the midst of extreme poverty. The city, which stands as the quintessential human habitation — civilized, diverse, cosmopolitan — is at the same time becoming the greatest threat to human well-being. "Of all the recognized ecological systems it is human urbanism which seems most destructive of its host" (Cook, 143). Cities are energy hogs, sucking energy from near and far to allow some city dwellers to live at the highest level of comfort and convenience ever known, while many others exist in squalor. Cities of twelve million or more are divided, to be sure by class, race and gender, but also by the space they own and the energy they can command. A spacious condo overlooking the harbour, with all the electronic devices desired, is the sign of the successful city dweller. But having transformed first nature so thoroughly into the built, utilized environment, we are no longer aware of nature as source, as that which feeds us every mouthful we eat and provides us with every breath we take. We can forget "first nature."

But *can* we? The answer appears to be no, in the judgement of

The United Nations Millennium Ecosystem Assessment, the work of over 1300 experts worldwide: "the first attempt by the scientific community to describe and evaluate on a global scale the full range of services people desire from nature" (UNEP, 16). The sobering conclusion of this recent, massive study is that out of twenty-four essential services provided by nature to humanity, nearly two-thirds are in decline. These services are numerous and all-encompassing, falling into three major categories: Provisioning Services (food, fibre, genetic resources, biochemicals and natural medicines, fresh water); Regulating Services (air, climate, water, erosion, disease, pest, pollination, natural hazard); and Cultural Services (spiritual and religious values, aesthetic values, recreation and eco-tourism) (UNEP, 17). As the Assessment states, "In effect, the benefits reaped from our engineering of the planet have been achieved by running down natural capital assets" (UNEP, 5).

Yet nature's services are seldom appreciated; they are often hidden, particularly from city dwellers, for whom clean water comes from the faucet and food from the supermarket. "First nature" provides these services "free" to the planet's inhabitants, but as the Assessment points out, as societies become more complex and technologically advanced, it is "easy to gain the impression that we no longer depend on natural systems" (UNEP, 6). The Assessment stresses the need for consciousness-raising: "We must learn to recognize the true value of nature both in an economic sense and in the richness it provides to our lives in ways more difficult to put numbers on" (UNEP, 5). Such true value ranges from the taste of a cup of clean water to the sight of snow-capped mountains. We are nature's debtors and nature's lovers.

THINKING DIFFERENTLY

The task before us — a qualitative shift in our attitude toward nature — is daunting. Yet this need appears to be the overwhelming conclusion coming from all fields that study planetary health. As botanist Peter Raven says: "It is also a fundamentally spiritual task"

(Raven, 25). After stating what geography, anthropology, biology and sociology can contribute to the planetary crisis, most scholars agree that an attitude change is "also" needed, a shift in values at a deep level. From the time of Aristotle to the eighteenth century, economics was considered a subdivision of ethics: the good life was understood to be based on such values as the common good, justice and limits. Having lost this context for how to live on our planet and substituting the insatiable greed of market capitalism in its stead, we are now without the means to make the qualitative shift in thinking that is required. With the death of Communism and the decline of socialism, Western society is left with an image of human life that is radically individualistic. The current major societal institutions in the West — government, economic, and religion — all support the assumption that the liberty, gratification and salvation of the individual human person is the appropriate view of who we are in the scheme of things. This is diametrically opposed to how we should think of ourselves within an ecological world view. It is impossible to imagine us acting differently — acting as "ecological citizens" — unless we internalize ecological values (Kjellberg, 46).

One of the distinctive activities of religion is the formation of basic assumptions regarding human nature and our place in the scheme of things. As theologians widely agree, all theology is anthropology. Religious traditions educate through stories, images and metaphors, creating in their adherents deep and often unconscious assumptions about who human beings are and how they should act. Religions are in the business of forming the imagination, and thus influencing the action of people. It is at this point that religions can make a significant contribution to the planetary crisis. For we live *within* the assumptions, the constructions, of who we think we are. As these assumptions, constructions, change, so might behaviour. To be sure, there is no absolute relationship between thinking and doing. While the Greeks thought that to know the good was to do the good, most of us would probably agree with Paul that this is not necessarily so. Nonetheless, our basic assumptions or world views influence, often in hidden and insidious ways, our decisions and behaviour. The ways we imagine ourselves in the world are critical to living in those ways. Thus, as many theologians and urbanists agree, utopian thinking — in addition to being a prophetic witness against "what is" — becomes a possible way forward toward more just and sustainable living. As various NGOs (non-government organizations) like to say, "a different world is possible." But how do we get there? How can it become possible?

One small contribution toward this possibility is to change the metaphor by which we think of ourselves in the world. The metaphor that is conventional and widely accepted in twenty-first century market capitalism is *the individual in the machine*. Human beings are seen as subjects in an objectified world that is there for our use — our needs, desires and recreation. The world is a "thing" to be utilized for human needs and pleasure. To see ourselves this way, however, is an anomaly in human history, for until the scientific revolution of the seventeenth century, as Carolyn Merchant and others have pointed out, the Earth was assumed to be alive, even as we are (Merchant). Throughout time, from the Greek Stoics to the medieval Christians and the First Nations peoples, the organic quality of the Earth was not questioned. But during the last few hundred years, it has become increasingly useful and profitable to think of the world more like a machine than a body. Since we always think in metaphors — especially at the deepest level of our world views — the nature of the metaphor becomes critical. If the machine model is dominant, then we will think of the world's parts as only externally related, able to be repaired like cars with new parts substituting for faulty ones, with few consequences for the Earth as a whole. With such a basic model in mind, it is hard for people to see the tragedy of clear-cut forest practices or the implications of global warming.

However, the "body" is re-emerging across many fields of study as a basic metaphor for interpretation and action. Geographer

David Harvey mentions "the extraordinary efflorescence of interest in 'the body' as a grounding for all sorts of theoretical enquiries over the last two decades or so" (Harvey, 97). As we have noted, this interest is hardly novel: from the Socratic notion of the body ("man") as the measure of all things to the Stoic metaphor of the world as a living organism and First Nations' understanding of the Earth as "mother" of us all, body language has historically been central to the interpretation of our place in the scheme of things. This is true of Christianity as well. As an incarnational religion, Christianity has focused on bodily metaphors: Jesus as the incarnate God, the eucharist as the body and blood of Christ, the church as the body of Christ.[1] To see bodily well-being as the measure of both human and planetary well-being is so obvious that it seems strange that it should need a revival. What is gradually surfacing once again is the realization that the appropriate metaphor with which to imagine our relation to the world is not *the individual in the machine*, but *bodies living within the body of the Earth*. The food chain supports the centrality of this model: our eating transforms the body of the world into our bodies. However, behind twenty-first-century destruction of the planet as well as the impoverishment of the majority of its inhabitants lies a very different assumption about human beings: we are individuals with external relations to one another and to the planet itself.

Before proceeding further with the body model (or any other model), we must note that all metaphors are partial, none is adequate, and all need supplementation from other metaphors.[2] Metaphors are not descriptions; rather, they are the principal epistemological tool available to us on matters having to do with our most basic assumptions about ourselves and our world. We judge metaphors not by descriptive agreement, but by a shock of recognition that follows initial disbelief. Thus, as Jacques Derrida points out, metaphor lies somewhere between nonsense and truth and we entertain the nonsense for a while to see if it has any truth (Derrida, 41-42). Thus to imagine the world as a machine or a body engenders an initial suspicion followed by an acknowledgment of possibility — and eventually, if the metaphor turns out to be an enduring model, with acceptance and familiarity. In addition, however, to this set of criteria for a good model, one other is crucial: what are the results of living within it? What does thinking within this model do to our acting within it?

We have seen the results of living within the machine model for several hundred years now, and the verdict is overwhelmingly negative. Is it time to return to the model of the world — and ourselves — as body? The body as measure, as the lens through which we view the world and ourselves, changes everything. It means that human beings as bodies, dependent on other bodies and on the body of the Earth, are interrelated and interdependent in infinite, mind-boggling, wonderful and risky ways. It means that *materialism* in the sense of what makes for bodily well-being for all humans and for the Earth, becomes the measure of the good life. It combines the socialist with the ecological vision of human and planetary flourishing. It means that the good life cannot be the hoarding by a few individuals of basic resources for their own comfort and enjoyment. Rather, if we desire to take care of ourselves, we must also take care of the world, for we are, in this metaphor, internally related and mutually dependent on all other parts of the body. The metaphor of body — not just the human body but all bodies (all matter) — is a radically egalitarian measure of the good life: it claims that all deserve the *basics* (food, habitat, clean air and water).

This model turns our thinking upside down, for it makes two claims at odds with the mechanistic model. First, it claims that we human beings can no longer see ourselves as controlling all the other "parts"; rather, we must acknowledge that as the creature at the top of the food chain, we are totally dependent on all the others who are presumably "beneath" us. Second, it impels us to acknowledge that the 20 percent of us who use 80 percent of the world's energy are responsible for the crushing poverty on our planet through our refusal to share resources equitably among all human beings and other creatures. In other words, this model helps us to see that sustainability and just distribution of resources are but two sides of the same coin: in order for the Earth to be healthy long-term, the basic resources of life must be shared equitably among all creatures.[3] In other words, the individualistic, greedy assumptions of market capitalism are false: human beings cannot flourish apart from the flourishing of all the constituents that make up the Earth. The Earth is more like a body than it is like a machine. Returning to the wisdom of our forebears and living within the body model rather than within the machine appears to be an appropriate move. This move, I believe, will help us in our central political task as expressed by Harvey: "Suffice it to say that the integration of the urbanization question into the environmental-ecological question is a *sine qua non* for the twenty-first century" (Harvey, 429).

GOD ENCOMPASSES THE WORLD

Is the model of the body also appropriate for thinking about the relationship of God and the world? If we were to imagine ourselves and the world in organic rather than mechanistic terms, what does this do to our concept of God?

As shocking as this question may seem, it is fully in keeping with the incarnationalism of Christianity. One of the most distinctive beliefs of this religion is that God became human, became flesh, in Jesus Christ. This incarnationalism is, however, also implicit in Hebrew with its understanding of Emmanuel — God with us, here and now, on the Earth. God is not a distant, unmoved Mover, as in Greek thought, but the One who suffers with, delights in, punishes and persuades the wayward tribe of Israel. Christianity claims that the Messiah has come — God has appeared in human flesh — in Jesus Christ. To see incarnationalism as the nature of God, that God is always with us on the Earth, and not simply in the one-time event of Jesus, has been a deep strand in historical Christian thinking and is emerging once again in the world view known as panentheism (not to be confused with pantheism).

Panentheism says that God encompasses the world: God is internally related to every iota of creation as its source and sustaining power, but God is more than the world.[4] God and the world are related on the analogy of a baby in the womb. Everything that is, is *in* God and God is *in* all things and yet God is not identical with the universe, for the universe is dependent on God in a way that God is not dependent on the universe. This understanding of the relation of God and the world is in contrast to both theism and pantheism. Theism says that God is "above" the world and only related to it externally as its creator and ruler, whereas pantheism identifies God with the world.[5] Panentheism, broadly understood, is widespread among process theologians, feminist and ecological theologians, as well as Hindu and First Nations religions. This theological perspective understands the transcendence of God to be radical immanence; that is, the glory and power of God is manifest not in distance from the world but in intimacy with it as its source, sustenance and renewal.

I would like now to investigate in more detail the contribution of the model of the world as God's body for twenty-first-century urban living. These contributions emerge from the two central streams in Christian thought: the sacramental and the prophetic, or the Catholic and the Reformed (or Protestant). The model of the world as God's body has both sacramental and prophetic dimensions.

THE SACRAMENTAL DIMENSION

If one lives within this model, one sees the world differently: not as an object or a machine or simply a resource, but as sacred, valuable and needing our care. As mentioned earlier, the model of the world as God's body rests on an incarnational view of creation. Rather than seeing creation as separate from and external to God, something that God manipulates and controls (and hence that we can as well), an incarnational creation view sees nature as intimately related to God, as "within" God. The world is God's body; hence, creation, nature, bodies, flesh — these are all "of God." The world, including nature, is not ours to do with as we wish. It all belongs to and tells us of God. The sacramental dimension claims that nature is an image of the divine; it is a reflection of God in all of God's diverse beauty.[6] Hence, while the sacramental dimension of the model connects us to God, it does so only through the millions of different bodies that make up God's "body." It suggests a celebration of bodies as well as concern for the care and feeding of bodies that underscores our respect for their intrinsic worth as part of God's creation.

The sacramental dimension of the model of the world as God's body prohibits us from folding first nature into second nature, since it suggests that nature, ours and everything else, does not belong to us in the first place. It is "other." The interpretation of nature as sacrament of God demands a different stance, one suggested by Henry David Thoreau's comment that "wildness" was in the second-growth forest at Walden Pond in Concord. "Wildness" is in the mind as well as in reality; it is our recognition of otherness. In the words of philosopher Iris Murdoch: "Love is the extremely difficult realization that something other than oneself is real. Love . . . is the discovery of reality (Murdoch, 51). In other words, "love" is not a sentimental emotion or an act of charity; rather, it is the "objective" recognition that others exist, have intrinsic worth, and rights to the basics of existence.

This sense of the "other" is evident also in the story of creation in Genesis. While Christianity has often been condemned as a major contributor to environmental destruction with its slogan from Genesis, "subdue and dominate," one should also note a very different sensibility within that text. After each creation — of the light and darkness, the waters and the land, the sun and the moon, all fish in the sea and birds in the air and animals on the land (including human beings) God says, "It is good." God says of creation "It is good," not good for human beings (or even for the divine self!), but simply "good." This is an aesthetic statement of intrinsic worth for each and every creature. This story supports both the intrinsic worth of others and their right to the basics of existence.

Such an attitude toward the world acknowledges that human beings have indeed constructed the world in which we live, that there is no uninterpreted, pristine or untouched nature left. Nonetheless, it is still possible to hold, if one lives within the model of the world as God's body, that a sensibility of appreciation of and care for "others" is an imperative — and that it is a realistic assessment, as well.

THE PROPHETIC DIMENSION

While the sacramental dimension of the model encourages us to appreciate and love others — realize their worth — the prophetic dimension focuses our attention on limits — the recognition that bodies, including the body of the world, are finite. The "prophetic dimension" does not mean predicting the future but, in line with the prophets of the Hebrew Scriptures, demanding justice for all of God's creatures. All life-forms must have food, fresh water, clean air and a habitat. The prophetic dimension stresses the limits of all bodies, the finitude of the planet, the need for a just and sustainable use of resources. The model of the world as God's body places severe limits on the excess, hoarding, greed and injustice of some parts of the body — namely, the well-off 20 percent of human beings who are contributing to the destruction of the planet and the impoverishment of fellow human beings.

The central issue at the Third World Urban Forum that met in June 2006 in Vancouver was the projection by the UN's latest evaluation of cities: that slum living is now among the fastest-growing legacies of "civilization" (Hume, A17). Given present trends, one out of three city dwellers will be doomed to the slums. The conditions in many cities — those pushing twenty million — are already dire. The needs of the doubling of city populations by mid-century from the present two billion to four billion are mind-boggling (Third Session of the World Urban Forum). Housing, public health, transportation, energy, food and water, education and medical services are simply the basics needed for minimal human existence. The Forum met in a city — Vancouver — widely praised as one of the most livable and well-built in the world; it epitomizes the "compact" city with its high-density population core of business and residential buildings, good public transit, numerous parks, and the greatest percentage of pedestrians and cyclists of any North American city. It is a dream city. But even Vancouver has "the lower East Side," an area of great poverty and drug addiction, an indication of things to come in the cities of the future according to the Forum. Vancouver is an example of the two sides of cities — the New Jerusalem and Babylon — with the latter projected as humanity's destiny.

Is the model of the world as God's body relevant to the upcoming urban crisis? The prophetic dimension of the model — the awareness of the finitude, limits and needs of bodies — suggests that it is. In fact, this dimension must take center stage. Our very survival may well rest on living within a different construction of nature — one closer to contemporary reality — in which second nature must be restrained. The model of the world as God's body, which sees all bodies as needing the basics, suggests a kenotic sensibility for twenty-first-century well-off urban dwellers, so that the projected slum dwellers may have space and place.

"A kenotic sensibility": "kenosis" means to empty, to pull back, to limit. The term is traditional in Christian theology as a way to understand both God's creation of the world and the incarnation in Jesus Christ. In creation, God allowed "space" for others to exist by divine limitation, not as a self-denying act but as affirmation of the other, in a way similar to the Genesis announcement "it is good." In the incarnation, according to the Pauline text, Christ "though he was in the form of God, did not regard equality with God as something to be exploited, but emptied himself, taking the form of a slave, being born in human likeness" (Phil. 2:6–7).[7] Kenosis is a unifying theme in Christian thought, extending beyond God's actions in creation and the incarnation to include the discipleship of followers. As Paul reminds his flock: "Let each of you look not to your own interests, but to the interest of others. Let the same mind be in you that was in Christ Jesus"; namely, follow the self-emptying Christ (Phil. 2:4–5). Kenosis — self-limitation that others might have place and space to grow and flourish — is the way that God acts toward the world and the way that Christians are to act toward one another. The notion of self-limitation for the well-being of others is widespread among many religions, as evident in the emptying God in Buddhism and Gandhi's notions of *ahimsa* and *satyagraha* (reverence for all living things, and soul or love force) (Cobb and Ives). In spite of differences among the religions on many issues, there appears to be no religion that supports "blessed are the greedy" (except, perhaps, the new "religion" of market capitalism). In both Buddhism and Christianity, compassion toward others is based on self-emptying, which, paradoxically, is also the way to true fullness: whoever would save their life must lose it.

For well-off city dwellers, the kenotic, prophetic sensibility also means that second nature, the built environment, must be minimized rather than maximized. It means small condos and apartments, not mansions; living spaces that go up, not out; hybrid cars, not Hummers; food that is grown locally, not half-way around the world. It means saying NO, saying "enough." Second nature is built upon first nature and first nature is, increasingly, a vulnerable, deteriorating body unable to support the Western high-energy-use lifestyle. This realization should impact us at all levels: what we eat, our means of transportation, what we wear, the places we live, the parks where we play, the offices where we work. One of the greatest challenges of the twenty-first century is decent, liveable conditions for the billions who will live in cities. We well-off city dwellers need to take up less space, use less energy, lower our desires for more, attend to "needs" before "wants" — become small, in other words. The prophetic, kenotic sensibility demands that prosperous urban dwellers retreat from expansion and accept simplification at all levels of existence. Justice and sustainability demand that whatever we build upon first nature be shared with all other beings and be done within the limits of the planet's resources.

In sum, second nature needs to acknowledge the base on which it is built and will continue to depend — first nature. A deep understanding of nature reminds us that we are *bodies* before all else. We cannot interpret or build unless we can eat. While we are at the same time interpreters and builders of our world, we are not its maker or master. There is something outside our interpretations and constructions: the air we must breathe, the water we must drink and the food we must eat.

A new Cascadian civil religion would include an attitude, a way of thinking and acting that underscores the beauty and intrinsic value of first nature as well as our inexorable dependence on it. It would help to situate human beings in an appropriate stance toward the world: a stance of gratitude and care, gratitude for the wonder of living on this beautiful planet (as the poet Rilke puts it, "Being here is magnificent"), and care for its fragile, deteriorating creatures and systems. We do not own the Earth, we do not even pay rent for it. It is given to us "free" for our lifetime, with the proviso that we treat it with the honour it deserves: appreciating it as a reflection of the divine and loving it as our mother and our neighbour.

Part Four

❧

CASCADIAN CULTURE

VOLCANIC CASCADIAN CULTURE. The three major cities of the
Pacific Northwest, Portland, Seattle and Vancouver, feature dramatic
views of snow-covered volcanic mountains, adding to the sense that
the region has both a geographic and cultural instability, even
explosiveness. Patricia O'Connell Killen believes spirituality is
present in Cascadia "like magma under the volcanoes."
This is Mount Hood near Portland, Oregon.

CAN'T ESCAPE WILDERNESS. In a not uncommon occurrence, this black bear wandering onto the North Vancouver yard of the editor's mother illustrates how nature imposes itself on the urban residents of the Pacific Northwest. Since they cannot defeat the region's wildness, most city-dwelling Cascadians are learning a healthy respect for the wilderness. (Photo Credit: Carla Ferguson)

SEATTLE LIGHTS. Eco-theologian Sallie McFague urges moving beyond simplistic, dualistic thinking that nature in our cities involves only trees, gardens and beaches — and that humans create the rest. Cities, where most Cascadians live, are dependent on the transformation of energy from nature, exemplified by electricity and fuel. "There is nothing," McFague says, "outside nature." (Photo Credit: Natalia Bratslavsky)

PACIFIC NORTHWEST DIVERSITY. Vancouver's giant Dragon Boat
Festival mixes together the region's ethnically diverse city dwellers, many
of whom arrived from elsewhere in search of a promised land. In addition
to reducing their ecological footprint, Philip Resnick urges Cascadians
to avoid hubris, overcome divisions through dialogue and show greater
respect for the accumulated wisdom of the past, East and West.
(Photo Credit: Norman Chan)

THE IDEAL SYMBOL FOR CASCADIA? Many say the evergreen tree is the best symbol for the Pacific Northwest. It can be found throughout the mountainous terrain, grows into one of the tallest trees in the world, feeds the crucial logging industry, provides habitat for wildlife and hikers and, as the indigenous people have long taught, is increasingly seen as sacred, especially now that it is under threat. These evergreens are in Washington's Olympic National Forest. (Photo Credit: Tashka)

THE SALMON. Symbols help a population define what is sacred. While some believe evergreens, mountains, rivers or beaches best symbolize Cascadia, many maintain that the self-sacrificial and highly mobile salmon captures the ethos of the region. Many Cascadians believe they will be saving themselves by saving the once-bountiful fish, which is both threatened and aided by human development — including this piece of engineering near Tumwater Falls, Washington. (Photo Credit: David W. Slocum)

PEACE ARCH AS ICON. Eleanor Stebner writes that Cascadia needs a human-made symbol instead of one that leans on nature. In the face of often-hysterical terrorist fears and heightened border security, Stebner believes that the International Peace Arch straddling the Canada-US boundary at Blaine represents the highest ideals of peace, a bi-national working together for the common good and a creative transformation of both the Pacific Northwest and the planet. (Photo Credit: Stuart Davis)

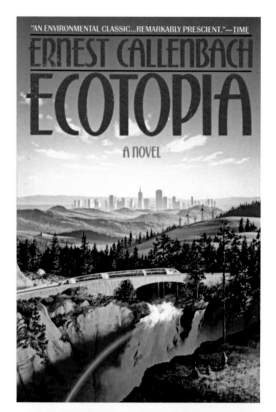

"THE DOUG." The most popular flag to represent the mythical free-standing nation of Cascadia is known as "the Doug." It's an image of a Douglas fir tree on a green (forest) and blue (ocean) background. Champions of a free-standing Cascadia nation have also created semi-humorous bumper stickers telling outsiders to keep their imperialistic hands off. The 1975 novel *Ecotopia* encouraged many Cascadians to envision the region as a futuristic, ecological Eden.

CHAPTER 10

❧

"The Divine Brushing Against the Natural": Pacific Northwest Magic Realism

PAULO LEMOS HORTA[1]

IN THE LATE 1970s, British Columbia author Jack Hodgins was experimenting with ways to convey a sense of Vancouver Island itself — the land and the people — and of the mythologies that people brought to that part of the world. He felt he had found the answer when he hit upon the idea of writing an account of one of the "many failed utopian colonies in Vancouver Island's not-so-distant past."[2] Close to where Hodgins lived, just south of Nanaimo, Brother Twelve had established the Revelation Colony in the 1920s, and one of Hodgins' high-school students lived in Brother Twelve's old house (whose basement still held the safe in which the colonist had stored his money and gold). Yet soon after beginning, Hodgins found himself frustrated in his attempt to piece together this episode in history because "people didn't want to talk about it." He decided to write it as fiction, instead.[3] Yet the switch to fiction did not resolve the fundamental problem of the discomfort of the locals to speak — well or ill — of Brother Twelve's religious and utopian enterprise. Hodgins perceived this resistance as part of a larger regional cultural configuration: on the one hand the West Coast seemed to him to be the Canadian region "most uncomfortable with (and even somewhat hostile to) matters of religion," yet on the other it had "a reputation for a disproportionate number of utopian colonies and new-age types of spirituality."[4]

He asked himself: What sort of fiction might overcome the reader's unease with the discussion of an episode inextricably linked to the related questions of faith and utopia? The task he had set himself as a novelist was complicated by his ambition to be read not merely within small literary circles but by the public at large. He was concerned with the possible rejection of his work, not only by "those who might feel implicated in, say, a story about a utopian colony" but by the "general reader" — that is, by readers he suspected might prove defensive either about their faith or their secularism.[5] How was he to proceed without alienating or embarrassing the very people he was writing about? He found the solution by abandoning the realism of his first manuscript novels (which had been rejected by publishers anyway) and embracing the prose style he had discovered reading the work of Gabriel García Márquez: magic realism — a style that seeks to capture "the marvelous that lies within" reality.[6]

Hodgins gambled that, with its "playfulness, humour, indirection and exaggeration," magic realism would allow the reader to "overlook certain serious underlying opinions relating to uncomfortable issues by imagining them as part of the fun," and allow him as author to put forward his "own points of view in a package palatable even to those who might be inclined to avoid a story that dealt with the issue more directly or uncomfortably."[7] Hodgins also felt that he had been favourably disposed to magic realism by an upbringing marked by the dramatic contours of the landscape of British Columbia. In magic realism, he had found what he was looking for — a style in his view uniquely attuned to both the landscape and the mythology of Vancouver Island.

Two decades later, in the late 1990s, the young Oregon author Gina Ochsner was also looking to find a way to write about the spiritual in a secular world. In her case she was seeking a modern register that might match the matter-of-fact tone that she identified with Old Testament accounts of miracles and the supernatural. Her Quaker upbringing and adopted Greek Orthodox faith were very much part of the stories she sought to tell. But which modern prose style would suit them? Her goal was to persuade readers to suspend their disbelief for a time and accept the spiritual preoccupations in the dark moral parables of her short stories. She argues:

> . . . disbelief is the necessary shadow of belief. The reader brings to bear his or her disbelief and the writer must build out of natural and healthy doubt to establish belief. It's a necessary negotiation that ultimately leads to balance within the story (between the characters who accept without question and the doubting Thomases) and without (between author and reader) so that the piece represents a balanced work of human imagination, logic and vision (faith).[8]

To make faith and the supernatural both comprehensible and credible to the sceptical reader, Ochsner, like Hodgins, had recourse to magic realism. Heeding Flannery O'Connor's caution that "if the readers don't accept the natural world, they'll certainly not accept anything else,"[9] Ochsner makes a realistic portrayal of nature a centerpiece of her magic realism. To create belief out of disbelief, she suggests, an author must "in a consistent and credible manner" use "the physical props and natural laws of the world (no matter how strange that world is)," for otherwise "internal logic fails" and "the story fails, too." The goal of her magic realist writing is to present in a credible fashion "the divine brushing against the natural."[10]

Starting from their wholly different vantage points, Hodgins and Ochsner share a sense that magic realism is a modern prose style uniquely attuned to the difficulties of portraying qualities of spirituality within the Pacific Northwest. Yet this linking of spirituality with regard to the history of magic realism as a form is not at all an intuitive assumption to make (one need only recall Salman Rushdie's satire of aspects of religion in *The Satanic Verses*, 1988). In fact, the spiritual quality present in much Pacific Northwest magic realist fiction may be its distinctive quality. Both authors are invested in the project of revealing magic within reality and the supernatural within the natural. A secular religion of nature suggests itself to Hodgins, not only on a personal level (given his scepticism of religion and religious utopias), but also as a sort of safe middle ground in the cultural configuration of the West Coast. Neither the aggressively secular nor the devoutly religious reader of the West Coast would object to the revelation of nature as magical. The spiritual qualities that Ochsner puts forward are not secular but orthodox and religious — quite a gamble given the secular audience for her stories when they are first printed in the pages of magazines such as *The New Yorker*, noted for their cosmopolitan sophisticated readership.

WHAT IS MAGIC REALISM?

Franco Moretti, a leading scholar of world literature, distinguishes between the study of space in literature (say, representations of the Pacific Northwest in the region's writing) and the study of the literature in space — such as the influence of magic realism across Pacific Northwest letters. It is this latter emphasis that interests me in this paper.[11] Moretti systematizes a distinction that many of us recognize instinctively in our literary practice of the everyday. For instance, Washington author Tamara Sellman keeps separate her blog of Pacific West Coast writing[12] (space in literature) from her online anthology of magic realism across the globe (literature in space).[13] Pacific Northwest letters have been particularly well served by the first type of literary geography in studies of the literary representation of the region's landscape and flora by Rudy Wiebe and Andreas Schroeder, Laurie Ricou and Jack Hodgins in his role as literary critic.[14] To look at magic realism in Pacific Northwest letters is to engage in the second type of literary cartography identified by Franco

Moretti, the analysis of literature in space. This analysis must be more attentive to international literary influences, as Geoff Hancock recognized when compiling an anthology of Canadian magic realism,[15] and also to how these influences take root within the context of distinct local influences and landscapes.

Stepping back for a moment, one can see that the concept of magic realism in its beginning was distinct from what one finds in Pacific Northwest magic realist fiction. In the early 1920s, German art critic Franz Roh defined magic realism to describe the return to realism and objectivity in the new schools of painting that followed Expressionism. In coining the term, Roh registered a discomfort with direct invocations of spirituality. He stated that he preferred "magic" to "mystery," and here he was signalling that he was describing not a religious mystery that descended literally to earth, but a magical quality that hides and palpitates within a reality that can be objectively observed.[16] Magic realism in Roh's sense meant a new realism that intimated a sense of disquiet and foreboding in natural landscapes and portraits of ordinary people and objects.

When the term began to be used in the Pacific Northwest, however, it soon took on a different meaning. George Bowering has noted that as it was applied to the Canadian painters Ken Danby and Alex Colville, magic realism came to mean the painting of "natural items in such a way that the meticulous detail and lighting suggested some sort of spiritual glow."[17] What we see here is a shift in the connotation of a critical term. For Bowering and others, Franz Roh's magic realism no longer appears antithetical to spiritual intimations.

Similarly, the postwar magic realist style of Gabriel García Márquez's *One Hundred Years of Solitude* (1967, first translated into English by Gregory Rabassa in 1970)[18] appears to be more open to the spiritual once it takes root in the Pacific Northwest. For the seminal practitioners of the prose style in Spanish, Portuguese, German and English — García Márquez, José Saramago, Günter Grass, and Salman Rushdie[19] — experimentation with magic realism coincided with a youthful flirtation with Marxism and a commitment to modes of secularism less sympathetic to the claims of faith and spirituality. For the writers of the Pacific Northwest, such as Hodgins and Ochsner, to understand magic realism as a style uniquely apt at stating the claims of faith is to reverse the terms of the equation inherited from García Márquez. Distinctively, the inaugural and definitive works of magic realism in the Pacific Northwest concern themselves with religious utopias and the dark moral parables of faith.

MAGICAL REALITIES AS FAILED UTOPIAS OR "EDENIC SWINDLES"

Mario Vargas Llosa, in his essay "Questions of Conquest" (1990), speculates that the early chroniclers of the discovery and conquest of the New World were in their own way the first practitioners of a magic realist style of writing. "In the chronicles we not only dream about the time in which our fantasy and our realities seem to be incestuously confused," he claims. "In them there is an extraordinary mixture of reality and fantasy, of reality and fiction in a united work. It is a literature that is totalizing, in the sense that it is a literature that embraces not only objective reality but also subjective reality in a new synthesis."[20] For Vargas Llosa the first chronicles of the new world — with their novel synthesis of reality and fantasy, objective and subjective reality — form the tradition from which the magic realism of García Márquez would emerge, and he notes that the Colombian author uses themes from the chronicles in his fiction. One of these is a longing akin to the yearning for utopia, "the promise of something new and formidable, something that if it ever turned into reality would enrich the world and improve civilization."[21]

British Columbia author George Bowering's novel *Burning Water* (1980), which fictionalizes the expedition of Captain George Vancouver to the Strait of Juan de Fuca, similarly connects the early explorers of the Pacific Northwest to the magic realism of modern prose fiction. It is a novel that seeks to convey the sense of strangeness felt by the explorers searching for a new world. Mario Vargas Llosa writes that because the Spanish chroniclers narrated events "under the passion of recently lived experience, they often related things that to us seem like naïve or cynical fantasies."[22] Similarly, the narrator of *Burning Water* relates matter-of-factly the experience of seagoing vessels crossing the Rocky Mountains:

> Then he felt the bow of the *Discovery* go up, and the surge of power as the sails caught and the waters dropped below and behind them. He braced himself while the craft bumped through the rocky air above the first peaks of the Coast Range. He saw the *Chatham* break through the cloud cover, and a few seconds later they were enveloped in grey cloud that turned white, and then they were through. The sun shone white over the miles and miles of cumulus, and picked out the moisture shining on the sails of the two ships alone in all that fluffy sea, coursing eastward effortlessly now, at home in the jet stream.[23]

Historically Captain Vancouver's expedition had sought to determine whether the famed Northwest Passage existed. It is possible to read the passage as a metaphorical realization of this quest. Here Bowering captures well the mixture of subjective and objective reality in the chronicles of the new world also noted by Vargas Llosa. As Bowering describes it, the explorers experience a sense of an unseen world always beyond the horizon that they should be able to reach. The many islands and fjords of the coast seem magical, a place where everything is possible.

Modern novelists of the new world are fond of comparing their task to that of the continent's first chroniclers and cartographers. Michael Ondaatje has stressed the shared goal of modern Latin American and Canadian authors of documenting a still unnamed reality and geography. In the introduction to his 1990 anthology of Canadian short stories, *From Ink Lake*, Ondaatje appropriates for a Canadian context a citation from Chilean poet Pablo Neruda: "there are rivers in our countries that have no names, trees which nobody knows, and birds which nobody has described. . . . Our duty, then as we understand it, is to express what is unheard of." As Ondaatje notes, "Canada, too . . . is still documenting and inventing itself" and naming "its fabulous mountain ranges and rivers."[24]

The comparison to the situation of the early chroniclers of a new and foreign world carries a particularly utopian saliency for authors who invoke the promise of the Americas as a new Eden. Evocations of the landscape of the Pacific Northwest as an enchanted setting for utopian quests draws on a tradition of representing the "marvellous reality" of the new world in Latin-American letters, widely disseminated via Haitian author Alejo Carpentier's novel *The Kingdom of This World* (1949) and its famous prologue.[25] For Carpentier, the fauna and flora as well as the history of the Americas were themselves larger than life. In his view, the land need not be made magical or transformed through artifice or a whimsical imagination; the writer need only find ways to do justice to a reality already marvellous. A larger-than-life nature demands a larger than-life-realism.

West Coast magic realists would concur with Carpentier's proclamation of the New World as a New Eden. "Certainly it is possible to get the impression that B.C. writers are like a lot of Adams gone mad in Eden, naming everything in sight," Jack Hodgins observes in the introduction to his 1976 anthology of West Coast writing, adding in a similar vein to Neruda, "It must be remembered that this is, in a literary sense, unexplored territory; writers are making maps."[26] Bill Gaston, another Canadian West Coast author, aptly defines this thread of magic realist writing in the region:

> It seems to me that the land itself is exaggerated — the trees and waves are so huge, and the weather is so big. The land doesn't have a sense of being settled at all yet. It still has a dangerous feel. Out west, people feel a bit puny and appear a bit absurd — especially self-important people. . . . It invites an absurd vision, an exaggerated vision. . . . In my fiction, very rarely does anything impossible happen. Things are just slightly larger than life — the reds are a bit brighter, the greens are a bit greener, and people smile a bit more crazily.[27]

Oregon ecologist and theologian Gail Wells cautions in Chapter 14 of this volume that "it can be limiting to have the landscape so thoroughly dominate the artistic consciousness," suggesting that "our dazzling scenery might be giving us a sort of tunnel vision, distracting us from the rich storehouse of human experience and human interaction."[28] Yet in the view of the magic realist authors of the Pacific Northwest this investment in landscape may signal a stronger and more universal empathy that comes from living in a landscape of overwhelming breadth and beauty.[29]

Hodgins himself frequently stresses the formative influence of natural landscape in his own magic realist writing on the region: "I believe the dramatic contrasts of mountains and forests, coastline and winding roads, etc, of northern Vancouver Island had as much to do with the way I see the world (and stories) as had reading Latin American fiction — in fact, this may have been a reason I so quickly responded to Márquez and others."[30] Thus, his reading of *One Hundred Years of Solitude* struck a chord for Hodgins because it reflected so clearly his own experience of life on Vancouver Island: "the gossip and memories of [his] parents' generation when they recounted their childhoods and early experiences of natural extreme dramatic elements."[31] While accepting the label of magic realism for his early fiction, Hodgins protests that he aimed merely at realistically "creating a world very close to the world in which [he'd] grown up" and that any exaggeration "was only the sort of exaggeration I heard on a daily basis from family and friends and public officials."[32]

Hodgins affirms he is a "magic realist" in the sense that he sees "the magic that's already there."[33] For Hodgins, those who share a similar connection to the land, and inherit via family history exaggerated accounts of its storms and of its failed utopias, do not think of this writing as magical but simply as realistic. The stories sound fantastic only to those with no connection to the land or its history. It is in this sense that Pacific Northwest writers saw magic realism as a way of escaping prairie realism and naturalism (the dominant forms to that point) with their sense of the land as an enemy that had to be fought and defeated. Instead, the land of the Pacific Northwest could be described as magical, enchanted with a multitude of possibilities, even a utopia.

What then does the magic realism in the Pacific Northwest in the 1970s borrow from the Latin-American tradition, and in what ways does this writing diverge from that tradition? The defining work of magic realism, *One Hundred Years of Solitude* (1967), famously opens with the invocation of a "world so recent that many things lacked names, and in order to indicate them it was necessary to point."[34] It is Gabriel García Márquez's wondrous discourse of an Edenic new world that Jack Hodgins would relocate to the Pacific Northwest in his novel *The Invention of the World*. *One Hundred Years of Solitude* and *The Invention of the World* are both narratives of failed utopias, or, to borrow Hodgins' phrase, Edenic swindles. While the utopias betrayed by the protagonists in García Márquez's novel are primarily political, scientific, and perhaps even technological,[35] Hodgins chose to privilege the tale of Brother Twelve's colony "just south of Nanaimo" rather than the "the Finnish socialist colony of Sointula,"[36] which might have more closely resembled García Márquez's Macondo.

The Invention of the World exhibits many of the characteristic traits identified with García Márquez's *One Hundred Years of Solitude*.[37] In both novels a series of key narrative devices recur with the effect of constantly revealing reality itself to be magical. A semblance of magic is introduced into routine life through the intermingling of events of a more ambiguous affiliation, for instance evasive and secret experiences and prophetic dreams that possess a distinct life (such as the dream that sets in motion the action of the section "Eden's Swindle" in Hodgins' novel). The introduction of unusual events suggests the existence of another reality governed, in Hodgins' words, by the "combination of energy, humour and a little exaggeration."[38] Uncanny events are not introduced as absurd but as the exaggerations of an objective reality, facts that exist subjectively in the credulity and imagination of the people (which in both novels are rural and eccentric small town folk). As these events are recalled in the past tense, often through nostalgia, the distance in time reduces objective reality and events are de-naturalized and appear imaginary. In collective memory, history becomes myth.

The Invention of the World begins in Irish mythology and ends with a wedding that the narrator has already begun to transform into a legendary event. Both novels employ similar tricks of persuasion to pass off the fantastic as credible, notably what Hodgins terms the humorous approach to issues of faith and the supernatural, and what Mario Vargas Llosa terms the alchemy of laughter and the fantastic in García Márquez's work ("prodigies lose their prodigious air in presenting themselves as games or pranks . . . paradoxically, the reader consents to play").[39]

The opening of "Eden's Swindle," the second section of *The Invention of the World*, is strongly reminiscent of García Márquez's work:

> It was Keneally's mother who started the whole deception, one hundred and fifteen years ago and thousands of miles away. When the ghost of Cathleen ni Houlihan appeared in a dream to predict that her child would be fathered by a bull-god from the sky, the poor girl was so alarmed at the prospect that she got all tangled up in her blankets, fell off the side of her bed onto the stone floor, and knocked every trace of memory right out of her pretty skull. She could not remember a thing: not her name, not the cause of the long white scar down the side of her throat, not even the nature of the dream which had caused her to lose her memory. She did not recognize her mother, a fat sharp-eyed woman who claimed an ancestry including the warrior-king Brian Boru, and who locked herself in a shed of stones rather than face the shame of a simple-minded daughter. Nor did she recognize her father, a man whose peasant instincts ran to less dramatic gestures than his wife's. . . . The least she could do for him, he said, was drown herself in a place where she had no name.[40]

Many of the elements of this passage are found in *One Hundred Year of Solitude*: the location of a magical or miraculous time in the distant past, a prophetic dream foretelling the birth of a mythological being, an amnesia attributable at once to a natural and a supernatural cause, the claim of a fabulous ancestry, the quick sketch of character via the presence or absence of "dramatic gestures," and an ostracism resolved via a journey to where one is unknown (such as the one that leads Aureliano to first found Macondo). The beginning of this section is unmistakably Márquezean in its structure.

This is not the place to offer a genealogy of magic realist authors, but briefly Hodgins' influence can be traced via patterns of friendship and mentorship in the subsequent magic realist writing of many British Columbia authors, such as Bill Gaston (*Deep Cove Stories*, 1989) and Gail Anderson-Dargatz (*The Cure For Death by Lightning*, 1996; *A Recipe for Bees*, 1998). Gaston's early fiction appears influenced by both the *Invention of the World* and Hodgins' second novel *The Resurrection of Joseph Bourne: Or, A Word or Two on those Port Annie Miracles* (1979), a novel in which Hodgins remembers "consciously working to give the story a 'magic' sense" while "keeping the reality of that part of Vancouver Island."[41] Anderson-Dargatz went to the University of Victoria specifically to study under Hodgins, who recalls that there was a clear presence of magic realism in the earliest draft pages she showed to him of her first novel.[42] Anderson-Dargatz's subsequent magic realist fiction, in particular *A Recipe for Bees*, bears also the trace of her own reading in Latin American magic realist fiction, notably Laura Esquivel's *Like Water for Chocolate: A Novel in Monthly Installments with Recipes, Romances and Home Remedies* (1993, first translated into English in 1995).

If one pans back to the larger context of late twentieth-century English-language fiction, it is fascinating to see magic realism take hold in Pacific Northwest letters via the influence of Hodgins' *Invention of the World* (1977) and Bowering's *Burning Water* (1980) before Salman Rushdie's Booker-Prize-winning novel *Midnight's Children* (1981) would make it fashionable to import magic realism throughout the English-speaking world and identify the style with the postcolonial predicament. British Columbia authors appear to have consumed and engaged foreign works crucial to the development of a regional magic realist style upon their first translation into English (Bowering recalls the early influence of Adolfo Bioy Casares,[43]

Hodgins that of García Márquez) — before they had been imported and adapted in English-language fictions by authors such as Rushdie and Ondaatje (in the 1983 memoir *Running in the Family*) to suit the metropolitan tastes of literary circles in London, New York and Toronto.

The depth of the appeal and autonomous influence of early magic realist fictions in the late 1970s perhaps helps explain why the style continues among authors in the Pacific Northwest after the waves of enthusiasm associated with magic realism in the academy and the media have passed. In 1993 Esquivel's formulaic novel *Like Water for Chocolate* and the film of the same year by Alfonso Arau[44] began the decline of magic realism as a creative force in Latin America. Its death can be found in 1996 in the *McOndo Anthology* and the *Crack Manifesto* conceived respectively in Santiago and Mexico City. Yet in the Pacific Northwest many works have continued to be penned in the unmistakable cast of magic realism: among them British Columbia authors Gail Anderson-Dargatz's *A Rhinestone Button* (2002), Anosh Irani's *The Cripple and his Talismans* (2004) and Pauline Holdstock's *Beyond Measure* (2003), which was published in the United States in 2005 under the more explicitly magic realist title *A Rare and Curious Gift*. South of the border there is Washington State author Diana Abu-Jaber's *Arabian Jazz* (2003) and Oregon author Kathleen Alcalá's Mexican trilogy *Spirits of the Ordinary* (1997), *The Flower in the Skull* (1998) and *Treasures in Heaven* (2000). As elaborated upon in the section that follows, the most original magic realism in contemporary Pacific Northwest letters is to be found in the short fiction of Gina Ochsner from Keizer, Oregon.

THE MAGIC OF REALITY AS THE POSSIBILITY OF GRACE

If Hodgins' early fiction inaugurated a tradition of magic realist writing in the Pacific Northwest a little over three decades ago, the future of this prose style in the region is well represented by the Flannery O'Connor prize-winning work of Oregon author Gina

Ochsner, who is not yet forty. Ochsner is atypical among accomplished magic realist authors, who have generally tended to be secular. The author of two short story collections, *The Necessary Grace to Fall* (2002) and *People I Wanted to Be* (2005), Ochsner has claimed and reinvented magic realism as a style particularly suited to her own religious beliefs.

Before proceeding further with Ochsner's fiction, it will be useful to consider a passage from Portuguese Nobel Laureate José Saramago's *The Cave* (2000) that captures the sense of the precedence of sensorial reality to speculations regarding the supernatural, which are shared by other seminal practitioners of magic realism such as García Márquez, Grass, and Rushdie:

> Note that when we are born our fingers do not yet possess intelligence, they acquire it little by little with the passing of time and the help of eyes that see. This is precisely why what they always have been known to do best is to reveal the occult. What the brain registers as knowledge of magic or the supernatural, whatever magic or the supernatural may mean, the fingers with their little minds have taught them. For the intelligence of the head to know what a stone is, it was first necessary for the fingers to have touched it, to have felt its roughness, weight and density. Only much later would the head understand that with a piece of stone one could make something which would come to be called knife and something which would be called an idol.[45]

While it is difficult to generalize about the complex literary productions of such canonical authors within contemporary world literature, at times the presence of magic realism in their work has coincided with attempts to historicize and de-mythologize the truth of revelation and scripture, as in the controversial examples of Rushdie's *The Satanic Verses* (1988) and Saramago's *The Gospel According to Jesus Christ* (1991) which led to the fatwa against Rushdie and Saramago's self-exile in the Canary Islands after the Portuguese government's rejection of his novel.

In a reversal of Saramago's emphasis on the precedence of physical sensation to intimations of the supernatural, Ochsner writes that belief "is the engine that makes perceptions operate." In her essay "The True World: When Consensual Reality Is Not Enough" (2005), Ochsner dates her attraction to magic realism to her childhood immersion in Old Testament accounts of the miracles and "many evidences of an unseen and sometimes seen God who could take any form he wanted whenever he wanted because he could."[46] She was struck by the matter-of-fact tone with which the Old Testament presents evidences of the supernatural: "These accounts of the strange, the wondrous, the magical are so seamlessly woven into the narrative, so completely organic, that they are not held apart as pieces of oddity, but rather as evidence of a parallel, invisible world that intersects ours, though we aren't always aware of it."[47] For instance, in the account of the aftermath of the conversations between Moses and God "face to face, as a man speaks to a friend," she is struck by the Israelites' request that Moses veil his face, for to gaze upon its residual radiance would be to risk blindness. For Ochsner the body of stories and belief she grew up with "so thoroughly suffuses" who she is and how she sees things that it determines the sort of stories she tends to read and to write and predisposes her to the magic realism of the writing of Gabriel García Márquez.[48]

Indeed in García Márquez's writing she admires the use of magic realism in the service of a realism that she takes as a model for her own fiction. As his fiction situates the unbelievable within a believable world and the credible reactions of ordinary and humble people, "we are forced to observe them and ask why they behave the way they do."[49] She suggests that readers of his short story "A Very Old Man with Enormous Wings" — in which the title character falls to earth and briefly invites the curiosity of a small town — will discover that the tale "was never about the angel" but about the "quirky, curious, easily bored, but ultimately believable townspeople."[50]

García Márquez's stories demonstrate to her that strange circumstances and unconventional means can best reveal "our essential human nature." In this context Ochsner eloquently privileges magic realism as a style, for "nothing better can reveal the Divine brushing against the Natural":

> In these stories, the extraordinary occurs in the context of the ordinary, pitched against the ordinary backdrop of ordinary human lives and human psychology and what we see is the supernatural overlapping, sometimes colliding with the Natural. The supernatural here is a fact, but it displaces nothing Natural. . . . The plot events, the background setting, the props all may be quite odd, even absurd, but people's reactions to very basic problems . . . are always and must be utterly human, and in this way, utterly credible.[51]

Rather than as a prescription or formula that might narrow the possibilities for fictional experimentation, Ochsner sees magic realism as exponentially multiplying the tools in her writer's toolbox, for while a "story told tight to only what can be proven as real must confine itself to just that — realism only," stories that partake of both magic and reality "extend the borders of both" and are thus "like arrows that outstrip the strength of the bow."[52]

Ochsner's story "Articles of Faith," from the collection *People I Wanted to Be* (2005), presents the riddle of whether a childless couple is being haunted by the ghosts of their miscarried children. Paraphrasing her reading of García Márquez, it can be said to be ultimately less about the ghost children than what they might reveal about the state of Irina and Evin's marriage. Their distinct responses to the ghosts (Irina cherishes them, and Evin seeks to escape their presence) tell the story of the cultural and psychological misunderstandings upon which their marriage was built, the deterioration of their relationship, and — via an ambiguous ending characteristic of Ochsner's stories — the possibility of new beginnings, with or without each other.

In the story, the ghosts are real enough to displace objects and play pranks but not, as Irina laments, "real enough to hold." Their uncertain affiliation as hallucinations or agents of the supernatural manifests perhaps the divine brushing against the natural. There are also spiritual undertones to Evin's experience of nature as he goes fishing to escape his wife's resentment of a childless marriage. Evin watches "for the possibility of grace, a bit of heavenly kindness dropped here on the flat surface of the water, shown there in the fierce span of an eagle's wings here in his tired heart, which still managed to want what it wanted."[53] He comes to this spot to fish because he seeks "a kind of healing" in the experience of inhaling "the sweet dampness that hung like a cloud over the dark water."

Characteristic of a magic realist text, a veritable intoxication of the senses precedes the story's introduction of the suggestion of the haunting by the ghost children:

> He loved his shed, a rundown shack of peeling tarpaper and shingles. He loved the smell of the fresh sawdust Irina spread over the floor, the drying rowan and cowberries hanging in the swatches. He loved the diesel fumes and the oil that beaded up as a dark resin along the old boards on hot days. He even loved the smell of the lake salmon and the scent of the mud from the lakes on the tips of his fingers. He was thinking of all this when he opened the door and instantly smelled something new: a clean brisk aroma, like the rush of air from a freezer when the door is yanked open.[54]

Here the real and the natural evoke the supernatural and the other-worldly. Evin registers the presence of the children as "sudden shocks of chilly updrafts or, if it was daytime, as shafts of light, motes of dust, scraps of sky."[55] Evin acknowledges the ambiguous affiliation of these sensations and of his conviction that he could sense a ghost in the still air "as if holding its breath." Are these sensations natural or supernatural? As he and his wife come to agree, "[i]t could be the cold," for "they both knew the air could make you clumsy, make you silly, wishing for the impossible" and "[t]he lowering frost could make you see things, make you parse figures from the shadows."[56]

The dark ambiguity of Ochsner's intimation of the divine brushing against the natural helps differentiate it from the sometimes more formulaic recent magic realism of other contemporary writers in the region. She remains interested in crafting stories that "ask us to see the world differently, as richer, fuller, malevolent, malignant, beautiful, wondrous." Against the cliché that magic realism offers the soothing enchantment of nature, she maintains that these types of stories "touch a subconscious yearning for the absurd told truthfully, the grotesque with meaning and meaningful consequences."[57] The only reassurance she offers the reader, a trace of the faith that motivates the stories' composition, is the intimation that perhaps we are not intended to figure things out or resolve riddles or conflict.

The malevolent, the malignant, the absurd, the ridiculous and the grotesque are of course present in the evocation of the natural as supernatural in the works of García Márquez, Grass, Rushdie, Saramago, and in the context of Pacific Northwest letters, Hodgins. Yet somewhere along the chain of subsequent imitations and popularizations of the form, the label has acquired the generic expectation of an obligation to uplift, reassure, and to countenance despair with hope (in Laura Esquivel, in the recent work of Isabel Allende, and in the context of Pacific Northwest letters in the work of Kathleen Alcalá). Ochsner's insistence on the dark, ambiguous and unfathomable essence of nature and reality makes her a worthy successor to the tradition of García Márquez and also a fitting contemporary to the Latin American authors of her generation who likewise refuse the path of the familiar and the formulaic.

Without representing a comprehensive map of magic realism in the region, the case studies of Hodgins and Ochsner offer suggestive snapshots of the genealogy and future of the form in Pacific Northwest letters. Magic realism in Pacific Northwest letters breaks from the tendency in the early magic realism of García Márquez, Grass, Rushdie and Saramago to conceive of the role of religion in opposition to that of the secular humanism they espoused. In the Pacific Northwest, the magic realists have found a path to re-enchantment, often via the landscape, visions of utopia, and faith. Hodgins, Bowering, Gaston and Anderson-Dargatz rejected the grim fatalism of earlier realistic fiction to celebrate the sense of "other worlds" on the coast. In her turn, Gina Ochsner conceives of magic realism as uniquely attuned to religious belief and sensibility. She is perhaps most original in refashioning the style for her own purposes, the revelation of "the divine brushing against the natural."

CHAPTER 11

℘

Let the Salmon Be Salmon:
The International Peace Arch
as Symbol and Challenge

ELEANOR J. STEBNER

CULTURES CREATE SYMBOLS. If Cascadia really exists, it must have shared symbols. One could argue that the plentiful natural symbols of this geographical bioregion work just fine as symbols. Think, for example, of the wild and brooding Pacific, or the soaring Douglas fir, or the snow-capped and stream-laden mountain range, or the plentiful and self-sacrificial salmon. Any one of these might serve as Cascadian symbols. Such natural phenomena take on cultural meanings. The ocean may come to symbolize the infinite untapped source of mystery, the trees may come to represent protection and shelter, the mountains may stand for longing, beauty and challenge, and salmon may represent subsistence or even plenty.

Some advocates of Cascadia propose that this region adopt a flag, one of humanity's most ancient means of expressing both inclusion and exclusion. The so-called Doug (or the Douglas Fir) flag and the flag of the Republic of Cascadia utilize natural symbols in advocating for a distinct Cascadia. The Doug Fir flag contains three horizontal stripes — the top stripe represents the sky, the middle white stripe represents the clouds and snow-capped mountains and the bottom green stripe represents the forests. Smack-dab in the middle stands a representation of the Douglas fir tree. The so-called Republic of Cascadia flag is designed like the American flag, but replacing the red stripes are blue wavy lines (representing the waves of the Pacific), and replacing the 50 stars is a stylized depiction of a setting sun (to represent the western edge of the continent), with its center on a fir cone; its background is divided into two colour zones, green on one side (to represent the lush vegetation of the area) and red on the other side (to represent its volcanic subterranean qualities).

All natural symbols take on social meanings, as anthropologist Mary Douglas has argued in her now classic work on symbols.[1] Some proponents of Cascadia may continue to argue for utilizing natural symbols to communicate the uniqueness of this area (and in so doing, idealize and anthropomorphize both the region and the natural environment). I suggest, however, that utilizing natural symbols inadequately represents a social people sharing a particular region of this continent. Why? The answer is simple: We humans do not exist without changing our environment. We build houses in which to live and roads on which to drive; we build museums and libraries, theatres and universities, bridges and bank towers. What we construct materially may better represent our values than the inheritance of our natural environment. Cultures need cultural symbols that represent a people's particular understanding of history, their geo-political realities and their future hopes. The etymology of the word culture means, after all, to cultivate and to till; in other words, culture implies changing what is natural for the perceived benefit of human society.

While some Cascadians may promote trees and mountains and water as representative of Washington, Oregon and British Columbia, cultural symbols may be more sincere or genuine. Perhaps railway hotels or lighthouses might be cultural symbols reflecting the Euro-American settlement of this area and the push for westward expansion. Or perhaps any number of dams might reflect the desire of humans to tame and control their environment. Or perhaps Starbucks or Microsoft, as corporate global success stories, might be cultural symbols showing the import of leisure and technology. Or perhaps what is needed is a symbol that reflects both the history of the area and the hope for future generations. Such a symbol ought to encompass both geo-regional and global concerns. Such a cultural symbol may be found in the International Peace Arch.

Over half a million people stop and visit the peace arch every year. They take time to wander the well-manicured grounds of grass, flower and sculpture. Hundreds of thousands of other people view it only in passing, as they drive through one of the busiest border crossings between Canada and the United States. Standing solid and stark — it was one of the first structures along the Pacific coast to be built earthquake resistant — this 67 foot/20 meter-plus high arch has one cement steel foot firmly planted in Canada and the other in the US. The building of this arch as a monument for peace was first suggested in 1915. American Quaker and businessman, Samuel Hill, made the idea into a reality, and its dedication, before at least ten thousand people, occurred in 1921. The historian of the peace arch, Richard Clark, summarizes its significance by noting that it has been the "setting of devotion and demonstrations, queens and quarrels, marriages and marching bands." He further notes that throughout "its history, so notably marked by variation ranging from violence to indifference, peace has remained its ongoing theme."[2]

In the post 9/11 context, the peace arch may appear as an ironic symbol. The Bush administration established the US Department of Homeland Security in November 2002, which in turn reorganized US Customs and Border Protection in March 2003 (renamed the Bureau of Customs and Border Protection in April 2007). Its purpose is to "secure" border crossings. Border "protection" staff has increased almost three-fold and border agents have been renamed border guards. Armed American border guards — and soon to be armed Canadian border guards (approved under the Stephen Harper government) — regulate the border crossings in a military manner. While NEXUS lanes have been established for approved low risk travellers, border wait times continue to increase. The American Terror-Alert coloured chart — ranging from green to red, with green meaning low risk to red meaning severe risk — keeps the US populace informed that an almost perpetual yellow — meaning elevated risk level — exists from threats of terrorism. American officials relentlessly urge Canada to increase its security measures, which it views as lax, and to change its internal immigration policies, which it believes "admits" terrorists. What used to be positively — even proudly — upheld as the only non-militarized border in the world is no longer. Passports are required and interrogation from guards is normal. Yet in the political reality of a post 9/11 world and the US-Iraq war, al-Qaeda and Afghanistan, the International Peace Arch may be a symbol that is absolutely needed to challenge the militarist vigour enhanced by an unrelenting war on terror.

The peace arch provides the region of Cascadia with an identity of import and reflects Cascadian culture, most especially its ideals in regards to spirituality and social change. But before these themes are discussed, it is necessary to say a few words about monuments themselves. Recent years have seen a growing intellectual interest regarding the roles that monuments play within human societies and cultures. As reflectors of the past, interpreters of the present, and signifiers of the future, monuments hold a significant amount of social history and political ideology. Furthermore, as art curator and historian Andrew Butterfield has written, the recognition of shared monuments is "one of the means by which an aggregate of individuals transforms itself into a community."[3] Needless to say, some monuments, especially those that contain exclusive or divisive religious symbolism or what may be considered inaccurate or biased historical interpretation, are also the targets of raging debates regarding the use of public space and public monies.[4] While the final verdict is not yet rendered regarding the overall status of monuments and memorials in public spaces, it seems clear that American historian and urbanization critique, Lewis Mumford, was wrong when he exclaimed in 1938 that monuments were dead in so-called modern societies.[5] The Vietnam Veterans Memorial, the opening in 2005 of Berlin's Holocaust Memorial (after years of debate), and controversies regarding how to mark the former site of the World Trade Towers in New York City, show the contemporary interest in monuments and memorials.

Recent years have also seen a growing interest in the International Peace Arch. Located at the border between Canada and the US and on a park shared by the towns of Blaine, Washington, and Douglas, British Columbia, the peace arch may indeed be a significant cultural symbol for Cascadia. It may show how a particular monument reflects not only the history of an area, but also, in its marking of something of worth, provides a continuous reminder of particular ideals shared by a geographical region, political entity or dominant culture.[6] While some people — journalists in particular, it seems — suggest that Cascadia is "united by a peculiar blend of trees and technology, fertile farms and urban sprawl, container ships and kayak tours,"[7] and while other people — sociologists in particular, it seems — suggest that it may be characterized by attitudes reflected in a term such as the "none zone,"[8] I suggest that if Cascadia exists as a geographical, social and cultural region, it needs a shared monument. The International Peace Arch may be it. While many monuments and memorials exist throughout British Columbia, Washington and Oregon, the peace arch is the only one shared across the 49th parallel separating Canada and the US. It thereby shows the binationalism of the Cascadian region, a political reality that cannot to be trivialized or ignored in any discussion of Cascadia.

So let me now give an overview of the origins of the peace arch, the views of its patron, Samuel Hill, and some of its most famous moments. I will then discuss briefly how the monument may reflect Cascadian sensibilities, especially in terms of how contemporary citizens understand it as a witness and a challenge, not only to people in this region, but to the entire world.

The building of the peace arch cannot be separated from the westward expansion and settlement of the continent by white Euro-Americans. Indeed, its patron, Samuel Hill (1857–1932), moved to Oregon to make his fortune. Initially trained as a lawyer, Hill found his wealth first in railways, then in gas and electricity and telephones and water power plants and in land investments. He even tried to organize (unsuccessfully) a Quaker farming community. He is perhaps best remembered for his building and promoting of highways throughout this region. While no Bill Gates, Hill was a financial wheeler-dealer. And although he lived in the Northwest and loved it, he thought of himself as an internationalist and travelled widely in Europe, Japan and Russia.[9]

Hill's motives in promoting and sponsoring the peace arch were mixed. No doubt, Hill was an egotist and, like other wealthy tycoons of his day, he loved to build monuments. He also was a Quaker by religious background and persuasion (although I have found no evidence that he was part of a Quaker meeting). He believed that all religions pointed toward the peaceful interrelationships of human beings. Yet the idea of the peace arch did not originate with him. Rather, it was first suggested to him in July 1915 when Americans and Canadians gathered at the border to celebrate the centennial of the signing of the December 1814 Treaty of Ghent. The treaty ended the War of 1812 and signalled peace between Great Britain and the United States. (It also ended any hope for Native American sovereignty and independence, for while historians note that neither England nor the US won the war, the greatest losers were the Native American people — but this is another historical strand that cannot be pursued in this essay.) The centennial ceremony was sponsored by Sam Hill and his Pacific Highway Association. Four thousand people attended, and mayors and religious leaders spoke. Hill spoke about the peace shared between the US and Great Britain: "We remember that no great teacher of the human race, whether

Brahma or Buddha, Confucius or Christ, has ever advocated war. We believe that in the future the nations of the world will reach their highest development physically, mentally, morally and spiritually along the lines of harmony, peace and goodwill, one toward another."[10] During the ceremonies, the suggestion was made to build a peace arch. Samuel Hill agreed. Construction started in 1920 (after the end of WWI) and it was dedicated in 1921.

A peace arch directly contradicted the military arches of triumph that were scattered throughout the world: from Hadrian's Arch in ancient Athens, to the Arc de Triomphe in Paris commissioned by Napoleon, to the soon-to-be completed (1924) Gateway of India arch in what was then called Bombay (Mumbai), and to the soon-to-be destroyed (1928) Red Gate in Moscow built by Peter the Great. Monumental arches were symbols of victory and the glory of war and power. A peace arch, therefore, twisted the values of conquest, and would have been especially evocative given the fact that the arch stood between two sovereign nations. Also common in this time period were so-called welcoming arches, built as either permanent or temporary structures. They were built to greet dignitaries, such as visiting royals, and to welcome arriving immigrants. Many such arches were erected at entrances to racial and ethnic communities, such as in various Chinatowns scattered throughout North America. Welcoming arches served to mark territory and to offer a formal extension of friendship to outsiders. The arch on the border between the US and Canada, therefore, not only projected peace rather than military might, but it also served as a two-way permanent welcoming gate. Indeed, it was a portal — in fact, the peace arch was initially referred to as the Peace Portal — having the role of moving people from one reality into another reality: people crossed from one country into another country, and from conflict into peace.

Arches share relatively uniform shapes and serve as gates or portals, and they almost always include inscriptions. The International Peace Arch is no exception. A number of statements are inscribed on it. Within the arch itself are two phrases: "1814 open one hundred years 1914," referring to the non-militarized border shared between Canada and the US; and "May these gates never be closed," perhaps referring to the two-faced Roman god, Janus, the god of doors, gates and portals. On the outside of the arch appear two more phrases, the one read from the south stating "Children of a common mother," and the one read from the north stating "Brethren dwelling together in unity." The latter phrase is most certainly a paraphrase from Psalm 133, verse 1: "Behold, how good and pleasant it is when brothers dwell in unity!" (RSV), but the origins of the first phrase are debatable.

While the "common mother" may refer to England and France, the Semiahmoo Indian Reserve lay almost adjacent to the Canadian side of the arch, making a purely European political meaning quite ironic, to say the least. Historian Richard Clark is not certain of the inscription's original meaning, but he suggests that the phrase be interpreted as meaning that we are all children of the Earth, which is our common mother. This kind of spiritual interpretation fits with Sam Hill's remarks at the 1921 dedication. Despite the fact that Hill spoke of the treaty as occurring between the "English-speaking race," he went on to say that its purpose was for all countries, in their "own faith," to recognize their unity with one another. In a speech given some eight years later, Hill made his position clear: while he believed in world peace, he believed it could only occur if it first appeared at "home" in the nation. Hill was, like many other people in the region, a political non-conformist, adamant, for example, about his opposition to both slavery and prohibition; to support either, he said, amounted to tyranny. Even though Hill was a strong individualist, he also upheld values of social justice.

The International Peace Arch has been the site of thousands of events through the years. It has been the location for annual events related to national ceremonies, such as Flag Days, and cultural celebrations, such as Icelandic picnics. Literally thousands of children and youth have visited the peace arch through school-sponsored trips and through national and international scouting organizations. Special ceremonies have been held there, from wedding ceremonies to a memorial service for John F. Kennedy. It has also seen numerous rallies and protests. During the 1950s, for example, singer Paul Robeson gave a total of four concerts from the American side of the arch, after the US government refused to allow him to leave his country. The concerts were amazingly popular, at least among people who supported civil liberties and workers' rights.[11] Protests against the Aleutian Nuclear Tests were held at the arch in the 1960s, and it was the location from which Jane Fonda and Tom Hayden staged a 1974 protest against the Vietnam War. During the 1980s the arch saw numerous peace rallies and prayer vigils for nuclear disarmament. During the last decade plus, folks have gathered at the foot of the arch to protest the North American Free Trade Agreement. In the summer of 2006, US and Canadian war protesters gathered, on the Canadian side, in opposition to the Iraq war and occupation. For the most part, these gatherings have been peaceful and nonviolent. Two events, however, did include potential violence. In 1940 two men got into a heated argument during an assembly of the Women's International League for Peace and Freedom, and in 1970 Canadian student protesters against the Vietnam War "invaded" the arch and caused minor damage to it.

Perhaps because of its location on a major thoroughfare and on an international border, the arch has received a fair amount of attention through the years. It has been anything but a dead monument. Indeed, it is legitimate to suggest that it has become a kind of cultural shared sacred space. It has connected people during the various decades in a whole variety of actions and causes. At the very least, it has worked as a symbol of unique Cascadian identity, especially in regards to issues of spirituality, protest and social change. In the years after 9/11 and in the midst of ever increasing means to secure border protection its role as a symbol is especially conspicuous.

Although the peace arch is quite respectable (how can a magnificent arch not be respectable?), it exhibits a rebellious, nonconforming attitude traceable to the life and words of Sam Hill himself and to its numerous supporters through the decades. While the arch exhibits religious qualities, these qualities are expressed in ways that today might be referred to as spiritual. The inscriptions themselves evoke spiritual ideals that exist at first glance between two nations but ultimately these ideals exist between many humans.

It is fascinating to regard two contemporary people who promote the peace arch. Take Richard Clark, for example, the historian of the peace arch. Clark started off as a Baptist minister, became an Anglican priest when he was dismissed by the Baptist convention for not believing in a literal Adam and Eve, and eventually left formal religion behind. Although born in the US and a resident of Blaine, Clark has lived and worked on both sides of the border. He regards himself simply as a human being who is an advocate for world peace and for Mother Earth. Politically active, Clark wrote a Proclamation for Promoting Peace that was adopted by the City of Blaine in 1998. He continues to push to establish a sister relationship between Blaine and Pugwash, Nova Scotia, believing that such a relationship would better promote peace on an international scale.

Or consider Christina Alexander. Alexander founded the United States Canada Peace Anniversary Association (USCPAA) in 1995 to honour the history and legacy of the peace arch. As a songwriter and activist, Alexander believes that the peace arch exists to promote peace throughout the world. She believes that the best way to accomplish this task is through educating people to be aware of "their differences" and thereby create a climate of understanding, respect and appreciation. The USCPAA emphasizes the education of children. Alexander's song, "Children of a Common Mother," states her perspective on the peace arch as a symbol, not only for the region of Cascadia, but for the entire world:

> Standing tall
> There for all
> A symbol of freedom, peace, and harmony
> Our fathers eyes
> Saw troubled times
> So they built a reminder
> For all the world to see.[12]

One-time president of the International Peace Arch Association, Nellie Browne Duff, suggested in 1961 that the peace arch was both "a symbol and a challenge." The symbol is one of peace and the challenge, as Richard Clark suggests, is to "empower the symbol with substance." Empowering any monument with substance is what keeps it from becoming dead. The International Peace Arch promotes social transformation and seeks to advance the common good, not only locally, but globally as well. In so doing, it provides a significant and provocative cultural symbol for Cascadia, rooted in its history and reaching for its ideals.

This is not to suggest that the physical features of Cascadia — its water, trees, mountains and fish — are not operable as symbols. But when dealing with human society, humans ought to look at the limitations and insights of our own cultural creations, and let them spur us into creating a more just and peaceable world. While the natural features of Cascadia may serve as symbols of the geographical ethos of the area and perhaps even evoke a sense of "the spiritual," I'd prefer to let the salmon be salmon.

CHAPTER 12

⤸

A Geo-indigenous World View
from the Far West Coast
of Cascadia

ELI BLISS ENNS

AS IS THE CUSTOM of my people, I shall begin with an introduction. My name is Eli Bliss Enns. I was born on Vancouver Island, on the west coast of the region sometimes known as Cascadia. My mother was a flower child that came to Clayoquot in the 1970s in search of a different way of life from the farm on which she had been brought up. On my father's side, my ancestry goes back thousands of years in a place known today as Clayoquot Sound.

The word Clayoquot is derived from the set of concepts *Tla-o-qui-aht* in the Nuu-chah-nulth language. The *Tla-o-qui-aht* are the indigenous people of Clayoquot Sound. My father gave me the middle name Bliss because this was his intention for me. He brought his little family out to live on a small island on the far west coast of our ancestral territory and endeavored to build a home for us there.

The Island where we lived for a few summers in my beginning years is named "rising out of the water" — in our language, Echachist. This place name captures centuries of observation and ancestral knowledge of place. More integrally, this place name is indicative of an intimate understanding of the transformative processes at work in our world, *Quay-qwiik-suup*, which forms part of the core of a world view.

The following pages capture briefly my personal truth concerning my spiritual world view as it develops from Clayoquot. I state this as a disclaimer, because although many, if not all of the elements of what I have written here come from the many teachers in my life, the synthesis is my own and may be somewhat unique to my family. I do not claim that this is an authoritative statement on the spiritual world view of any broader group of people. That said, it may be appropriate to note that many of the underlying values are shared in some form or another by many of the indigenous peoples of Cascadia.

Although my person originates from the Cascadia region, I consider my world view to be one that is geo-indigenous. Where applicable, I will make the appropriate connections between elements of this world view as reflected in manifestations in the natural world of Cascadia. Before I move into the body of my work, I will first provide some clarity on terms used and on the format that I have chosen to convey my thoughts:

- Spirituality for me embodies all of the intangible elements of self including emotional, psychological and intellectual elements.

- A spiritual world view to me refers to the explanatory, orienting and prescriptive elements of the discussion on what it means to be human — the connection our spirituality has with our people of the past, present and future, and the role we have in the universe.

- "Geo-Indigenous world view" is a term that I use to convey the simple idea that as a species, we are all indigenous animals to the planet Earth and related to all other beings through our common ultimate source of creation.

The format that I have chosen is straightforward. The Nuu-chah-nulth concepts listed down the centerline of the following pages form the frame work of the piece. Following each concept, I provide elaborations in English. In conclusion, I will recap with a few words on implications/applications.

For the sake of clarity, my use of and interpretations of words and phrases of the Nuu-chah-nulth language, my native language, are my own personal recollections that have been passed down to me within my own family. Other speakers may have other under-standings as a result of their family's teachings. It is our belief that we all hold an important piece of the puzzle equally valuable to the whole.

First, a few words on Clayoquot Sound: Tla-o-qui-aht is the confed-eration of historic native groups that once lived all around the lake system called Ha-ooke-min. Tla-o-qui-aht has been translated to mean "different people." However, it means much more than that. To begin with, *Aht* means people, and Tla-o-qui is a place in Clayo-quot Sound presently known as Clayoqua. In this way Tla-o-qui-aht can be understood to mean the "people from Clayoqua."

This understanding of Tla-o-qui-aht speaks of the history of our people dating back to the early to mid 1600s. As mentioned, in for-mer times, our ancestors were in fact not one tribe but many small tribes and family groups who lived all around Ha-ooke-min, which is now known as Kennedy Lake and which is where Tla-o-qui is located.

The defining event that changed the face of Tla-o-qui-aht forever is eternalized in the name of the Esowista Peninsula. The war of Esowista was the first Great War that Tla-o-qui-aht engaged in as a single force. The people who once lived on the peninsula from Long Beach to Tofino and further north had kept tight control of ocean resources, and had made it a common practice to raid the sleepy fishing villages of Ha-ooke-min to take slaves and other commodities. In our language Esowista means "clubbed to death."

Tla-o-qui-aht maintained their presence in this part of the Sound until our first contact with Europeans in the late eighteenth century. Having already been engaged in trade with neighbouring communities, the extension of this practice to the newcomers was a natural transition. For the most part, trading relations were peaceful until the early 1790s when an American trading vessel called the *Columbia* fired on Tla-o-qui-aht's principal village, Opitsaht. In summary, Tla-o-qui-aht, different people, are the people from Tla-o-qui; they are a confederation of many different smaller groups who once lived a very different lifestyle at Ha-ooke-min. Understanding this history is an important prerequisite to understanding the geo-indigenous world view I am about to present because it provides a context for the teachings.

Wii-cosh-naas
Honoring our mutual source of creation:
Everything that exists is born from a common creative source.

Wii-cosh-naas Ha'wiih
Our most highly esteemed Ancestors providing
us guidance today:
Our highly esteemed Ancestors epitomize the
creative source, and they are charged with the responsibility of
employing that power in the stewardship of us all.

Wii-cosh-naas Hahoulthee
Our Ancestral lands providing everything that we need to live:
The ancestral lands that have provided everything our people
of the past, present and future need are endowed by
the common source of creative power.

Wii-cosh-naas Teechmis
The core of our being: physically & spiritually:
The core of our being forms the crux of the physical
and spiritual elements of the creative power.

Quu-us
We are real live human beings with links to the people
of our past, present and future:
As human beings we are medicine stewards, a critical
link among past, present and future generations. As a link,
our critical role is to handle/manage the life-sustaining medicines
that we have inherited from our ancestors for the purpose
of sharing them in the present and passing them on to future
generations. These medicines include air, love, water,
knowledge, salmon, laughter, cedar, stories and whale songs.

Quay-qwiik-suup Quu-us
The great dual process of transformation
is forever at work in the universe:
The dual process leaps forth from the common source
of creation and consists of a physical and a spiritual element.
Human beings, like other beings, represent an intersecting
point between these dual forces of transformation.

Hishuk-ish Tsawak-nish
Everything is one and interconnected:
Spreading horizontally outwards among our present people,
including all other beings, is an interconnecting relationship that
is equivalent to total present oneness, the sum of which comprises
a current expression of the common source of creation.

Wii-tsiki-ach-cu
Harnessing the total-power of the moment to empower ourselves:
Each moment holds the power to change forever. The power
of the moment drives the process of transformation.
Take the moment to contemplate alternative paths forward.
Empower yourself to choose a path. Be aware that every
moment that has come before has led to this moment:
the present moment. Take the moment to explore your options.
As you do so, you empower yourself to choose the direction of
your life and your community's history.

Eli Bliss Enns / 211

Iisaak
Moving through life with respect:
Whatever path you select, move forward with
humility and respect.

In conclusion, one can say that in former times, and still today, to one degree or another, ideas of spirituality, self and the land go hand in hand. The complication that has been introduced is an imposed world view which has had a tendency to see the natural world in terms of commodities or merely as a part of the background to man-made infrastructures such as buildings and roads. The key difference is whether we see ourselves as apart from or a part of the rich dynamic world around us.

Islands, lakes, rivers, mountains and other topographical features were given names with much consideration to function, origin, practical use and in relation to significant stories in human history. It was not a custom to name places after oneself, as is the custom in some other cultures. For example, Kennedy Lake is known as Ha-ooke-min to my people. Ha-ooke-min is a descriptive term. This name speaks of the bounty of fish and other resources that once filled that lake before the mass interruption of natural cycles. Upper-Kennedy River is named Winche, which also describes the types of resources that were found there.

On the other hand, people are often named after places. This practice is a part of the traditional land titles law. Land titles were passed down through the generations from titleholder to successor and so on with the passing of names.

As an example, in my own family there is the name Tsee-iism. It describes a height of land, westward slope and beachfront area that is now known as Radar Hill. As the name Tsee-iism has been passed down from my great-great grandfather's time, so has the title to that land. My nephew Preston now holds that name. As a part of his education, Preston/Tsee-iism is taught that ownership of the land implies a responsibility to protect it and use its resources prudently.

He does not have the right to exploit it or otherwise misuse it.

I understand that all places on this earth are experiencing the process of transformation. It is also understandable that this process is more pronounced in some places than others. Cascadia and in particular Clayoquot Sound are among those places where the effects of the transformative process are most pronounced. These changes are clearly having an effect on the world view of the people who have lived in Clayoquot from time immemorial. One can only hope that the grounding principles of our spiritual vision will continue to influence the transformations now underway.

CHAPTER 13

∽

Conjectures on Workplace Spirituality in Cascadia

MARK WEXLER

PLACES IN THE IMAGINATION that have a kernel of reality always possess an economy. It is the engine that turns the gears, moves the levers and puts bread and wine on the table. In reality, the striving and aspirations of both religion and spirituality, particularly when not enveloped in escapist (or seclusionist) doctrine, must marry the sacred with the instrumental, or work and the workplace with the spiritual. This is my thesis in this paper. I pursue it in an imaginary place, with a claim to be real and within it a very dynamic clustering of economic forces.[1]

FRAMING THE ELUSIVE UTOPIA
In this compilation, Cascadia is depicted as an elusive utopia. It is a region both real and imagined, of contradictions and alluring possibilities. In depicting it, the contributors to this book focus on the

relationship between nature and spirituality. Cascadia is conceived of within five interrelated frames — 1) a bioregion, 2) a cultural zone, 3) a mythic place, 4) a regional history, 5) a model of the future — and now, in this discussion, as 6) an economic cluster in which nature and spirituality loom large. I briefly discuss each before attending to Cascadia as an economic cluster.

A bioregion

The alpha and omega of Cascadia, its origins along the Northern Pacific Coast, its salmon rivers, its temperate rainforest and its thick backbone of the snow-laced Rocky Mountains all provide a backdrop to a region nestled in a shared geography. It is a geography that inspires a reverence for nature, a nontraditional attitude towards religion and a shared sense of place. Cascadia is a bioregion, especially if it serves to separate a people from others — as one observes in island cultures and those set aside by impenetrable mountains or high altitudes. Bioregions create the conditions wherein residents relate to one another as having a common destiny. It provides those in it with a strong sense of place. Even if those within the bioregion do not develop a common sensibility, outsiders may treat residents of the bioregion as if they were similar. Thus one could conjecture that humour bandied about in Toronto regarding Vancouver's flaky flirtation with organic foods, tree hugging and corporate retreats into the forest are echoed in jokes about the residents of Portland and Seattle as told by New Yorkers or Chicagoans. The sense of sharing a spectacular, and at times, insulating bioregion such as Cascadia facilitates the emergence of distinct regional cultural images, styles of architecture, leisure pursuits and the like.

A cultural zone

Cascadia has an identifiably unique demographic. It attracts some. But others cannot imagine living beneath recurring rain and learning to build it into their songs, paintings and world view. Some are drawn to Cascadia to sleep and dream at the edge of the sea; others imagine this as far too damp a place to raise a healthy family. It is too dangerous: nightmares abound where the green of the temperate rainforest juts into the blue of the roiling Pacific. The tides rise and fall. Nothing seems permanent. Decay accelerates. There are indigenous peoples' tales of the great tsunami that will obliterate all in its path. Some are willing to live in a region whose ground may quake and open any minute, swallowing buildings — plate glass plummeting from high towers slicing through objects on the streets below. Others cannot. It is in this way that bioregions help carve out people who share a culture and an attitude and who are later seen by those eager to hock their goods and services as a unique demographic zone. In this regard I recall my personal experience when I first moved to Cascadia (Vancouver) from Toronto in 1976 as a vegetarian: I found, much to my surprise, that what I had thought of as my relatively idiosyncratic eating patterns were well-established in my adopted region.

A mythic place

In adopting a region or adapting to it, individuals and groups shape and fashion a mythos about their bioregion and shared culture. The myth of Cascadia emanates from a marriage between a unique landscape and a reverence for its placement — not in art but in the quest, often experienced as a spiritual yearning, to live close to, in and with nature. Myth is a ritualized form of embodiment. It locates the sacred. Some, such as contributor Eleanor Stebner, see it in the Peace Arch; to others it is embodied in the salmon. It is borne in the song and ritual dance of indigenous people, in the majesty of the soaring ancient redwoods, in stories of the left-leaning wobblies riding the rails and in the old mission ships visiting the isolated native communities and lumber camps. It is tied to the cowboys and ranchers rolling up their bedrolls and moving the cattle closer to market. It is borne in the tales of the old railway hands and in the mouth-to-CB radio stories of the long-haul truckers, and in the ferry workers moving freight and/or the population around Puget Sound or through Georgia Strait. The mythos of a region distinguishes it from others and provides it with recognition of its unique history.

A regional history

Cascadia, as this book argues, is also an area with a unique history. A place is discovered, made and invented by people who live there and who come, sometimes pushed, sometimes pulled, from elsewhere. The telling of the history of a place is a form of modern cosmology. This is where we came from. This is the story of our place. These are the events that have shaped us as a people. History, unlike myth, unfolds with a self-conscious version of a fact pattern. As the local predisposition of the people gives way to a regional attitude, a shared history of the region emerges. This history is distinguished from the histories of other regions. Not surprisingly, the history of Cascadia is often told "sadly," as a tale of depleting resources — of fish, lumber, minerals and the failure to achieve a sustainable balance with nature. Sometimes, more happily, the history of Cascadia is told as the building of a great experiment in postmodern fusion, a mixture of East and West and a willingness to move into the new service economy — fuel cells, software, digital entertainment and eco-tourism. The story of the origin and evolution of a region aids its inhabitants in producing a sense of and belief in its future.

A model of the future

Both variants of the history of Cascadia lead to a similar sense that inhabitants have about it as a model of the future. If the history of Cascadia is told as the depletion of a region of its resources, then the future addresses Cascadia as a purveyor of environmental sustainability, a strong advocate of both corporate social responsibility and a champion of the triple bottom. In this sense, the future is an antidote to a misspent past. The Cascadian future embraces both hubris and confidence — the confidence to restore the rivers and oceans to their lost plenitude, to clean the polluted air and to turn back the seeming inevitability of global warming. In this experimental future, Cascadia is a postmodern fusion of East and West — the right- and left-brained. The quest is to place the machine in the garden and see to it that each, in harmony, thrives. In this model of the future, the region no longer speaks to an economy of fishers, lumberjacks and miners — but to a regional cluster for the aggregation of young, leading-edge knowledge workers committed to designing solutions to key problems gripping the planet.

An economic cluster

In presenting Cascadia as an economic cluster, I look at work and the workplace as centers of instrumental human activity and as a vital force giving shape to a unique and "elusive" notion of workplace spirituality in Cascadia. An economic cluster may be thought of in two interrelated ways. First, an economic cluster can be viewed within the notion of an industry: firms which are interdependent and rely upon the same knowledge base, whether they emphasize strategies of competition or co-operation. Second, in regional studies, an economic cluster is a group of firms that develop within and become interdependent with a region and its economic future.

Workplace spirituality is to be understood as the quest for meaning and spiritual identity that predominates within a particular economic cluster. In this paper, workplace spirituality occurs within the nature-oriented spirituality and the unique history and mythos of the bioregion known as Cascadia.

ECONOMIC CLUSTER/WORKPLACE SPIRITUALITY

Before I indicate how workplace spirituality manifests itself specifically in this place known as Cascadia, I invite the reader to examine Figure 1, my basic four-cluster model of workplace spirituality. This model simplifies some complex notions. The scholarly pedigree of this representation of economic clusters and their guiding world view is spelled out more fully in my book *Leadership in Context: the Four Faces of Capitalism*. The four economic clusters are the market, the planning, the adaptive and the innovative clusters.

In any region, including Cascadia, each cluster seeks to increase its influence. In secular contexts where instrumental behaviour strongly influences the prevailing world view, the nature of the economic cluster within a dynamic or changing region impacts that region's notion of workplace spirituality. Contemporary Cascadia is

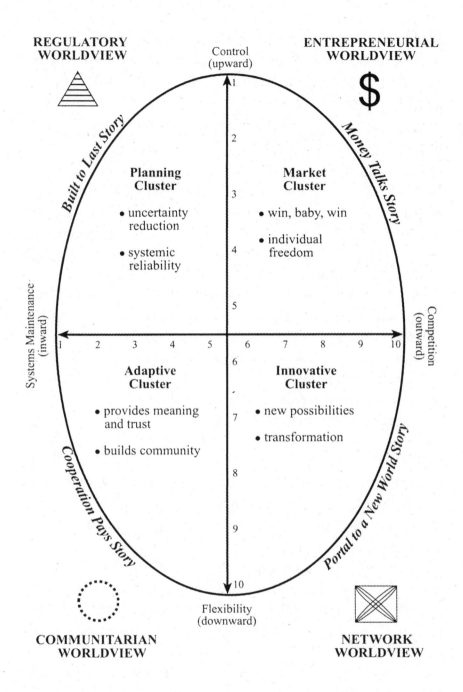

REGULATORY WORLDVIEW

Control (upward)

ENTREPRENEURIAL WORLDVIEW

$

Built to Last Story

Money Talks Story

Planning Cluster

- uncertainty reduction
- systemic reliability

Market Cluster

- win, baby, win
- individual freedom

Systems Maintenance (inward)

Competition (outward)

Adaptive Cluster

- provides meaning and trust
- builds community

Innovative Cluster

- new possibilities
- transformation

Cooperation Pays Story

Portal to a New World Story

Flexibility (downward)

COMMUNITARIAN WORLDVIEW

NETWORK WORLDVIEW

Figure 1

riveted, as I shall argue, with strong and contradictory images of spirituality and nature formed by forces within its economic cluster. These forces point to Cascadia as a visionary hotbed of grassroots movements that embrace the sanctity of nature — doing battle with an equally visionary group of design-based innovators embracing the sanctity of a leading-edge built environment rooted in a celebration of the knowledge-based global economy.

Market Cluster

In the market cluster bolstered by the entrepreneurial world view, the "money talks" story prevails. In economic terms, it is symbolized by the dollar sign (Euro, Pound Sterling, Baht, etc.); in terms of workplace spirituality, it is denoted by elevating the notion of *immersion*. It is focused on action. In Figure 2 it is represented by "the hand." When the market cluster contends for regional centrality, workplace spirituality strongly emphasizes the ideals of strong individualism, making an impact and using one's gifts to raise oneself above the fray and achieve a sense of tranquility and self-realization through success. The workplace in a region dominated by the entrepreneurially minded market cluster lionizes the self-made individual and has as its mantra Nike's slogan "just do it." (As most readers know, Nike originated in Oregon.) Action, particularly when deemed successful within a competitive context, confers privilege. The entrepreneurs in the market cluster look askance at the rule-based bureaucratic disposition of those in the planning cluster.

Planning Cluster

Second in the model (see Figure 1) is the planning cluster, with its regulatory world view. In economic terms the planning cluster is represented by the bureaucracy of credentialled experts housed in relatively large hierarchical organizational structures. In regions dominated by the regulatory world view government agencies and large bureaucratically structured organizations somewhat sheltered from the market (oligopolies or monopolies) prevail. In terms of workplace spirituality, the regulatory-rooted planning cluster bows

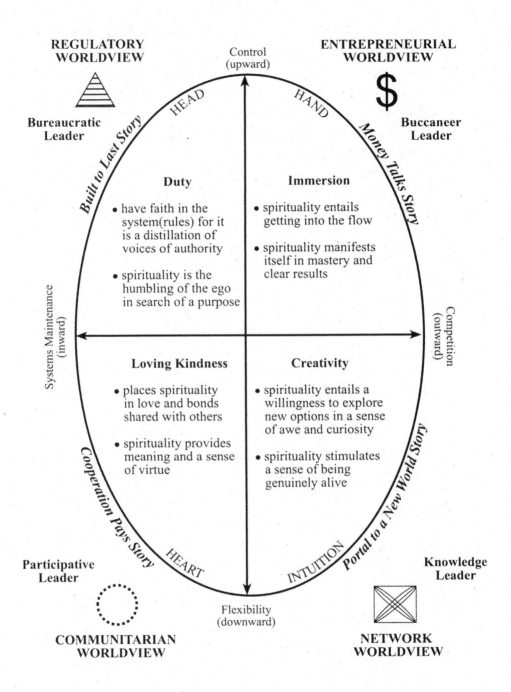

REGULATORY WORLDVIEW

Bureaucratic Leader

Built to Last Story

HEAD

HAND

Control (upward)

ENTREPRENEURIAL WORLDVIEW

$

Buccaneer Leader

Money Talks Story

Duty

• have faith in the system(rules) for it is a distillation of voices of authority

• spirituality is the humbling of the ego in search of a purpose

Immersion

• spirituality entails getting into the flow

• spirituality manifests itself in mastery and clear results

Systems Maintenance (inward)

Competition (outward)

Loving Kindness

• places spirituality in love and bonds shared with others

• spirituality provides meaning and a sense of virtue

Creativity

• spirituality entails a willingness to explore new options in a sense of awe and curiosity

• spirituality stimulates a sense of being genuinely alive

Cooperation Pays Story

HEART

INTUITION

Portal to a New World Story

Flexibility (downward)

Participative Leader

COMMUNITARIAN WORLDVIEW

Knowledge Leader

NETWORK WORLDVIEW

Figure 2

down to and spiritually acknowledges the notion of *duty*. This duty is to the authority of the system. In a region in which the planning cluster takes root, government and large organizations in the private sector attempt to reduce uncertainty, rather than maximize profits, as is the case with the entrepreneurially minded market cluster. Reducing uncertainty entails prudence and deference to authority. Rules as indicators of precedent are privileged as forms of rationality. It is due to this faith in rationality and the rules of evidence that it is represented as "the head" (see Figure 2). The slogan "just do it," so prevalent in the market cluster, is replaced by the much more prudent and tradition bound "tried, tested and true." Champions of the duty-based planning cluster are uncomfortable with the cavalier nature of risk extolled by entrepreneurs in the market cluster and, as will be seen, the reverence for dialogue, sharing and trust extolled by advocates of the adaptive cluster.

Adaptive Cluster

This cluster is rooted in non-governmental organizations (NGOs), not-for-profit-organizations, foundations and private sector firms that promote corporate social responsibility, sustainability and, more often than not, niche market goods or services to those with a distinctly communitarian value system. It shapes community. In the cut and thrust of winner-takes-all markets, and in the midst of the cold impersonal objectivity of the duty-bound planning system, the adaptive cluster provides individuals with a sense of meaning and trust. Regions dominated by the adaptive cluster strongly emphasize egalitarianism and attempt where and whenever possible to give voice to those unable to make themselves heard. This "co-operation pays" story is depicted by the workplace spirituality of *loving kindness* and is represented in Figure 2 by the heart. The ideology is communitarian and the quest is for a genuine diversity grounded in dialogue. The slogan of practice is "may a thousand flowers bloom." The adaptive cluster embraces a notion of the community as organic and natural. This occurs while expressing extreme discomfort with the market cluster's emphasis upon winning and individualism, the planning cluster's adherence to a hierarchical notion of rules, and the innovative cluster's celebration of new possibilities embedded in the aesthetics of the synthetic (or built).

Innovative Cluster
The fourth quadrant of the model (see Figure 1), the innovative cluster invests heavily in research and development as a means of exploring new possibilities to transform our planet, and through the use of new technologies and science formulates a synthetic environment which greatly improves upon our past habitat. In regions dominated by the innovative cluster there is a strong push towards globalization and a celebration of the emerging knowledge-based economy. The innovative cluster's story is in fact an optimistic rendering of the portal to a new world — one in which the anxieties of global warming may be diminished by the creation of temperature-controlled cities and a reliable high-rise, hydroponic food source. Workplace spirituality in the innovative cluster entails a willingness to explore new options with a sense of awe and curiosity. Discovery is a blessing. Faith is placed in the human capacity to solve problems with insight and panache. In Figure 2, the innovative cluster with its reverence for *creativity* is designated not by the hand, head or heart but by the visceral ability to mobilize intuition. Those imbued with the workplace spirituality of creativity look askance at those heavily invested in the duty-bound planning cluster, the nature-is-sacred adaptive cluster and the win-at-all-costs short-term thinking of those immersed in the market cluster.

I would like now to discuss in more detail the forms of workplace spirituality that develop in each of the clusters.

Workplace Spirituality of Immersion in the Market Cluster
At the center of the market cluster is the workplace spirituality of *immersion*. It is a form of spirituality in which individuals self-consciously employ mindfulness as a means of increasing their capacity to win. For example, athletes talk about getting into the "flow." This entails the Zen-like notion that once one learns how to shut off the head and pay attention to the "here and now," one becomes far

more effective. Hard-bitten land developers or labour negotiators talk about getting into the "zone." In Cascadia, Nike is joined in the market cluster by such iconic entrepreneurial firms as Starbucks, the Jim Pattison Group, Columbia Sportswear and Nordstrom's. In these organizations, concentration and focus are tied to action. The market cluster formulates a spirituality of results. Immersion, as seen in Figure 2, is symbolized by the hand. With it men and women make things happen. One finds in this cluster, family businesses and larger profit-maximizing entities which tend to be either owner-operated, or controlled by a small group of actively involved share-holders. Immersion suits the self-made. It is ruggedly individualistic. It is results oriented. It addresses individual freedom for one's business — it is like one's castle — and in it one can do what one wants when one chooses. Immersion can be practised without authority figures. It is not a communal practice. It is and can be thought of as creative, but the creativity is tied to the individual and his or her ability to move swiftly rather than, as is the case in creativity in the innovative cluster, to introduce originality.

Workplace Spirituality of Duty in the Planning Cluster
In the planning cluster, where rules are prevalent and the system thick with signals about what is and is not appropriate, workplace spirituality focuses upon *duty*. The workplace spirituality of duty calls on individuals to have faith in the system and its rules. This is not a world celebrating the self-made, but one extolling authority. This authority is not necessarily one to which one gives blind obedi-ence; rather one has faith in the voices of authority as the distillation of rational experience within the system. These systems are hierar-chical. Large government agencies and heavily regulated industries such as banking or bureaucratized utilities predominate. The plan-ning cluster is exemplified in such Cascadian organizations as B.C. Hydro, Safeco, Weyerhaeuser and Puget Sound Energy. Here infor-mation is always written down. All meetings are encoded in their minutes. These systems are information retentive. At the top of the organization we have men and women who have proven that they

have the experience to use the best rules of the past (precedents) and apply these to the present data to come up with sound and rational procedures. The workplace spirituality of duty, its adherents argue, diminishes the ego. It is not about "self," but about adhering to the spirit of the rules and, when you do, you will be rewarded. Security comes to those who take to the routine and flourish in the often-repetitive rounds of work that prevail in the planning cluster. In rewarding duty, seniority — the demonstration of loyalty over time — is highly prized.

Workplace Spirituality of Loving Kindness in the Adaptive Cluster

Whereas God is in the details in the "built-to-last-story" of the duty-bound regulatory world view, the same cannot be said for the *loving kindness* in the "co-operation pays" story within the adaptive cluster. The adaptive cluster is embodied in organizations like the Bill and Melinda Gates Foundation, Doctors without Borders, Greenpeace, World Vision, Mercy Corps and in a more business-like fashion at B.C.–born Mountain Equipment Co-op, VanCity Savings Credit Union, Powell's City of Books, and Recreational Equipment Inc (REI). Contemporary Cascadians, as we are seeing within this volume, are drawn to the civil or natural religion of loving kindness and the natural, apparently genuine communities of the adaptive cluster.

At the center of the adaptive cluster one finds neither the dollar sign nor the rule of law. Rather, one locates the gift. The gift and gift-giving entail trust and both speak to the recognition that in giving one creates communal bonds with others. These bonds are grounded in two notions — reciprocity and philanthropy. In the former, one extends the gift or loan to another, who in time can be expected to repay it. The gift or loan is understood as a kindness or favour. The favour involves A providing B with something B wants but cannot easily attain without the assistance of A. In reciprocity it is expected that, in time, B will repay A, but not necessarily with the same favours he or she received. Reciprocity is rooted in communal norms and cultural understandings. Philanthropy is a form of gifting wherein those with adequate resources give to those who either lack resources or who have been victimized or traumatized. If the slogan in the action-immersed market cluster is "just do it," and in the duty-bound planning cluster is "when in doubt, don't," the slogan in the adaptive cluster is "let a thousand flowers bloom."

Workplace Spirituality of Creativity in the Innovative Cluster
If the notion of diversity is highlighted in the adaptive cluster as an end unto itself, it is also celebrated in the innovative cluster, but only when it bolsters *creativity*. The innovative cluster is one Cascadians increasingly present as their model for the future. It is embodied in such Cascadian firms as Microsoft, Amazon.com, Sierra On Line, MacDonald Detwiller and Electronic Arts. But it struggles with and contradicts contemporary Cascadians who embrace the adaptive cluster. Of the four clusters the innovative is the most compatible with the call to globalization. Creative people dwell on the edge of dynamic pools of knowledge. These can be located anywhere on the globe. However, once a region succeeds in attracting a particular type of creative person in a critical mass or number to a region — as for example Hollywood for movie-making, Seattle or Redmond for software and Vancouver for video games — then others are drawn to build upon that growing knowledge base. Each and every age has its notion of leading-edge industries. Thus Northern Michigan (Detroit, Pontiac, Lansing and Dearborn) were clearly part of a leading edge innovative cluster in the early 1900s.

The future, insist those in the innovative cluster, has yet to be correctly designed. There is not a reverence for the past, so clear in the workplace spirituality of duty. Nor is their much respect for the workplace spirituality of loving-kindness, with its explicit admiration of the design of nature as the template for the healthy, sustainable community (social capital). Unlike immersion in the market cluster, with success measured in dollars (financial capital), creativity in the network world view highlights intellectual capital as expressed in the originality of design embedded in patents, genomic mapping, software and all forms of intellectual capital.

WORKPLACE SPIRITUALITY SHAPES CASCADIA

From my perspective and that of many contributors to this book, to make sense of contemporary Cascadia — at least from the perspectives of nature and spirituality — one can frame Cascadians as: a) embracing a civil religion more strongly than is typical in other regions, b) expressing a reverence for nature and the natural, c) advocating a strong desire to heal the planet through environmental awareness and the pursuit of sustainability, d) possessing a weak sense of history but a strong sense of place, and e) presenting their region as a model for a technologically informed and designed future.

All but the last of these stem from the framing of Cascadia as a predominantly adaptive cluster imbued with the bond of community and intimacy or loving-kindness as the prevalent form of workplace spirituality. However, the last point e) deeply contradicts point c) and frames Cascadia as an innovative cluster partial to a workplace spirituality of creativity.

In this section, I will address points a) to e) and discuss the conflict between e) and c). I will conclude this discussion with suggestions on what seems most relevant for those interested in exploring workplace spirituality in Cascadia.

Let us turn first to how an examination of workplace spirituality, albeit from a somewhat personal perspective, helps us make sense of some of the major themes in this book.

The fact that Cascadians are more likely than those in other regions to turn away from formal religion and embrace spirituality tells us a great deal about how Cascadians see the regulatory world view. The planning culture imbued with the workplace spirituality of duty is not particularly well-developed in Cascadia. Institutionalized religion, with its clear lines of authority, hierarchy and rules is part and parcel of the regulatory world view in the planning cluster. One may ask: Why are Cascadians less enamoured with the regulatory world view than are residents of other regions? In other words, why do Cascadians in large numbers turn away from formal organized religion? There are I believe five major reasons.

First, the region is primarily one in which branch plants flourish. The inhabitants of Cascadia associate authority as something distant. The second reason is that no church or organized religion dominates the region and claims it as its turf. Third, the mobile immigration into Cascadia is more often than not motivated by a desire to get away from constricting forms of authority present elsewhere. The fourth reason is that organized formal religions in the church, temple, synagogue and mosque have not customized their doctrine or services to the inhabitants of this region. The fifth and last reason is that high mobility into and out of the region has played havoc with the ability of the church, mosque, temple or synagogue to provide a stable center and to develop a strong core of patrons and sponsors.

I caution, however, that recognizing the absence of a strong tie to the church, mosque, temple or synagogue and simultaneously a strongly stated preference for spirituality over a religion does not mean that we understand what form of spirituality dominates in Cascadia. In the compilation of readings in this book there has been an assumption that the civil religion focuses upon nature. I do not dispute this.

However, I would suggest that we are not sure whether the individual or group in Cascadia that reveres nature does so within the workplace spirituality of immersion (the market cluster), loving-kindness (adaptive cluster) or creativity (innovative cluster). We do know, and in this volume, accept that Cascadians do not embrace the deference to authority that prevails when the planning cluster is strongly ensconced in a region.

The Market Cluster in Cascadia: Many Are Getting into the Flow
Those Cascadians who revere nature within the workplace spirituality of immersion will see nature as a means of getting into the flow, of self-actualizing. Hiking, skiing, kayaking, white river rafting, mountain climbing, sky diving and the like are all means to challenge oneself and enhance one's growth, development and happiness. The focus is upon nature as a personalized experience.

In this entrepreneurial world view, nature can be revered in its developed form or as wilderness. In its developed form it is revered in the design of ski runs, golf courses, running circuits and nature-based resorts that are aesthetically pleasing and challenging. The idea of a green entrepreneur is no contradiction to those imbued with the combination of the "money talks story," and the workplace spirituality of immersion. Green roofs, LEED certified buildings, locally grown organic food and energy-efficient housing all are bought and sold. The buying and selling of these commodities is understood as protecting nature and helping those with a desire to consume and immerse or achieve a sense of spiritual well-being. Wilderness, for those who follow the immersion model, is a place to take on challenges which emphasize survival, rugged individualism and the ability to improvise and think on one's feet. Indeed organizations like Outward Bound seek to market themselves to executives and high-achieving youth as a means of developing their skills and challenging themselves against and in nature.

In the market cluster, imbued with the workplace spirituality of immersion, the landscape of Cascadia is seen as a means of drawing in consumers or tourists. The cruise ship industry and ecotourism share the idea that the landscape of Cascadia is like a magnet. The cruise ship industry in particular seeks to immerse people along the scenic route skirting the Pacific, weaving in and out of the fjords and terminating in Alaska. Eco-tourism immerses people interested in getting closer to nature than their urban experience can typically provide. They can come close to the whales. They can observe the totem poles on the Queen Charlotte Islands and examine the unique landscape of glacier streams emptying into the blue waters of the Pacific. Those in the market cluster look at the landscape of Cascadia as a resource. The salmon along Washington's coast and the beaches along the Oregon shore carry clear economic value; the former is diminishing while the latter increases in value.

Some in this cluster seek to suggest that nature and the landscape, if left intact but accessible to the public, may be worth far more in the long term than parking lots or shopping malls. This argument is rooted in relative returns on investment, and is open to debate, since some in the market cluster would like their return on investment in a shorter time frame than that proposed by their more conservation-minded colleagues.

The Planning Cluster in Cascadia: Feeling Duty to the Long-Term

The duty-bound planning cluster looks at the unique Cascadian landscape as a portfolio to be monitored. The regulatory world view seeks to distribute the landscape in such a manner that the constituents in Cascadia feel comfortable with who gets what, where, when and why. Thus, it is difficult to locate eco-tourism near territory devoted to mining or aggressive forestry practices. Similarly, it is foolhardy to place working farms rife with the sounds and smells of livestock and fertilizers close to the ever-growing enclaves of subdivisions encircling metropolitan areas. Then, too, deep-sea fishers in search of wild prey are uncomfortable with the allegedly disease-carrying farmed fish.

In the regulatory world view, one has a duty to ensure that real estate, which is typically how landscape is understood, is integrated and planned — so that the region can still function based on rules regarding what can be done on each parcel of land or bit of river, lake and ocean. As well as zoning, the duty-based planning cluster increasingly grapples with the notion of sustainability. This is neither because it is a particularly imaginative group (as is the innovative cluster), nor because it is a particularly committed or passionate group (as is the adaptive cluster), but rather because it feels a sense of duty to take into account the big picture and the long time-frame. Today, however, within Cascadia it is the adaptive culture that passionately champions sustainability, while the planning culture remains aloof, yet aware of its importance for their mandate.

The Adaptive Cluster in Cascadia: Loving Nature and Kindness

While the reverence of Cascadians for nature can be understood in the market cluster, and as a duty to be fulfilled in the planning cluster, so too can it be framed within the adaptive cluster, where workplace spirituality is practised as loving kindness. In the adaptive cluster, nature and the natural are the basis for a healthy community. In this community intimacy and the ability to trust and enter into dialogue flourishes. Human communities which act on the natural cycle and with the rhythms of nature become less drug addicted, less violent and less prone to the exploitation of the marginal, powerless and ill. This occurs because the rhythms of nature, when observed and built into the community, lend themselves to recognition that all of us — rich and poor, men and women, young and old, white, coffee-coloured and black — join the whale, the badger, the ptarmigan, the river system, the glacial estuary and the weather system as part of the community in nature. Nature, in the communitarian world view, is the great chain of being. In revering it, as in a secular form of pantheism, Cascadians believe that they are slowly learning to heal the region. One first acts locally, then globally. With loving kindness one heals the world. In so doing, adaptive cluster Cascadians do not turn their backs on technology; they become selective. Cascadians choose technologies which enhance community in the great chain of being: the bicycle over the SUV; organic foods over genetically modified foods; and public transit or carpooling over the individual in the automobile. With the advent and growing attention to global warming, the "co-operation pays," approach to workplace spirituality has gained new adherents in large numbers.

The Innovative Cluster in Cascadia: Drawn to Creativity

The civil religion of Cascadia with its reverence for nature collides with but accommodates the innovative cluster and therein those imbued with the workplace spirituality of New Age creativity. The collision occurs because creatives in the innovative cluster believe that it is possible to improve upon nature. Indeed it is nature that needs repair. Seeking to return to or emulate the "natural" cycles of nature requires that we radically reduce world population size and return to a far more primitive lifestyle. Thus, the best minds of the innovative culture use their creativity to develop, for example, genetically modified foods. From the point of view of the adaptive culture, these foods do not enhance trust nor develop intimacy in the community. They are unnatural. If there is a civil religion in Cascadia from the communitarian world view, it is quite clear that genetically modified foods violate the secular premises of this religion. On the other hand, genetically modified foods patented in the innovative cluster and disseminated by the market cluster lower the price of food. They can be grown on far less land and (arguably) permit growers to fine-tune the nutrient value to the health needs of inhabitants in specific regions. The land saved from intense organic agriculture can then, advocates of the innovative cluster insist, be turned over and used for public enjoyment.

One of the reasons that the innovative cluster is becoming so important to Cascadia is that the area has no strong industrial base. In essence, Cascadia's economic development has gone from its roots in the primary industries of farming, forestry, fishing and mining has by and large bypassed the factory and now is focusing upon such services as tourism (specializing in eco-tourism) and computer-based software, video games and explorations in biotechnology. The movement from a primary industry base to a tertiary service sector economy has required that Cascadia both educate its population and seek wherever possible to attract a new population of people with highly developed skills and creativity. This has made for a region with a special history — rooted in indigenous peoples, timber and mining communities, the gold rush and the independent fishers — but it has not made for a strong memory. The sons and daughters of the forest workers, miners and fishers are looking for work elsewhere.

The new entrants into Cascadia bring with them a sense of rootlessness, a questioning of authority and willingness — if they do not fall on fertile ground within Cascadia — to move on. This population, without a deep sense of their shared history, shares a fascination with the clearly unique landscape of the temperate rain forest on the west coast, the Rockies in the interior and, in amongst the valleys, pockets of desert here and steppe-like micro regions elsewhere. This landscape is celebrated in all four economic clusters. Each, however, sings quite a different song about the supernatural nature of Cascadia.

IN CASCADIA, THOSE LOYAL TO LOVING KINDNESS COMPETE WITH THOSE WHO CHAMPION CREATIVITY

Those in the adaptive cluster, with their workplace spirituality of loving kindness, are passionate and fully committed to what is natural in Cascadia. They do not see nature as landscape, resource or portfolio to be managed. Rather, as we have observed, they imbue it with the spirit of a civil religion. This is one of the reasons that Cascadia is a hotbed of social movements, giving birth to environmental NGOs and grassroots activist groups. Cascadia is an excellent recruiting ground for radical environmentalists. Radical environmentalists can be understood as willing to break the law, a sort of principled civil disobedience, in order to enhance the common good and develop the community by protecting what one holds dear — nature and the landscape.

What has helped the adaptive community develop its passion for environmentalism rests, I believe, upon three features. First is the relative affluence of the population. People with good jobs have the time not only to improve the world but do so without fearing the loss of their jobs. This leads to the second point. When most of the jobs are not industry-based, but rooted in the service sector, it is far easier to rail against industrial externalities like pollution. Third, the relatively recent founding of urban centers in Cascadia (late 1800s, early 1900s) has made cities that are easy to get out of. The urban population in Cascadia enjoys the rural landscape without too much fuss. The urban Cascadian embraces the rural environment far more easily than the residents of Toronto, New York or Boston. This of course is a mixed blessing. Cascadia has sprawl. Its cities are more auto-dependent than their more subway friendly eastern variants. This has created a tension regarding the landscape of Cascadia. How is a Cascadian city to be designed so that it is less intrusive on the countryside?

To answer that question, Cascadians increasingly turn to the innovative cluster — and in line with their distrust of authority, by and large bypass the planning cluster. The problem for the innovative cluster in Cascadia is how to best put the machine in the garden without destroying the beauty of this super "natural" bioregion. It is a difficult task, not made easier by those in other economic clusters seeking to influence the design.

At present, the innovative cluster is quite confused. In the early days of the Internet and the development of the mobile phone and telecommunication systems it was thought that the need for urban density would diminish. Marshall McLuhan, a favourite of Canadians, wrote early and often about the global village. His intimations of a globe laced with small communities all in touch through the new media has not come to fruition.

Indeed, the super cities on the globe are growing in number and size. Cascadia is a region that, due to the relative youthfulness of its conurbations, remains aloof from imminent super-city worries, but is chock-full of suggestions on how Portland, Vancouver or Seattle can serve as a model for the future. The design community in Cascadia embraces the problematic nature of urban sprawl and uncontrolled growth in two ways.

The first is to densify the city, increase the presence of high-rises with commercial outlets at grade, move the population to row houses in lieu of the single family homes, increase the parks and park-like amenities and carefully sculpt out view corridors enabling the population to see the mountains, rivers and ocean. The second, much more radical in scope, is to contain the cities of the future in temperature-controlled enclosed platforms or urban biospheres. This solution will encase the city and separate it from sprawling into the countryside. It will serve as a foil for some aspects of global warming. It will enable cities to be built on or over bodies of water and will, in time, lead to a reliance on temperature

control and nutrient controlled soil or water (hydroponics) biospheres for the agribusinesses needed to feed the urban spheres. In
the innovative cluster there is a decided recognition that landscape
is increasingly designed: nature enhanced by the built environment. The garden has its place in the machine-based future, but it
is not at its center.

The study of economic clusters and workplace spirituality in
Cascadia suggests that this region, still relatively brash in its boast-
ful image and demeanour, is internally divided on how it ought to
present itself to others. Each economic cluster presents a strong
and largely competing version on how to frame spirituality and
what this means in the context of Cascadia. These views are particularly reflected in the works within this volume which portray Cascadia as a place of contradictions, ironies and great hopes. Cascadia
is just that and more.

In the bioregion loosely built into the present geographical boundaries of Oregon, Washington and British Columbia, one finds an
interesting combination of traditional farming, ranching and fishing meeting New Age variants of these old occupational categories.
It is a mythic zone in which tales of indigenous peoples mix with
the urban cultures' pursuit of drugs, rock 'n roll and plain old excess.
It is a cultural zone in which great wealth expresses itself in contradictory fashions. On the one hand, there is a tale about the beautiful nature of simplicity; on the other, the codex of secret handshakes
and nods of Rolex watch wearers. In my opinion, the elusive utopia
that is Cascadia is a combustible mixture of a reverence for nature
and a keen desire to design a new future. It is where the organic
farm must have a WiFi Internet connection.

CONCLUSION

Cascadia is a work in progress. To those in the market cluster, it is a
haven for rugged individualism, a deeply libertarian region immersed in a market ideology. In this region, freedom prevails to
them. Government, big business and labour must be kept off the

backs of the people. It is a home to fundamentalists, cults and sects. People fearful of the impending apocalypse seclude themselves and prepare for the end. Others in the hills of British Columbia, Washington and Oregon prepare themselves to withstand blackouts, food depletion and the cessation of government as we know it. This is the world view in which Cascadia is home to a people who believe that their homes are as castles were to kings. These rugged individualists, born and bred in the market cluster view, see the world in Darwinian terms. It is a struggle in which natural selection favours those who are quick to adapt, who are not frightened of contrarian positions and who distrust authority. In a sense, Cascadia serves to those in the market cluster as an imaginary frontier to those from other regions seeking freedom.

This view of Cascadia is not offered up by those in the planning cluster imbued by the workplace spirituality of duty. Theirs is a Cascadia in which systems are robust and affluent. Trains, ferries, buses and planes run on time. Law and order prevail. The public utilities, banks, educational system and health services are state-of-the-art and, as the euphemism goes, world-class. From the cradle to the grave those who live in Cascadia can plan and act in a rational manner so as to achieve security. Cascadia is well governed. This is not accomplished by a cavalier search for freedom as is so prominent in the market cluster. Rather, it is achieved by incremental rational planning, the creation of policies and rules that are seen as legitimate, and recognition that genuine freedom is only possible if the population recognizes that rights must be balanced with duties. To those in the planning cluster, Cascadia presents itself as a region which provides its inhabitants and those eager to move into it with the infrastructure and wherewithal to achieve security.

Cascadia also presents itself, as is clear throughout this book, as a region deeply invested in creating a sustainable community in harmony with nature. To this influential group, it is a region passionately interested in becoming a model for the environmental movement. It is extremely critical of those who fail to recognize how fragile the community is and are willing to trade off short-term wins for more sustainable environmental gains. The loving-kindness-based adaptive culture, at times with a sense of its own moral superiority, chastises those who would sell our birthright for security. It is a region of spiritual seekers, and it laments those who are willing, in the name of competition, to let the wealth between winners and losers get out of hand. To the adaptive culture, the healthy community is not one that is at peace with the proliferation of the homeless. The healthy community is one in which trust and dialogue thrive. The butcher's mentally disabled son is taken care of by the village after the butcher and his wife die. The healthy community is a compassionate one.

Cascadians also highlight the region as a model for the new knowledge-based global cluster of innovators. The innovative cluster, imbued with the quest for creativity and respect for the fruits of the labour of creatives, is one of the models of the future that Cascadians put forward. Like that of the fusion of east, west and north, it has a kernel of truth. Cascadia is a region increasingly attractive to young creative individuals. The combination of lifestyle, freedom and compassion is a magnet for creatives. Also, the existence of networks of project-based organizations working in leading-edge fields like software development, digital communications, ergonomics and fuel cell technologies, create a drawing card. The universities in the region are supportive of these applied creative ventures. Capital is relatively plentiful. These innovative creatives increase the degree to which Cascadia is a mobile population, new to the area and like all converts to a new thing, frequently smitten by the place and all it has to offer.

To me, Cascadia is largely a place in the imagination. As a hypothetical territory, Cascadia presents itself much as do the inkblots in a Rorschach test. With the diminished intensity of the call to orthodox religiosity, Cascadia has developed a cluster of competing secular or workplace spiritualities. With its diversity and lack of a dominant religious or spiritual model, Cascadia has become a projection onto which people throw their experiments. I view the experiment in workplace spirituality in Cascadia as a fusion: Western materialism meets Eastern mysticism; forest workers glide by video game designers; dumpster divers share urban spaces with vegetarian meditators; and genetically modified seeds are planted across the road from the organic farmer's fields.

What, I suggest, makes Cascadia an elusive utopia is its openness to contrasts. In it, workplaces are imaginary spaces where the instrumental meets the search for meaning, the ineffable and the sacred. Cascadia is a place in the mind for those seeking to experiment with boundaries, who are unafraid of stark contrasts and who enjoy the adventure of living by the crashing sea, the impassable snow-filled passes and the presence of others who not only march to a different drummer, but proudly seek to bring this into their work.

CHAPTER 14

ↂ

Nature-Based Spirituality in Cascadia: Prospects and Pitfalls

GAIL WELLS

I RECENTLY PICKED up an issue of the *Oregon Historical Quarterly* devoted to the role of earthquakes and tsunamis in shaping the Northwest (*Oregon Historical Quarterly*, Summer 2007). One of the articles had "Cascadia" in its title, and I thought, How serendipitous! This author and I are both deep in thought about this place called Cascadia. Then I realized that the author was using the word more literally, to refer to the Cascadia subduction zone, an offshore fault that has triggered intermittent upheaval and remoulding of the Northwest's physical landscape. I also realized that, in our metaphorical use of "Cascadia" in this book, we are talking about a similar restless process, an upheaval and remoulding of our cultural landscape. The essays contained herein are all, in various ways, attempts to detect and chart this tectonic movement.

In this essay I want to talk about one of the key indicators of seismic change in this quasi-mythical geography we are calling Cascadia, and that is the phenomenon of spirituality expressed outside conventional religious forms. Mark Shibley and Patricia O'Connell Killen, also contributors, have studied and written extensively about "secular but spiritual" people, those who answer "None" to queries about their religious affiliation, but who nevertheless venerate something other than "God" as conventionally understood. For many, that "something" at the center of their spiritual focus is nature.

I have heard it said that nature-based spirituality is leading the way toward the healing of Cascadia's environment, and of its inhabitants as well. I've heard it implied that, because they love nature, people who practise nature-based spirituality have better environmentalist credentials than other people — particularly adherents of conventional religion. Indeed, I've heard conventional religion blamed for the environmental degradation that the Northwest has suffered in its short history of European-American settlement.

Is nature-based spirituality really capable of leading us toward a better nature, in both senses of that term? I think it goes without saying that a love of nature is a necessary condition for right environmental behaviour. How can it not be? Moreover, speaking as a "conventional" Christian, I know the church has fully participated in transforming the Northwest into the economic powerhouse it is today, and I am uncomfortably aware of its encouragement of, cooperation with, or tacit acquiescence in the environmental and human costs of that development. I know many people who maintain, along with the American cultural historian Lynn White, that traditional Christianity is to blame for the exploitative actions that have caused so much environmental damage.

My intention here is to offer a gentle yet sceptical meditation on claims to environmental enlightenment made on behalf of nature-based spirituality. I realize it will be a struggle to grab hold of "nature-based spirituality" and define it in useful terms, because at this moment in its history there is nothing discrete or codified about it, no flying-buttressed edifices, no countable congregations, no pastors, deacons, creeds, catechisms or articles of faith. One "spiritual but not religious" person might embark on a spirit quest in a grove of ancient redwoods; another might chain herself to a logging bridge; a third might plant native dogwoods along a degraded stream. So my characterization, besides being subjective, will necessarily be incomplete.

In taking a sceptical glance I do not mean to insult people who feel a reverence for nature. I feel that reverence myself, and it is far from my intention to criticize anyone's spiritual practice. Rather, I want to explore what I perceive to be the intellectual threads that make up a philosophy of nature-based spirituality, discuss where these ideas come from, and suggest ways in which they might promote or hinder effective environmental action. From my early Bible training I remember the epistle of James, where he says, "Faith without works is dead." What kind of works are coming out of Cascadian-style faith in nature?

First, I should define my terms as best I can. By "nature-based spirituality," I mean the set of philosophies, attitudes and practices embraced by people 1) who say they are spiritual but not religious, and 2) whose spiritual expression is centered in nature. Such a person's life is made richer and more meaningful by a sense of awe and wonder in the presence of the natural world, and his or her response carries with it a strong urge to protect the natural world from abuse.

This could describe a lot of people, including many good Catholics and Baptists. One could go further and say nature-based spirituality includes a conviction that nature represents ultimate reality and, as such, offers both a source of ethics and a framework of meaning for life. For its most passionate adherents, nature-based spirituality answers those two central questions that religion tries to answer: "What is real?" and "How shall we then live?"

Nature-based spirituality has been called a "civil religion" of this region — an idea well developed by Sallie McFague in her chapter — and indeed it seems to have a peculiarly Cascadian flavour. Its first widespread literary expression that I know of was the 1975 novel *Ecotopia*, by Ernest Callenbach, which portrays a mythical nation along the American west coast that has split off from the decadent and dystopian United States, and whose inhabitants revere nature, prize individual autonomy and enjoy free love.

Nature-based spirituality seems to be an organic outgrowth of our region's geography and history. There are many reasons, as Patricia O'Connell Killen explains, why the Pacific Northwest offers such a fertile environment for alternative spiritual expression. To begin with the obvious, we are blessed with stunning natural beauty, and the marks left on it by settlement and economic development, while profound, are relatively light compared to environmental impacts on many other regions of the country. The Northwest also has an abundance of easily accessible public land. These facts have given Cascadia's citizens a certain proprietary attitude toward their landscape, a sense that nature's beauty and grandeur belong to everyone, along with a tacit understanding that the claims of legal landowners are encumbered by this larger moral claim.

The Pacific Northwest's historical role as a resource colony, together with its relatively recent settlement history, has given it an appealing origin myth, which does not immediately appear to fit with nature-based spirituality. The West was seen as a frontier ripe for conquest, a land where harsh nature would ultimately yield to the strength of men. Nevertheless, elements of this story emerge in nature-based spirituality, as we shall see, in sometimes surprising ways. The frontier story celebrates individual achievement, even though survival on the real frontier depended more often on cooperation than on competition. As the writer Wallace Stegner has pointed out, the West's origin myth romanticizes "boomers," those restless individuals always chasing the next big strike, and downplays the role of people who stuck around and engaged with others in the hard work of making communities. Hollywood's durable plot line of lone-hero-takes-on-the-establishment is a frontier theme, and you can read it in all kinds of modern real-life dramas, including many accounts of environmental activism; the two-year so-journ of Julia Butterfly Hill in the top of a California redwood tree is a famous example (www.ecotopia.org/ehof/hill/index.html); Hill stayed in the tree from December 10, 1997, to December 18, 1999.

In part because of its frontier history, the West has weaker social ties than those of longer-settled areas, and this opens a hospitable niche for unconventional religious expression. I realize that to equate nature-based spirituality with religion, as Thomas Dunlap does in his excellent book *Faith in Nature*, might provoke an argument from some of the people we are talking about, many of whom are refugees from traditional religion and would not want to be called "religious." Nevertheless, I stand by the aptness of the comparison. When people say they are "spiritual but not religious," it implies some sort of correlation between spirituality and religion, even as the speaker expresses it as a negative. When I say, "I am A, not B," that implies that A and B are similar kinds of things.

Without settling the question for now, I am going to argue that both nature-based spirituality and conventional religion have the potential to play an important, subversive role in what has actually been Cascadia's dominant culture: the scientific-rational-secular-liberal culture of North America. That role is to offer an alternative way of thinking about what is real.

The writer Thomas Moore, in a series of books including *The Soul of Sex* argues that a pervasive scientific-rational world view has turned the modern world into a landscape of atomized objects stripped of subjectivity, numinousness, relationship, mystery, magic and miracle — a literal-physical and metaphorical-philosophical landscape reduced to its mechanistic functions, in which the workings of the gears and sprockets are assumed to be the only reality humans can claim to know.

Religion posits a different reality by asserting that there is something more, something "really real," something "out there" or "in here" that cannot be detected solely from the mechanics of the universe, but that is manifest in some mystical way within those mechanics. Robert A. Orsi, a professor of religion at Harvard and a practising Catholic, ponders the ways in which religious scholarship — taking its cue from scientific scholarship — dismisses or disregards or explains away what Orsi calls abundant events (Orsi, 34–43), such as physical or emotional responses to holy objects, experiences of the efficacy of prayer, and the uncanny awareness of sacredness clinging to a particular spot on Earth. These are the phenomena that our modern thinking wants to sidestep by reducing them to hallucinations or delusions, or to dismiss with the polite demurral, "Well, I understand that what you saw and felt was real *to you*." And yet these experiences (some in much more subtle guise) are essential to a spiritual life under any definition I can think of. The very center of a "spiritual experience" is an event, or unfolding of events, both inexplicable and utterly real.

People who embrace the reality of such experiences — whether they are conventionally religious or "spiritual but not religious" — live their lives, as Orsi puts it, at "an acute and deeply consequential angle of difference to the modern world." They live with an askew perspective that can lead them to imagine an alternative way of living in the world.

Over its long history, conventional religion has codified people's collective experience of the "really real" into commonly held cosmologies, theologies and systems of ethics. Nature-based spirituality seems to be an attempt to make a *personal* meaning out of one particular manifestation of the "really real," namely, an overwhelming sense of awe and wonder in the presence of the natural world, accompanied by a loosening of the grip of ego and a new sense of belonging, acceptance and union with the divine. Nature-based spirituality also offers a certain kind of comfort — not the comfort that comes from hope of heaven, or from collective worship of an agreed-upon deity in an agreed-upon way, but the comfort that comes from laying down the restless search for meaning, from finding a touchstone against which to measure one's individual life.

Nature-based spirituality shares a wide tent (to use a metaphor often applied to churches) with many other occupants of the Cascadian environmentalist universe. Here are examples of some of the others:

- People who pay extra for "green" electricity, recycle their cans and bottles, shop at the farmer's market, write letters opposing oil drilling in the Arctic National Wildlife Refuge, and generally practise an ethic of reduced consumption.
- Members of groups like the Sierra Club, the Wilderness Society, Defenders of the Earth, the David Suzuki Foundation, Greenpeace and 1000 Friends of Oregon, each focusing on its own suite of environmental issues.
- Members of any of hundreds of local grassroots organizations working on everything from toxic chemicals to sustainable forestry to songbird habitat to environmental justice.
- Members of groups like The Nature Conservancy, Sustainable Northwest and Ecotrust, which seek to work within the capitalist economic system to achieve sustainable environmental policy.
- Small-scale organic farmers who work to develop a community-supported agricultural system.
- Members of aboriginal tribes who base their land management on traditional practices, such as the Hoopa in northern California and the Yakama in Washington.
- Families who own forest land and harvest timber from it, and who care about sustaining it as forest land.
- City councillors, such as those in Bellingham, Washington, who adopt "green" building codes.
- Land managers for federal agencies who work within the progressive-conservation tradition to do their best for the people and the land.
- Land developers who seek to create compact communities with ample green space and farmland nearby.
- Some recreationists, such as hikers, hunters, anglers and surfers.

I have tried to make a spectrum out of these environmentalist expressions, but I could not do it; the relationship among them is not so much a line as a web. To make things more complicated, some of the people I mentioned may also embrace nature-based spirituality. However, in my typology, their environmental activism, whatever form it takes, does not depend on it.

The Cascadia to which these environmentalists devote their energy also resists neat definition. It occurs to me that calling it "Cascadia" begs a question. The name may ring sweetly in the ears of those sympathetic to nature-based spirituality, but it is rare to hear it on the lips of anyone from Weyerhaeuser or the US Forest Service (unless they are talking about subduction zones). I say this as a reminder that every label is an argument. The very concept of Cascadia as expressed in this book is an argument, an "askew" look at mainstream assumptions, definitions and boundaries.

The Sightline Institute, in its 2006 *Cascadia Scorecard*, defines "Cascadia" in bioregional terms, as "the watersheds of rivers that flow into the Pacific Ocean through North America's temperate rainforest zone." In the conventional calculation that attends the division of land into separate holdings, rivers commonly define boundaries — the Columbia divides Oregon from Washington, the Snake divides Oregon from Idaho. Cascadian geography turns that idea inside out: a river is not the boundary of a territory but its very heart, the bright thread that stitches the land together.

A map of Cascadia may look identical to a map of the Pacific Northwest, but the difference is in the eye of the beholder. In the Cascadian map the center of the territory, not the edges, is the feature of interest. The Cascadian map thus suggests that what draws a region together is more important than what separates it from its neighbours. This is an "askew" look at the world that embodies a profound ethical principle, unity of landscape and life, and opens possibilities for positive change in how we treat the Earth.

In the culture of Cascadia, nature-based spirituality has a distinct and lively presence, especially in the artistic and literary realms. It permeates the writing of prominent Northwest authors including Rick Bass, David James Duncan, Kathleen Dean Moore, Barry Lopez and Gary Snyder. Farther afield in the West are Wallace Stegner, Edward Abbey and Terry Tempest Williams.

In fact, mining nature for one's material has come to be almost *de rigueur* for a Northwest writer, and a reverential tone seems always to be expected. This is not necessarily a bad thing. We writers do feel blessed to live in a spectacular natural setting, and letting it guide our aesthetic journeys seems the least we can do in return. And some glorious writing has come out of it.

Yet it can be limiting to have the landscape so thoroughly dominate the artistic consciousness. Consider Barry Lopez, by all accounts (mine included) a wonderful writer. The landscape is such a presence in his work that it comes to function almost as a character; think of his *Arctic Dreams*. But when I compare his themes with the broad humanistic questions posed in the work of John Irving, or Margaret Atwood, or Alice Munro, I wonder if our dazzling scenery might be giving us a sort of tunnel vision, distracting us from the breadth of human experience and human interaction. This is a theme that Paulo Lemos Horta explores richly in his discussion of magic realism in this book. To be sure, the best Northwest writers convey "a stronger and more universal empathy towards people and creation," as Horta puts it, without lapsing into uncomplicated reverence — they show us a nature that illuminates and echoes the beauty and horror of the human condition, and vice versa.

Another place where nature-based spirituality abounds is in conferences and workshops and gatherings of thinkers. Kathleen Dean Moore, a philosophy professor at Oregon State University and a renowned nature writer, started the Spring Creek Project for Ideas, Nature and the Written Word. The Spring Creek Project brings together writers, scientists, musicians and artists to share their reflections about the natural world and the human role in it. A few years ago Spring Creek put on a conference called "Nature and the

Sacred — A Fierce Green Fire." The allusion is to the words of Aldo Leopold as he watched the fierce light fade from the green eyes of a dying wolf. The symposium was devoted to the different ways one could re-imagine the human relationship with nature. This re-imagining potential is an important strength of nature-based spirituality, and I will come back to it in a little while.

First, though, let me point out a few ironies in the fact that nature-based spirituality has found such a hospitable niche in Cascadia. The metaphorical Cascadia, centered as it is on rivers and watersheds, may exemplify a principle of unity, but the rockier part of its geography — specifically, the ridge of mountains slashing it in two from top to bottom (what Philip Resnick calls, in this book, the Cascade Curtain) — complicates the picture. The left, or west, portion of this divided territory is the wet side, a strip of oasis that runs approximately from Skagway, Alaska, down to Eugene, Oregon. The right, or east, portion, larger by far, is another world entirely.

I grew up on the left side, on the shore of the Pacific Ocean. I have always known I was a westerner — I absorbed that identity with my baby food. When I was seven or eight, though, I had a geographical epiphany that complicated this understanding. I was watching a cowboy movie on TV, and I asked my dad, "Where is this West, where these cowboys and Indians are?" I was puzzled that I did not see any of them around Coos Bay, and how much farther west could you go? He had to tell me that the West portrayed in the movie was actually quite a ways east of us. (I learned later that there are indeed Indians in Coos Bay, although no cowboys that I know of.)

The fabled country of western movies and literature is not the moist strip of Cascadian rainforest, but rather that wide swath between the Cascades and the Rockies whose defining characteristic, as John Wesley Powell, Bernard DeVoto, and Wallace Stegner have observed, is that it is dry. We who live here on the wet side, conditioned as we are by our lush, abundant, fuzzy-edged, forgiving environment, may have a hard time relating to that "West."

The vortex of nature-based spirituality may actually be in the drier region to the south of that wet strip, Jackson and Josephine counties in southern Oregon, and centered specifically on the pretty town of Ashland, with its well-stocked marketplace of personal philosophies and spiritual entrepreneurs. But this does not change the larger geographical split between wet and left (in both senses of the world) and dry and right (in both senses of the word). So we should keep in mind that Cascadia's geography can be as divisive as it is unifying, depending on the eye of the beholder.

The economics and politics here are similarly complicated. Cascadia is strongly urban — four out of five Northwesterners live in a city — and there is an urban-rural divide that is about as sharp as the mountainous spine I just mentioned. The urban parts of Cascadia embrace nature-based spirituality much more readily than do the rural parts, even though rural dwellers are physically closer to less-developed portions of the landscape and might be assumed to experience them more often.

Moreover, the wet side of Cascadia is well off relative to the drier parts to the east. The wealth, no surprise, tends to be concentrated in the urban areas. One sees a lot of Suburbans and Hummers and monster Chevy "Duallies" on the road in Portland, and even in eco-friendly Corvallis, Eugene and Ashland. Big houses and condos are sprouting all over the green hillsides, and many of them are built with lumber imported from British Columbia. It is a strange coals-to-Newcastle situation when a state so blessed with timber has to import lumber from another country because it cannot or will not produce enough of its own. That implies a contradiction between what people say they believe and what they actually do. In fact, as we all know, this disconnect is huge and pervasive, and while it is not confined to the Left Coast of Cascadia (the human capacity for self-delusion being universal), it is telling that nature-based spirituality is so much at home in this land of mini-mansions and SUVs.[1]

In what ways has nature-based spirituality influenced environmental activism in Cascadia? There is much truth to the cartoon picture of the Pacific Northwest as a land of "tree-hugging dirt worshippers," as Douglas Todd noted in his introduction to this book. Environmentalist philosophy, policy and practice have had significant impacts on the landscape and culture of the Pacific Northwest. Because of the huge federal presence on the US side, some of the most lasting environmental reforms have come through changes in federal land use law and policy. These changes have been brought about by action at all levels, from street demonstrations, citizen activism, lobbying efforts and political organizing, up to acts of Congress and rulings from federal courts.

Here are a few examples of actions at the federal level that have greatly influenced the Northwest's environment, on the US side at least:

- Laws regulating pesticides in the 1960s
- The Wilderness Act of 1964
- The Endangered Species Act of 1973
- The suite of laws governing management of federal forests that passed in the 1960s and 1970s. These include the Multiple Use-Sustained Yield Act of 1960, the National Environmental Policy Act of 1969, which required environmental impact statements and provided for appeals of decisions, and forest planning laws in 1976 that required accounting for biological diversity
- The Northwest Forest Plan in 1994, supposed to resolve the conflict between logging and environmental protection (but it has not)

In my state of Oregon, which has a sometimes-deserved reputation for progressive public policy, there also have been significant efforts on behalf of the environment. These too have come from action on many levels:

- The Oregon legislature declared the beaches as a public highway in 1913, thanks largely to the Canadian-raised Governor Oswald West, who firmly believed in the right of the public to regulate private property.
- State forest-practice rules were first enacted in 1948. They were strengthened considerably with the Forest Practices Act in 1971 and have undergone periodic upgrades since then.

– The Bottle Bill of 1971, bitterly opposed by the beverage industry, created a system of deposits and returns on beer and soft-drink bottles, and greatly reduced roadside litter. There are now efforts to extend the law to cover plastic water bottles and other containers not covered by the 1971 law.
– Oregon has passed significant environmental laws targeted mostly at industrial pollution and water quality.
– A comprehensive statewide land-use planning program was created by the legislature in 1981. A successful initiative petition two years ago posed a serious challenge to the system, and a subsequent referendum restored some restrictions. Now Governor Kulongoski and the legislature are grappling with how to reorganize the system in a way that protects property rights and still keeps public support for land-use planning.
– There have been increasing legal restrictions on agricultural open-field burning over the past decade.
– In the 1990s, Governor John Kitzhaber spearheaded the Oregon Plan for Salmon and Watersheds, hoping to forestall a federal listing of the coastal coho salmon under the Endangered Species Act. It did not work — the coho was listed — but the plan led to new ways for people to organize themselves around environmental problems, such as watershed councils of landowners along a stream and new partnerships among state agencies, industry and private citizens.

These few examples show that the people of Oregon have participated in many efforts at every level to improve their natural environment. The role of nature-based spirituality in these efforts is hard to discern. The battle over old-growth forests may be the most conspicuous and illustrative example. That battle took place over two decades, within a context of shifting public attitudes about the value and the meaning of forests. Nature-based spirituality may have been in some respects a driver of this shift and also in some respects a consequence of it. In any event, the battle ended in a draw, and that is where things sit today. Timber companies and environmental organizations circle each other warily, the Forest Service is struggling to refine its mission, and the Northwest spins its wheels for lack of a coherent policy on federal forests.

Because lasting environmental gains require broad public support, it is reasonable to say that most of the people involved in the efforts cited above did not profess or practise nature-based spirituality as such. More likely, they were motivated either by the progressive-conservation ethic, which is the conviction that we should take care of the Earth for the benefit of ourselves and future generations. Or they were motivated by the stewardship ethic arising out of the Christian and Jewish tradition, which is the conviction that we should care for the Earth because God created it and called it good, and also because God told us to. Many of the people who worked for these reforms may have had strong leanings toward nature-based spirituality, but it is hard to tease out the direct influence of those sentiments on the outcomes of these environmental efforts.

Does nature-based spirituality have what it takes to lead Cascadia toward environmental wholeness? I believe it holds promise, but some of its elements strike me as problematic and a potential hindrance to effective environmental action.

First, its radical emphasis on the *self* — the personal quest, the individual experience — gives me pause. The phrase "I am spiritual but not religious," Robert Orsi declares is "a mantra of modern men and women in the United States." It means, he says, that "my religion is interior, self-determined, free of authority . . . and my ethics are a matter of personal choice, not of law; I take orders from no one" (Orsi, 37).

For most of human cultural history, religious expression has been manifest mostly at the level of community. While a personal mystical union with the divine may feel to the believer like the fulfillment of an ancient yearning, the notion of an *individual* relationship with God is a relatively modern Christian invention (Beard, North and Price) and, I believe, a close cousin to the radical individualism that has come down to us from our frontier story. (The appeal of the sovereign individual is not lost on global commerce, whose mission it is to get us to buy more things than we need. "Have it *your* way!" the ads proclaim, offering us a vast array of meaningless choices.)

Because it is defined primarily by a person's individual aesthetic response, nature-based spirituality may, for some, amount to a private religion, offering solace and comfort at the risk of self-absorption and disconnection from the larger community. This works against the vision of connectedness that informs the Cascadian metaphor. More practically, it cuts a person off from the shared learning of a community and the accumulated wisdom of a faith, traditional hedges against error and hubris.

Certainly, many people whose spiritual lives are centered on a personal response to nature do become involved in communal efforts to heal the Earth. Mike Carr shows us some examples in this book. Yet the community of conventionally religious people, having already a semi-cohesive social structure, may have an advantage over nature-based spirituality when it comes to putting boots on the ground for the environment. Mainstream Christianity and Judaism have a long history of working toward progressive social change. Churches and synagogues played a major role in ending slavery in the United States, agitating for women's right to vote and other rights and liberties, securing civil rights for people of colour, and promoting care and stewardship of the Earth. At many critical moments in history (unfortunately not all), the church has risen to the occasion and stiffened its collective moral backbone to speak truth to power in an organized fashion.

The church is no model of unity, to be sure. Western Christianity, with its dozens of denominations, suffers from a long-standing liberal-conservative split that runs through the whole body. In America, left-leaning churchgoers have historically been the leaders of environmental activism within the faith community, although lately, in a heartening development, they are being joined more and more by their conservative evangelical brethren. Nature-based spirituality, while it may have the right instincts, does not yet have much of a track record.

My second concern is that, in its embrace of a mythical landscape, nature-based spirituality is by and large ahistorical. Assumptions are made about nature, wilderness and indigenous land traditions that are often not critically examined — for one, the myth that indigenous people lived lives of environmental innocence in a pristine Eden. A glance at actual indigenous practices, which included some dramatic manipulations of the landscape, such as the buffalo jump and the burning of the prairies, would help lay this story to rest. These practices were emphatically not done in the same spirit as our capitalist exploitation of nature. But they serve to show that native peoples met their material needs with their own technology, and that it is our own muddled psychological projection that makes us imagine that they "revered" nature in the same Romantic sense that we do.

This is in no way to deny that indigenous people may have much to teach us today about sustainable land management. A historical memory will help us learn from them without invoking the noble savage cliché, but it will also make us face our past errors and the painful realization that we are all complicit in our environmental messes.

Like radical individualism, this lack of collective memory unwittingly draws on the frontier story, with its recurring themes of progress and conquest in the creation of a glorious future. For some adherents of nature-based spirituality, that future is nature restored to primal innocence, before it was sullied by the human hand. It is instructive to note that the phrase "civil religion" has been used before in a frontier context. As Philip Resnick explains in this book, it once conjured the idea that America was God's new Israel, a nation plucked by his hand from the messy exigencies of history and planted in a timeless mythical landscape. If nature-based spirituality is a "civil religion" in this sense, then it may be subject to the same myth-induced collective amnesia.

Third, in its preoccupation with wilderness, its sacralizing of places where human beings *aren't*, nature-based spirituality has a frankly imperialist dimension. We in the "have" countries are fortunate to be able to sequester our landscapes for our own aesthetic and spiritual benefit while obtaining our material resources from someplace else. In his critique of American-style "deep ecology," the Indian ecologist Ramachandra Guha says that Americans "possess a vast, beautiful, and sparsely populated continent and are also able to draw upon the natural resources of the globe by virtue of their economic and political dominance" (Guha, 72–83). In its sometimes-myopic focus on untouched wilderness, nature-based spirituality enables us to deny our roles as consumers and material creatures.

Fourth, nature-based spirituality can lead to moral absolutism. "No compromise in defense of Mother Earth," said the American "deep ecologist" Dave Foreman of Earth First! This tenet has been particularly troublesome in the struggle toward a sustainable forest policy.

Every lasting political solution in a free society involves some compromise; otherwise you have theocracy or tyranny. Abraham Lincoln, perhaps the most revered of American presidents, did not shrink from compromise when he judged it necessary. "My paramount object in this struggle is to save the Union, and is not either to save or to destroy slavery," Lincoln wrote in 1862, a few weeks before signing the Emancipation Proclamation. "If I could save the Union without freeing any slave I would do it, and if I could save it by freeing all the slaves I would do it; and if I could save it by freeing some and leaving others alone I would also do that. . . . I have here stated my purpose according to my view of official duty; and I intend no modification of my oft-expressed personal wish that all men everywhere could be free" (Wikipedia online). Despite his passion for ending slavery, Lincoln had the guts to stay focused on the finish line in a heartbreakingly high-stakes race. More practically, he knew a rupture of the Union would do the slaves no good.

In the same way, a rigid insistence that forests are best served by locking them up and walking away not only disregards the needs of the human community, it does not serve the land well in the long term. A sense of practical compromise and the acceptance of appropriate hands-on management would carry nature-based spirituality much further toward sustainability in its thinking.

Fifth, I sense in nature-based spirituality a touch of anti-scientific truculence. Nature is seen as a teleological force, a conscious purpose that is working itself out independent of, or (paradoxically) pitifully vulnerable to, the exploitations of human beings. In this view, any manipulation of nature is by definition an assault.

Sacralizing everything dismisses science's appreciation for fine distinctions, and it resists the systematic unshrouding of mystery that science must do. It dismisses the power of technology to make things better for people and the Earth. I have heard some adherents of nature-based spirituality blame science, as some blame religion, for its contribution to environmental damage. But science, practised in the right spirit, is an ally of environmental activism, not an enemy.

Finally, nature-based spirituality can become a fad, something people pay lip service to but do not really believe. In a 2006 *Rolling Stone* article, the writer Kurt Vonnegut is quoted as saying, "Evolution is a mistake. Humans are a mistake. We have destroyed our planet" (Brinkley). Now, I'm never sure how seriously to take Kurt Vonnegut, but I cannot believe he means that. If he really believes evolution was a mistake and humans are a mistake, he would not be able to live. That is just too much of a cognitive dissonance.

Such fashionable angst, such a categorical denial of all that is good in human endeavour! And from such an influential figure. It is too easy, too glib, and it feeds into the nihilism of disaffected people, of whom there are far too many today.

Now that I have gotten these gripes off my chest, maybe I should hedge them a little, because it occurs to me that what bothers me about nature-based spirituality is the same as what bothers me, often, about conventional religion: the lack of historical memory, the hostility to science, the faddishness, the tendency toward self-absorption and extremism, the denominational squabbling, the disavowal or ignorance of the broad humanistic values that inform our faith traditions at their best.

And yet the most hopeful feature of nature-based spirituality is also something it shares with other faith traditions, something that lies in the realm of the imagination, and that is its own particular "askew" perspective on the world. By drawing others into that vision, nature-based spirituality can energize them to imagine the world in a different way. That, I believe, is its strongest potential contribution to the healing of the Earth.

Although it might offend people who consider themselves anti-religious, I believe nature-based spirituality has much in common with the emotional expressiveness of Pentecostal and charismatic worship. In these communities the touchstone of authentic spirituality is not theology, not dogma, but experience — experience of the divine, or, in a common phrase, a born-again experience.[2]

In the broadest non-sectarian sense, a born-again experience is a radical wrenching of the self from old habits and attitudes. A born-again experience is a call to imagine oneself and the world in a radically new way, and a call to act on that imagining. Anyone can have a born-again experience, including those who revere nature.

In the Christian context, a born-again experience is a call to repent and get right with God. "Get right" means get into reality. When I am right with God, I know what is real. As a Christian, I accept that God is sovereign and I am subject. God does not depend on me; I depend on God. In a similar way, when I am right with the Earth, I accept that the Earth and its processes are sovereign and I am subject. The Earth does not depend on me; I depend on the Earth. That is real. That is scientific fact.

Some might object to the word "sovereign" to describe the relationship I am talking about, and I acknowledge the risk that the root metaphor might be offensive to people who feel they have struggled with the "angry old man in the sky" image of God. In her chapter, Sallie McFague offers a more organic metaphor to frame the relationship between God and the world, which I am posing as an analogue to the relationship between the natural world and the human beings who inhabit it.

When McFague tenderly describes panentheism as the view "that God encompasses the world . . . but God is more than the world . . . the universe is dependent on God in a way that God is not dependent on the universe," she emphasizes that the natural world is a creature of God, just as we are. But panentheism also suggests nature does not care about us in the same sense that God cares about creation. This is part of the romantic idea that I am challenging: the notion (often unexamined) that nature is kindly disposed toward humans; or at least that it has some sort of intentionality toward humans. Panentheism, it seems to me, addresses this fallacy by saying that God is not co-equal with nature, that God is in nature but is bigger than nature.

In the context of such a relationship between God and nature, a human's born-again experience leads to repentance, which leads to changed behaviour. When I'm right with God, I put away pride and self-seeking and try to do what I discern to be God's will. When I'm right with the Earth, I put away fantasies of conquest and domination and seek to co-operate with nature's ways.

A born-again experience is a spiritual awakening. When I wake up to the staggering fact that God *is*, I wake up to gratitude for the miracle of existence, for my extraordinary good fortune that there is something to wake up to, when there could just as easily have been nothing. I wake up to the amazing grace of matter in motion, spinning away from its source, spiralling into nebulae, pulsing with energy, ever evolving, ever sustaining, ever renewing, a secular holy trinity.

The born-again experience is what the charismatics and Pentecostals are talking about when they talk about faith. Faith sufficient to move environmental mountains comes in many flavours, ranging from the burning-bush experience to a slower, unfolding apprehension of the divine, a spiritual experience "of the educational variety," as William James put it. Some people are able to express a sense of wonder about the natural world without resorting to mystical terms. I am speaking now of Rachel Carson, and another writer I admire, the geneticist Ursula Goodenough, author of *The Sacred Depths of Nature*. These two scientists describe the glorious complexity of the real world in awe-filled but completely naturalistic terms.

I believe effective environmental action requires faith in some form, because it is faith that gives the vision. Faith does not have to come from nature-based spirituality. But in this world in which conventional religion has turned off so many people, nature-based spirituality is an avenue to the divine that works for them.

I believe the most effective environmental action comes when faith is combined with a practical consideration of politics and science. Politics is about how things can be — it is "the art of the possible." Science is about how things actually work. Faith gives the vision of how things *should* be.

I believe that, while faith may not be sufficient for healing the environment, it is necessary. Purely secular, purely technical solutions are also needed, but often they are just another way for humans to exert their power over nature. Faith, by getting us right with the Earth, by constantly reminding us of our real relationship with nature, can help curb that hubris.

Paul, in his first letter to the Corinthians, writes, "When I was a child, I spoke like a child, I thought like a child, I reasoned like a child; when I became a man, I gave up childish ways" (1 Corinthians 13:11). The older faith traditions have had many centuries to develop a collective story and a collective call to action. Nature-based spirituality is young, and so is this land of Cascadia, where it has found a pleasant home. It may be that, in coming to grips with the critical environmental problems of the next two or three decades, nature-based spirituality will put away its childish ways, move out boldly in response to that born-again experience, and engage with others of the Cascadian community in a common and noble and absolutely necessary mission.

POLICE ON BICYCLES PROTECT STARBUCKS. The economics, politics and recreational culture of Cascadia are illustrated by these bicycle-riding police officers guarding Starbucks during the 1999 protests against the World Trade Organization conference in Seattle. Christians on both sides of the border were key organizers of what later became dubbed "The Battle of Seattle," one of the first mass protests to declare that consumerism threatens the planet's ecology.

PIONEER LOGGER AND CLEARCUT. The boom-and-bust resource economy of the Pacific Northwest is part of the reason organized religion has had trouble putting down roots. The mobility of loggers, fishers and miners made it hard to establish communities, writes Patricia O'Connell Killen. As an outsider to the region, Mark Silk picked up a hint of Cascadian nature reverence when he first saw the "desecration" wrought by clear-cut logging in Washington State.

PARASAILING NEAR VANCOUVER. Cascadians' passion for parasailing, windsurfing, kayaking, skiing, hiking, camping and other outdoor activities fit into what several contributors consider the region's "civil religion of nature." Health and recreation also make for idealistic businesses. They have turned Oregon's Nike, Vancouver's Mountain Equipment Co-op and Seattle's Recreational Equipment Inc. into industry leaders. (Photo Credit: Ian Smith)

CASCADIAN INNOVATION GOES GLOBAL. Business ethicist Mark Wexler
maintains that the Pacific Northwest's powerful high-tech industries,
such as Microsoft, Amazon and Electronic Arts, reflect a form of
"workplace spirituality" that believes creativity and innovation will solve
the world's difficulties. This ethos clashes with another form of
Cascadian spirituality, exemplified by Greenpeace and various
eco-tourist businesses that emphasize nature, loving kindness and
the building of sustainable communities.

BILL REID'S MYTHICAL CANOE. Canadians and Americans have embraced the aboriginal mythology and nature reverence inherent in this magnificent sculpture by the late Haida sculptor, Bill Reid. The giant Jade Canoe is the artistic centerpiece of Vancouver's award-winning International Airport, a black version titled "The Spirit of Haida Gwaii" dominates the Canadian Embassy in Washington, D.C. and, since 2004, Reid's image has graced the back of the Canadian $20 bill. (Photo Credit: Mark van Manen)

TRANSFORMING JACK SHADBOLT. This major 20th-century Pacific Northwest painter delved into many of the themes explored in *Cascadia: The Elusive Utopia*. With a devotion to freedom and justice, Jack Shadbolt was an early immigrant from England who admired West Coast wilderness and aboriginal mythology and transformed it. Like contributor Gail Wells, Shadbolt did not romanticize nature or aboriginals, but kept a firm grip on what was scientific and real.

DALE CHIHULY'S FLUID WORLD. The sensual glass sculptures of the famous Washington State glass artist, Dale Chihuly, flow from the region's fecund forests and oceanic depths. Intense and daring, Chihuly's glass abstractions of nature have been exported around the globe. These floating water lily bulbs enliven the grounds of a botanical garden in Missouri.

Douglas Coupland

Jack Hodgins

Gina Ochsner

PACIFIC NORTHWEST WRITERS. Douglas Coupland's novel *Life After God* causes Patricia O'Connell Killen to reflect on how the author has a "profoundly liturgical" sense of nature, while others worry that Coupland's emphasis on the future illustrates a lack of historical memory. Paulo Lemos Horta is struck by how B.C.'s Jack Hodgins and Oregon's Gina Ochsner adopt magic realism to delve into Cascadian themes of utopia, religion and the dark divinity of the natural world.

CASCADIAN

CONTEMPLATIONS

Cascadia

GEORGE BOWERING

HAVE YOU EVER NOTICED a pattern in the way Easterners make fun of West Coasters? In the US, people in Oregon are always depicted as flying *out of* the cuckoo's nest. They munch granola and wear logger shirts. Easterners call these "lumberjack" shirts. Oregonians make their own houses out of railway ties and recycled domes, and live with big dogs back in the hills. In Toronto, that's pretty much the way they imagine B.C. people: weed-smoking folk in granny glasses and vegan footwear.

The point is that those people out there in the mushroomy rain forest (they like this image, though most of Oregon, Washington and British Columbia are the next thing to a desert) are flaky. They eat flaky food and write flaky books. They are outside religion as we know it here in civilization. Religion means how we do things. We go to work every morning religiously. Out there on the edge they have no discipline, no get up and go. They fill their hot tubs with Perrier water,

But in Cascadia, in the Pacific Nation, we prefer spirituality to religion. We like to be breathed into, to be, as they say, inspired. Not all of us — there are some who watch television sent via air from the east. There's a lot of religion on that television, but not much vision.

Let's look at some more abstract words to sense the difference I'm trying to scare up. What I've been calling religion (perhaps not fairly) you could also call humanism. Humanism can be very nice. It gave rise to the Italian Renaissance, after all. But it also told us that we are privileged, that nature, for instance, belongs to us if we can name it, that we can use it as a backdrop for human portraits. In Ontario and Pennsylvania they have these things called woodlots. These are tiny bits of surviving forest or more often planted trees *owned* by farmers or agribusiness. You could never get lost in one. They are the opposite of clear-cut patches. Both these things are humanism in action. If you really want to see the results of unchecked humanism, go and look at what's happened to the ironically named Everglades or the massive river dams in China. Or look at the giant parking lots around those huge evangelical churches in Texas.

But have you ever been lost in the woods, or as we call it, the bush? That's where your brain skids a little, your heart is in your throat, and your lungs would like a little air. You are surrounded by beauty and you'd better start by breathing some in. Good sense and training suggest that you find a creek and follow it downhill. But another voice tells you that there's something here that you need all the time.

Whatever You Do

GEORGE BOWERING

Whatever you do, do not
slam the year open with a bang,
waken the child
sleeping under that tree
into terror, that tree
dying in our back yard,
birds lining up to mourn. You

wanted a cheer for new
lang syne? Have you looked at the under
cutting of the North Shore mountains,
have you heard four-wheel drives
passing your sweet coupé
on the rain slick of Burrard?

Let that babe sleep, let
chainsaw rest in watershed,
tell politico it's all right to be short,
tell him forget auld acquaintance,
have a look at this
sleeper 'neath our tree,
wake this sweet bairn if need be
with a cup of kindness, two handles,
show this dear drowsy head
the home-made paper you're holding —
it's the deed, hand it to that kid,
say keep this here, don't
let them take it anywhere, south or up the tower.
That's right, *companero*, and say, that wee critter
looks powerful like you, you
must be proud, lucky dad.

As an Earthquake rocks a corpse
its coffin in the clay
so are you rocked in your desire,
so do you meet a living January,
so does nature, call her that again,
depend on your doting, how we have
reversed our lot, oh Death
we address not, but list with new ear
to the Spirit herself utter her fear
for us.

      Look, we've wakened the child, how
can we teach her to be not us,
how give her power and sweetness,
and tell her what acquaintance should
be forgot?

      Spread a rictus along your jaw,
Dad, help raise a whoop and pretend
this will one day all be hers,
poor orphan, whose face even now
is shaded by that dead branch.

West Coast Mythistorema

PHILIP RESNICK

> *Our country is a shut-in place, all mountains*
> *And the mountains roofed in by a low sky, day and night.*
>
> — SEFERIS MYTHISTOREMA X

I

Sometimes the mountains shut out the sky
and throat-pipes constricted
we gasp for air.
Other times clouds lift
and the sheer extent of heaven
makes us land-sick,
losing our balance where the river treads
a cold grey line down through Alpine passes.
Already those who came before
knew there was no going back,
no westward haven to which,
like the refuge cities of old
one could run in one's hour of need,
no further parting of the sea
leading to some promised land.
Those who put down roots here
knew how thinly they grew,
top-soil washed away by salt and snow,
ghost towns where gold-seekers came to dwell,
settlers from Earth's four corners,
never quite sure why they had come,
what restless energy drove them on,
their skeletons consigned to graves
with moss for sheets
and stone markers, often in an alien tongue.

II

You can hear the shamans at night
amidst the numerous inlets that dot the coast
but all must be still,
no motor boats, cruise ships sailing north,
ghetto blasters wafting garbled sounds
of a centaur civilization, half-chaotic,
half-addicted to the code of work.
Plosives, guttural sounds, an occasional cry,
blend with gulls along the shore,
or the smooth flight of eagle,
wings streamlined, almost motionless against the sky
that in the distance seems to meet a point
where killer whale holds land and sea
suspended on its back.
Bear and beaver have been summoned to this ancestral rite,
and raven, tricking the first children who crawled
from the gelatinous mucous of a giant clam
deposited by the tide
to revel in the sand.
Before the fire dies down
and the young have drifted off to sleep,
legends are indented into logs,
carvings to keep the founding myths intact,
even as the shaman's voice grows mute.

III

No Argonauts sailed this way,
no warriors in hot pursuit of an absconding slut,
nor does the landscape bear the mark of overlain ruins.
We are so young,
and explorers whom our civic texts
try desperately to celebrate
could be down the block, cutting the lawn,
walking the dog,
or leading groups of twelve-year-olds
for camping trips
along the West Coast Trail.

IV

Religions come to us from far away;
those who are self-sufficient
have grown to do without.
For others, there is the fervour of rekindled faith,
a desperate need to relate
to a creed rooted in another age,
to mime the words, observe the formal rituals.
There is no burning bush by Jericho Beach,
nor do the fish in Okanagan Lake
redeem miracles the Gospels speak about,
even if one keep vigil for forty days,
or fix the sun where it sets towards the west.

V

As for politics,
the Persian Wars, the fall of Rome,
the yoke of feudal lords, Bastilles and sundry revolutionary wars
are foreign to these shores.
We do grow passionate in our hates,
the Right with its nasty streak
for elevating private greed into an affair of state,
the Left with its utopian zeal
for an eco-welfare paradise.
There are Mammons to be served,
cult goddesses and social trends,
bonds of commerce stretched
across the great expanse of water
that has displaced an earlier sea.
Yet in our hearts
we go on searching
for a mythic space.

Afterword

DOUGLAS TODD

AND SO YOU HAVE IT. The diverse visions of Canadian and American scholars, thinkers, ecologists, pollsters and poets on how this fresh place called Cascadia — branded as it with volcanoes, salmon, bicycles and cosmopolitan cuisine — is evolving, perhaps into something great.

Despite multiple perspectives, the contributors to this book are united by a sense that something special is going on in this brilliant green corner of the planet, so grand yet fragile. We have tried to stretch the imagination of readers, to highlight dangers facing this increasingly urbanized region, and to hold up ways to harness its incredible potential to foster respect for both nature and the beloved city, which are inextricably connected.

The contributors have been realistic about geopolitics and power in Cascadia. Still, we tend to believe there is more to the future of Cascadia than the proverbial bottom line, defined by economic absolutism. Many mistakes have been made — including too much logging, too many strip malls and too casual an acceptance of the chasm between the elite and the disenfranchised. But Cascadia is young and relatively unspoiled. It may be a forgiving place.

This book is subtitled *The Elusive Utopia*, not because we believe Cascadia will ever be a secular-but-spiritual New Jerusalem, for the word "utopia" was never intended to mean "absolutely perfect." The root meaning of "utopia," first coined by Sir Thomas More in 1516, is "no place." In other words, utopian dreams are always meant as ideals, as possibilities held up to draw something more out of us. As it says in the Book of Proverbs, "Without a vision, the people perish."

In this way, the book hopes to contribute to Cascadia's elusive utopian project. We do not want Cascadia to become just another place, indistinguishable, except for all the rain, from suburban Milwaukee, Calgary or San Diego. We oppose homogenization. We think the richest culture, values and spirituality grow out of a deep understanding of place, of wonder and gratitude toward the region in which we find ourselves, in all its particularity.

We know it is best to hold lightly to the desire for utopia. Most of the contributors to this book do not even believe in the inevitability of progress, that things are sure to get better in Cascadia or anywhere else if we just keep our motives pure and work hard enough. But we do believe in creative transformation — that we can raise the likelihood of bold choices being made, choices that respect the land, sea, air and all their many creatures while nurturing greater health and enjoyment for the most people.

Can young Cascadia grow up — offering something fruitful and sustainable to the world? It has been our attempt to raise possibilities that could help us answer positively that urgent Cascadian question. The reader is free to accuse us of being hopeful.

CONTRIBUTORS

JEAN BARMAN

"A product of northwestern Minnesota, I collected graduate degrees from Harvard University and the University of California at Berkeley before coming to my senses and moving to Vancouver in the early 1970s. Ever since, I have been intrigued by the history of this magical place called British Columbia and, more generally, by the links between it and the adjacent United States."

Jean Barman is a prominent Canadian scholar, historian and public intellectual with a passion for social change. She has written many books, including a bestselling general history of B.C., *The West beyond the West*, which appeared in a third edition in 2007. One of her current projects, in collaboration with fur trade historian Bruce Watson, focuses on French Canadians in the making of the Pacific Northwest. She is Professor Emerita at the University of British Columbia and a Fellow of the Royal Society of Canada.

GEORGE BOWERING

"I was born and brought up in the 'greenified' desert valley called the Okanagan, so every time it rains on me in Vancouver I consider it a personal insult or attack. I have lived here off and on since I quit the RCAF and enrolled at the University of British Columbia in the fall of 1957. For a time I joined the British Columbia Forest Service. Then I went back to UBC. I am now living in West Point Grey, and when the leaves hit the pavement around here I still think I'd better quit fooling around and attend my classes. I came to Vancouver to go to university, and here I am still. I got away for a while, to Alberta and Ontario and Quebec. To Italy and Germany and Denmark. I have lost my raincoat and rain hat, but it looks as if I'll stay a while. I don't know whether my connection with Cascadia is spiritual or chemical or correctional. I have never been up Grouse Mountain or on Gabriola Island, but I remember riding the Interurban train from New Westminster to Vancouver with my grandma. I do it all the time now, especially when the sun is shining."

George Bowering became a member of the Order of British Columbia while he was the Parliamentary poet laureate of Canada. He has published *Bowering's B.C.*, a history of the province, as well as three historical novels set in B.C. He was the first professor to teach a course in B.C. fiction at Simon Fraser University. He is the official Loud Mouth fan of the Vancouver Canadians baseball team.

MIKE CARR

"I was born and grew up in Toronto but moved to Vancouver in 1981. I came to British Columbia like many other eastern Canadians attracted by the meeting of mountains and ocean. I arrived at the end of June, and that summer I hung out on the beaches all around the mouth of the Fraser River, blown away by the incredible beauty here. Nevertheless, thanks to the incessant autumn and winter rains, it took me three years before I felt this was home. I have never grown accustomed or habituated to this awesome place. Eventually, I decided I had to learn more about ecology. So, in 1987 I returned to Toronto to do a masters degree in Environmental Studies at York University. Unable to find good work when I returned to this region, I did my doctoral studies on the bioregional movement at the University of British Columbia's School of Community & Regional Planning under Dr. William Rees. I have been an activist for social justice and ecological sustainability with many different groups in civil society for over thirty years."

Mike Carr has taught a range of courses at SFU and UBC for the past eight years, including First Nations Studies, Bioregionalism and the Natural World, Bioregional Mapping, Urban Sustainable Development, Planning and Policy, Urban Geography, the Geography of Colonial B.C., Regional Planning, Ecology and Social Thought, the History of Urban Form and the Formation of the Neo-Liberal Corporate World Order. He has published a number of articles and the book *Bioregionalism and Civil Society: Democratic Challenges to Corporate Globalism*.

PETER DRURY

"I was raised on Bainbridge Island, Washington, where each day I played with kelp, dug clams and looked for crabs and critters underneath rocks. I went on to pursue graduate education (master's level) in three fields: theology/ethics, social work, and business/economics. I laugh when discussing my three graduate degrees, but insist they are all part of a single education: to love, to share and to lead well. My parents, grandparents and great-grandparents enjoyed lives in Cascadia (Oregon and Washington), with their ancestors travelling from either Norway (Bergen) or Scotland (Orkney Islands) to arrive here. Dating back generations in Orkney, my father's family has been filled with builders and civil engineers."

Peter Drury is an ordained Protestant minister who for ten years served a vigorous, multicultural parish in urban Seattle. Today he is Development Director at Sightline Institute, Cascadia's premier sustainability think-tank.

ELI BLISS ENNS

"My life, like my genetics, has been divided between two distinct regions of Canada: the Assiniboine River valley in south-western Manitoba and Clayoquot sound on the west coast of Vancouver Island. Being of mixed ancestry, I was born with a sociological perspective and developed a natural passion for international dispute resolution issues. These passions have led me to focus my education on the comprehensive land claims process in British Columbia."

Eli Enns holds a political science degree from Brandon University in Manitoba and furthered his studies there with the Justice System Certificate. Most importantly, Eli is a father; he has five children aged one to fourteen years old. In his work, Eli strives to balance nine-to-five responsibilities with family values. At the moment he is working primarily in the Tla-o-qui-aht Tribal Parks initiative. Additionally, Eli volunteers his time for non-profit organizations, including the Tonquin Foundation and Indigenous Cooperative on the Environment.

ANDREW GRENVILLE

"I was not born in Cascadia. Nor have I ever lived there. And I have seen less than one percent of the land mass of the breathtaking region. That's probably why I thought to make a map of it — so I could figure out where it is. I am pretty Cascadia-poor. But that's okay. I live in Toronto, which we all know is the center of the universe. If you Cascadians are lucky, maybe your mayor will some day call in the army because it snowed. Maybe you too will become insecure enough to boast that your region is 'world class.' I hope not. It wouldn't be very Cascadian."

Andrew Grenville is Chief Research Officer at Angus Reid Strategies, which means he gets to ask lots of questions and find out what people think, which is fun if you are a research geek, as he says he is. He has not written any books. He has written bits and pieces of books — as he has with this one — on such things as out-of-body religious experiences, surveillance and the private nature of faith. He has also published articles in medical journals on what he calls "obscure" topics. "You probably don't want to read them," he says, "because they're pretty dry. Much better to luxuriate in the verdant oasis of a book on Cascadia."

PAULO LEMOS HORTA

"Born in Budapest, I lived as a child for several years each in Brasilia, London, Santo Domingo, and Montevideo before coming to Vancouver in time to graduate from high school and complete a BA and MA at the University of B.C. I would leave Vancouver for Rio and Toronto only to return years later to teach at Simon Fraser University. I suppose the openness of Vancouver to 'third culture' or nomad specimens such as myself is part of its appeal — it is no surprise Vancouver has ranked first in the world according to the UN as a welcoming place for foreigners to live. Mine was a decidedly urban introduction to the region's nature. As a teenager I lived downtown and snuck up the fire escapes of high-rises to rooftops with friends to enjoy the spectacular views. The region continues to attract me for its cosmopolitanism. Indeed, if we were to start sharing each other's stories, rather than producing and consuming them separately, this could prove a key cultural focal point in the twenty-first century."

Paulo Horta is the first professor to teach in World Literature at Simon Fraser University, a program he helped found and design. He has published literary and academic translations from the Portuguese in addition to articles on the novelists and translators of world literature.

PATRICIA O'CONNELL KILLEN

I grew up on the rich farmland of the Tualatin Valley in Western Oregon, with the Coast Range Mountains and the Pacific Ocean to the west, and the Cascade Mountains to the east. The daily view of five snow-capped volcanoes and blazing red summer sunsets over hills that progressed from green to purple to black shaped my psyche. So too did the rhythms and rituals of Catholic liturgical life. My family, mostly Belgian and Alsatian, with a bit of Irish, was part of a larger ethnic farming community made up mostly of Dutch and Belgian Catholics. I spent my summers working in the fields. In the end, the life of the mind called me away from the land and the immigrant enclave: I became an academic. Returning to the Pacific Northwest nearly twenty years ago after sojourns of study and teaching in California, Tennessee and Chicago, I knew I was home. Since returning I have been studying the religious complexity and possibilities of Cascadia. In the experiences of memory, innovation, and resistance of historic faith traditions here are clues for how faith communities might contribute constructively to the future."

Patricia O'Connell Killen is Professor of Religion and Provost of Pacific Lutheran University, in Tacoma, Washington. She is the primary editor of *Religion and Public Life in the Pacific Northwest: The None Zone*. She is the author of two award-winning books: *The Art of Theological Reflection* (with John de Beer) and *Finding Our Voices: Women, Wisdom, and Faith*. In 2001 she received the Paul Bator Memorial Award from the Canadian Catholic Historical Association and, in 2006, the Excellence in Teaching Award from the American Academy of Religion.

SALLIE MCFAGUE

"Although an American by birth, I have Canadian roots. My grandparents met at Acadia College in Wolfville, Nova Scotia, and our family summered at a cottage on the Bay of Fundy during my childhood. I thought of Canada as a land of beauty, excitement and adventure. After many years teaching at the Vanderbilt Divinity School in Nashville, Tennessee, I have returned to Canada, but now to the West Coast, to Vancouver. I still retain my feeling that Canada is a place of beauty, excitement and adventure. Every morning I walk in Jericho Park, and on a late February day I can see new cherry blossoms against the snow on the coastal mountains. To live in this place is a great privilege and responsibility, for it is here that we face, in unavoidable terms, the challenge of climate change, which is forcing the question whether we can have just, sustainable city living."

Sallie McFague is the Distinguished Theologian in Residence at the Vancouver School of Theology. She has taught and published in the area of religion and ecology for many years, with her latest book published in 2008: *A New Climate for Theology: God, the World and Global Warming*.

PHILIP RESNICK

"Like many other residents of Vancouver, I was born thousands of kilometers away from Cascadia. Growing up in Montreal, I subsequently spent a number of years as a graduate student in Toronto and in Paris, before joining the University of British Columbia's political science department in 1971. It was never my original intent to make Vancouver my permanent home. There were many summers and even years in Montreal and in Europe, reinforced by the feeling that Cascadia, for all its physical attractions, lacked the cultural, intellectual and political gravitas of older, long-settled and much-fabled places. With time, I began to find the physical habitat in which the residents of Cascadia reside becoming a part of me. Proof that I had finally come home occurred in 2002–2003, when I was spending a year in Paris as the Chair in Canadian Studies at the University of Paris III. Living in the Latin Quarter, around the corner from the Luxemburg Gardens, I was conscious of the pollution, the noise and the crowdedness of a city that I had often mythologized in the past. I began to miss the vista of mountains and sea, the soaring first- and second-growth forests, which give the west coast of Canada its particular character. Perhaps it was my version of an epiphany — I no longer had the feeling of being a spiritual stranger in a place where nature speaks louder than the recorded past."

Philip Resnick teaches Political Science at the University of British Columbia. He is the author of a number of books, including *Letters to A Quebecois Friend, The Masks of Proteus: Reflections on the Canadian State, Towards a Canada-Quebec Union, Thinking English Canada, 21st Century Democracy, The Politics of Resentment: B.C. and Canadian Unity* and *The European Roots of Canadian Identity*. His current research interests revolve around the character of multinational states and the question of what constitutes North American identity.

MARK SHIBLEY

"As a fifth-generation Oregonian, I spent childhood time on my grandfather's homesteaded farm in the Cascade Mountain foothills southeast of Portland. I bucked hay, explored the nearby woods, caught crawdads in the creek with my cousins, and slept under the stars on warm summer nights. That farm is now mostly forest, for which I have some ownership and responsibility. I came of age hiking the wilderness areas of the Oregon Cascades, but graduate school drew me to southern California for a Ph.D. in sociology in 1993. Then at Loyola University in Chicago I launched a career as a sociologist of American religion. But there I also cultivated a collaborative, community-based research program focusing on urban environmental health issues. For a Northwesterner, that was a profound re-education on the meanings of environment and environmentalism. Family and place pulled me home to Oregon in 1998. Here my investigation into the relationship between religion and nature is happily punctuated by fishing trips with my boys, mucking around in coastal tide pools and grafting new apple varieties into my orchard."

Mark Shibley is Professor of Sociology and Environmental Studies at Southern Oregon University. He wrote two award-winning books: *Resurgent Evangelicalism in the United States: Mapping Cultural Change since 1970* and *Building Community: Social Science in Action*, as well as many articles on evangelical Protestantism, the Christian Right and religious environmentalism in the US. Mark's recent work on this region's "unchurched" population was published in *Religion and Public Life in the Pacific Northwest: The None Zone*. With his students he continues to investigate and write about the social and cultural dimensions of environmental issues in the Pacific Northwest.

MARK SILK

"I am a native of Cambridge, Massachusetts, but was raised mostly in a New Jersey suburb of New York City. My young adulthood was spent back in the neighbourhood of my birth, but in due course I headed south, plying the journalistic trade in Atlanta, Georgia, for nearly a decade. Since the 1996 Olympics, I have been back in New England, teaching and running an academic center. The family summer place is on Mt. Desert Island, in Maine. In short, I've never lived in state that didn't have an Atlantic coast. I am about as far from being a Cascadian as it is possible for an American to be."

Mark Silk's job title is director of the Leonard E. Greenberg Center for the Study of Religion in Public Life and Professor of Religion in Public Life. He was trained to be a medieval intellectual historian but has spent the past three decades writing largely about the contemporary United States. His books include *Spiritual Politics: Religion and America Since World War II*, *Unsecular Media: Making News of Religion in America*, and (with Andrew Walsh) *One Nation, Divisible* — a book about religion and region in the US.

ELEANOR STEBNER

"I'm a relative newcomer to Cascadia, but I have roots here. My grandfather first moved to Vancouver in 1925 as a teenager. He returned to the prairies in the early 1930s, married my grandmother, and they moved back to Vancouver in 1937. My grandparents spent some of their happiest years of their lives here — hiking Grouse Mountain, playing softball and participating in the young peoples' group of their small but vital ethnically based Christian denomination. My father — their first child — was born in Vancouver before they returned to Alberta in the early 1940s and became farmers (a liveli-hood they neither desired nor excelled at). At any rate, I grew up in Alberta hearing loads of stories about the West Coast mountains, the Pacific Ocean and trees so large that one could barely walk around them, let alone see the tops of them. It seemed like paradise, a bit too perfect, much too beau-tiful, and way too temperate to really exist on Earth. But it does exist, and what do we make of it?"

Eleanor Stebner holds the J.S. Woodsworth chair at Simon Fraser Uni-versity. She researches North American Christianity in the nineteenth and twentieth centuries, political activism, women's history, the social gospel movements and religious and social institutions. Devoted to making a link between academia, religion and social betterment, she is the author of several publications, including *The Women of Hull House*.

DOUGLAS TODD

"In Cascadia, non-aboriginals are considered to have deep roots if their family members have been here a century. If you're from elsewhere, try not to laugh. I am one of the minority of Vancouverites actually born in the city. My four grandparents moved to Vancouver between 1910 and 1920 — from Wales, England, Ireland and Ontario (being United Empire Loyalists forced out of Boston, Massachusetts). I was raised in a West Coast forestry-industry family, with three generations of log scalers. I feel privileged to have been raised in this rugged, spectacular place. But I also lived in Los Angeles and Toronto and recognize that, even though Cascadia is geographically over-whelming and has its cosmopolitan aspects, we have a way to go to be-come great. Still, B.C. novelist Douglas Coupland, author of *Generation X* and *Life after God*, and I once decided we liked each other because we'd both played as teenagers in the jagged canyons of North Vancouver. We were also raised in thoroughly non-religious families, which is common in Cascadia. We agree there's something remarkable going on here. It has to do with the vast wilderness, lack of institutional history, dearth of clear codes to live by and soaring potential — but it also seems to have some-thing to do with an emerging nature-rooted spirituality."

Douglas Todd is an award-winning spirituality and ethics writer. As well as working for the *Vancouver Sun* newspaper and *Canwest News*, he is the author of *Brave Souls: Writers and Artists Wrestle with God, Love, Death and the Things That Matter*. In 2006 Todd served as Simon Fraser University's first Jack and Doris Shadbolt Fellow in the Humanities, an adventure during which this book was born.

GAIL WELLS

"I grew up in a small timber town on Oregon's south coast. There was not much in the way of culture: we had no symphony, no opera, no professional theatre, no art museum, no dance company. We mostly didn't miss these things because we got our recreation and our aesthetic and spiritual sustenance from the woods, the mountains and the ocean. Nature was all around us, and I thought everybody's family was similarly blessed. Then I went to college and met people who'd never camped in the woods, but who knew every artist in the museum and could hum the themes of all of Beethoven's symphonies. Many of these people were raised outside the Pacific Northwest. I thought to myself: well, I guess they have culture and we have scenery. It took me longer to realize that, here in Cascadia, in some ways at least, our scenery is our culture. For many of us, nature is right up there with art and literature and music in addressing the deep human questions about life and love, goodness and beauty, pain and death."

Gail Wells is a science writer, editor, and essayist living in Corvallis, Oregon, USA. She is the author of *The Tillamook: A Created Forest Comes of Age, Lewis and Clark Meet Oregon's Forests* (with co-author Dawn Anzinger) and *The Little Lucky: A Family Geography*. A dominant theme in her writing is the relationship of humans with the natural world.

MARK N. WEXLER

"I was born on the corner of Du Bullion and Rachel streets beneath the shadow of Mont Royal in *la belle ville du Montréal*, and now live on the corner of Chilco and Alberni streets alongside Lost Lagoon in Stanley Park, Vancouver. I walk the Stanley Park seawall, pick up my books at Joe Fortes Library and get my daily ration of caffeine from Bo Jangles Café. I became a convert to Cascadia in 1976 and now can be discovered looking longingly, eyes out to sea, in search of elusive pods of whales."

Mark N. Wexler holds the Endowed University Chair in Business Ethics in the Segal Graduate School of Business at Simon Fraser University. He is a four-time teaching award winner, the Price Waterhouse Cooper LIME (Leader in Management Education) award recipient for 2005 and an Astra-Zeneca Applied Ethics Scholar. Mark's work has appeared in more than one hundred refereed outlets. He has a new book entitled *Understanding Corporate Scandals: Who are those Monsters?* to be published by Edward Elgar Press.

NOTES & WORKS CITED

✑

CHAPTER ONE: MARK A. SHIBLEY (PAGES 33–52)

Works Cited

Albanese, C.L. *Nature Religion in America: From the Algonkian Indians to the New Age*. Chicago: University of Chicago Press, 1990.

Cole, M. "Soda Mountain Devotion Pays Off," *The Oregonian* (June 10, 2000): A11.

Cole, M. and J. Brinckman. "NW Areas on Monument List Soda Mountain: One of the most biologically diverse landscapes in North America," *The Oregonian* (June 1, 2001): A01.

Cronon, W. "The Trouble with Wilderness; or Getting Back to the Wrong Nature," *Uncommon Ground: Rethinking the Human Place in Nature*, edited by W. Cronon, New York: W.W. Norton & Co., 1996.

Hoagland, E. *Hoagland on Nature: Essays*. Guilford, CN: The Lyons Press, 2003.

Kosmin, B.A., E. Mayer and A. Keysar. American religious identity survey. The Graduate Center: City University of New York, 2001. www.gc.cuny.edu/faculty/research_studies.htm#aris_1 (accessed July 15, 2005).

Oates, D. *Paradise Wild: Reimagining American Nature*. Corvallis: Oregon State University Press, 2003.

O'Connell, N. *On Sacred Ground: The Spirit of Place in Pacific Northwest Literature*. Seattle: University of Washington Press, 2003.

Ressner, J. "The War of the West," *Time* (July 16, 2001): 26–28.

Shibley, M.A. "Sacred Nature: Earth-based Spirituality as Popular Religion in the Secular Northwest." Unpublished manuscript under review with *Journal for the Scientific Study of Religion*. 2006.

Thomas, C. "The Sacred Tree." In *Intricate Homeland: Collected Writings from the Klamath Siskiyou*, edited by S. Cross. Ashland, Oregon: Headwaters Press, 2000.

Wuthnow, R. *After Heaven: Spirituality in America Since the 1950s*. Berkeley: University of California Press, 1998.

CHAPTER THREE: PATRICIA O'CONNELL KILLEN (PAGES 65–85)

Notes

1. This chapter draws heavily on the following: Patricia O'Connell Killen and Mark Silk, eds. *Religion and Public Life in the Pacific Northwest: The None Zone*; Patricia O'Connell Killen, "The Geography of a Minority Religion: Catholicism in the Pacific Northwest"; Patricia O'Connell Killen, "The Religious Geography of the Pacific Northwest"; Patricia O'Connell Killen, "The Metroscape's Post-Modern Religious Life." I am grateful to Douglas Todd and Ronald Hatch for their critique of earlier versions of this chapter. I also want to acknowledge my colleague Samuel Torvend, chair of the Department of Religion at Pacific Lutheran University, for conversations on memory.

2. In the US the increase in "Nones" seems to have levelled off in the early 2000s. William Stahl in "Is Anyone in Canada Secular," argues that the rise in "Nones" among young Canadians may well be temporary. I suspect not. See also, Yves Lambert, "Religion in Modernity as a New Axial Age: Secularization or New Religious Forms?"

3. On re-brokering of attachments, see Robert Wuthnow, "Reassembling the Civic Church: The Changing Role of Congregations in American Civil Society," in Richard Madsen, William M. Sullivan, Ann Swidler and Stephen M. Tipton, eds. *Meaning and Modernity: Religion, Polity, and the Self.*

Works Cited

Archives of the Archdiocese of Seattle. Letter Books of A.M.A. Blanchet. Series A, Volume 2.

Archives of the Archdiocese of Seattle. Parish Reports.

Barcott, Bruce. *Northwest Passages: A Literary Anthology of the Pacific Northwest from Coyote Tales to Roadside Attractions*. Seattle, WA: Sasquatch Books, 1993.

Burkinshaw, Robert K. *Pilgrims in Lotus Land: Conservative Protestantism in British Columbia 1917–1981*. Kingston, ON: McGill/Queens Press, 1995.

Burns, Jeffrey. "Building the Best: A History of Catholic Parish Life in the Pacific States," in *The American Catholic Parish; a History from 1850 to the Present; Volume 2: The Pacific States, Intermountain West, Midwest*, edited by Jay Dolan. New York: Paulist Press, 1987.

Clark, Warren. "Patterns of Religious Attendance." *Canadian Social Trends*. Ottawa: Statistics Canada (Winter 2000): 23–27.

Clark, Warren and Grant Schellenberg. "Who's Religious?" *Canadian Social Trends*. Ottawa: Statistics Canada (Summer 2006): 2–9

Coupland, Douglas. *Life after God*. New York, NY: Pocket Books, 1994.

Duncan, David James. *God Laughs and Plays*. Great Barrington, MA: The Triad Institute, 2000.

Farley, Edward. *Deep Symbols: Their Post-Modern Effacement and Reclamation*. Philadelphia, PA: Trinity Press International, 1996.

Howell, Erle. *Methodism in the Northwest*. Nashville, TN: The Parthenon Press, Printers, 1966.

Killen, Patricia O'Connell and Mark Silk, eds. *Religion and Public Life in the Pacific Northwest: The None Zone*. Walnut Creek, CA: AltaMira Press, 2004.

Killen, Patricia O'Connell. "The Geography of a Minority Religion: Catholicism in the Pacific Northwest," *US Catholic Historian* 18 (Summer 2000): 51–71.

——. "The Metroscape's Post-Modern Religious Life," *Metroscape* (Summer 2006): 6–11.

——. "The Religious Geography of the Pacific Northwest," *World and World* 24.3 (Summer 2004): 269–278.

Lambert, Yves. "Religion in Modernity as a New Axial Age: Secularization or New Religious Forms?" *Sociology of Religion* 60 (Fall 1999): 303–333.

Leighton, Caroline C. *West Coast Journeys, 1865–1879*. Seattle, WA: Sasquatch Books, 1995.

Madsen, Richard, William M. Sullivan, Ann Swidler and Stephen M. Tipton. *Meaning and Modernity: Religion, Polity, and the Self*. Berkeley: University of California Press, 2002.

Noll, Mark. "What Happened to Christian Canada," *Church History* 75.2 (June 2006): 245–273.

O'Hara, Edwin Vincent. *Pioneer Catholic History of Oregon*. Patterson, NJ: St. Anthony Guild Press, 1939.

Pasquale, Frank L. "The 'Nonreligious' in the American Northwest," in *Secularism & Secularity: Contemporary International Perspectives*, edited by Barry A. Kosmin and Ariela Keysar, 41–59. Hartford, CT: Institute for the Study of Secularism in Society and Culture, 2007.

Schoenberg, Wilfred P., S.J. *A History of the Catholic Church in the Pacific Northwest, 1743–1983*. Washington, DC: The Pastoral Press, 1987.

Stahl, William A. "Is Anyone in Canada Secular?" in *Secularism & Secularity: Contemporary International Perspectives*, edited by Barry A. Kosmin and Ariela Keysar, 59–73. Hartford, CT: Institute for the Study of Secularism in Society and Culture, 2007.

Statistics Canada. *Religions in Canada.* 2001 Census: analysis series. Ottawa, 2003.

Szasz, Ferenc. *Religion in the Modern American West.* Tucson, AZ: University of Arizona Press, 2000.

CHAPTER FOUR: JEAN BARMAN (PAGES 89–104)

Notes

1. This essay draws on Jean Barman, *The West beyond the West: A History of British Columbia*, 3rd ed., and Jean Barman and Bruce Watson, *Leaving Paradise: Indigenous Hawaiians in the Pacific Northwest, 1787–1898.* I am grateful to Douglas Todd and Ronald Hatch for their comments on an early version of the essay.

2. In "Cascading Concepts of Cascadia," 117, Smith describes the various possibilities from a political and economic perspective.

3. A variant of this perspective can be found in Joel Garreau's influential *The Nine Nations of North America.*

4. An example of this perspective is the lush colour-illustrated volume entitled *Cascadia: A Tale of Two Cities, Seattle and Vancouver, B.C.* by Morton Beebe and containing essays by, among others, Jim Sutherland of *Western Living* magazine and Daphne Bramham of the *Vancouver Sun* newspaper.

5. It is also the case that some American scholars limit the Pacific Northwest to the United States, as with Carlos Schwantes, *The Pacific Northwest: An Interpretive History.* .

6. Typical of this perspective are Robert Bunting, *The Pacific Raincoast: Environment and Culture in an American Eden, 1778–1900*, and Dale D. Goble and Paul W. Hirt, *Northwest Lands, Northwest Peoples: Readings in Environmental History*, which assume that the natural feature discussed in the volumes cease at the United States' northern boundary; and William G. Robbins, ed., *The Great Northwest: The Search for Regional Identity*, which includes a single essay extending to British Columbia as a kind of afterthought, along with one on Alaska, under the subsidiary heading "The Greater Northwest."

7. Among the books written or edited from this perspective are the following: Robert E. Ficken, *Unsettled Boundaries: Fraser Gold and the British-*

American Northwest, this despite its title; John M. Findlay and Ken S. Coates, ed., *Parallel Destinies: Canadian-American Relations West of the Rockies,* whose perspective is captured in its title; Sterling Evans, ed., *The Borderlands of the American and Canadian Wests: Essays on Regional History of the Forty-ninth Parallel,* which highlights the borderlands motif; and Paul W. Hirt, ed., *Terra Pacifica: People and Place in the Northwest States and Western Canada,* whose essays tend to summarize earlier research rather than strike out into new ground.

8. William H. Gray testimony in *In the Supreme Court of Oregon Territory, January Term, AD 1889. The Corporation of the Catholic Bishop of Nesqually, in the Territory of Washington v. John Gibbon, T.M. Anderson and R.T. Yeatman.*

9. George E. Baker, ed., *The Works of William H. Stewart* (New York 1982) 3, quoted in James R. Gibson, "The Sale of Russian America to the United States," in Frederick Starr, ed. *Russia's American Colony,* 194n.

10. Edouard De Stoeckle, Russian Legation head in Washington DC, Russian Minister of Foreign Affairs Alexander Gorchakov, 1867, quoted in Gibson, "Sale of Russian American," 286, 292, in Starr, *Russia's American Colony.*

Works Cited

Barman, Jean. *The West beyond the West: A History of British Columbia,* 3rd ed. Toronto: University of Toronto Press, 2007.

Barman, Jean and Bruce Watson. *Leaving Paradise: Indigenous Hawaiians in the Pacific Northwest, 1787–1898.* Honolulu: University of Hawai'i Press, 2006.

Beebe, Morton. *Cascadia: A Tale of Two Cities: Seattle and Vancouver, B.C.* San Francisco: Abrams, 1996.

Bunting, Robert. *The Pacific Raincoast. Environment and Culture in an American Eden, 1778–1900.* Lawrence: University Press of Kansas. 1997.

Duff, Wilson. *The Indian History of British Columbia.* Vol 1. Victoria: Provincial Museum, 1965.

Elliot, Gordon R. "Henry P. Pellew Crease: Confederation or No Confederation," *BC Studies* 12 (Winter 1971–2).

Evans, Sterling, ed. *The Borderlands of the American and Canadian Wests: Essays on Regional History of the Forth-ninth Parallel.* Lincoln: University of Nebraska Press, 2006.

Ficken, Robert E. *Unsettled Boundaries: Fraser Gold and the British-American Northwest.* Pullman: Washington State University Press, 2003.

Findlay, John M. and Ken S. Coates, eds. *Parallel Destinies: Canadian-American Relations West of the Rockies.* Seattle and Montreal: Centre for the Study of the Pacific Northwest in association with University of Washington Press and McGill-Queen's University Press, 2002.

Franklin, Lady. *Lady Franklin Visits the Pacific Northwest.* Victoria: Provincial Archives of British Columbia, 1974.

Garreau, Joel. *The Nine Nations of North America.* Boston: Houghton Mifflin, 1981.

Goble, Dale D. and Paul W. Hirt. *Northwest Lands, Northwest Peoples: Readings in Environmental History.* Seattle: University of Washington Press, 1999.

Goldberg, Michael A. and Maurice D. Levi. "The Evolving Experience Along the Pacific Northwest Corridor Called Cascadia," in *Enterprise for Americas Initiative,* edited by Roy E. Green. Westport CT: Praeger, 1994.

Gray, William H. *Supreme Court of Oregon Territory, January Term A.D. 1889, The Corporation of the Catholic Bishop of Nesqually, in the Territory of Washington, v. John Bibbon, T.M. Anderson and R.T. Yeatman* (no publishing data).

Harris, R. Cole, ed. *Historical Atlas of Canada.* Vol. 1. Toronto: University of Toronto Press, 1987.

Hirt, Paul W. *Terra Pacifica: People and Place in the Northwest States and Western Canada.* Pullman: Washington State University Press, 1998.

Ireland, Willard. "First Impressions: Letter of Colonel Richard Clement Moody, R.E., to Arthur Blackwood, February 1, 1859," *British Columbia Historical Quarterly* 15 (1951).

Lamb, Kaye W., ed. *The Journals and Letters of Sir Alexander Mackenzie.* Toronto: Macmillan, 1970.

Lamb, Kaye W., ed. *The Letters and Journals of Simon Fraser 1806–1808.* Toronto: Macmillan, 1960.

Merk, Frederick. "The Genesis of the Oregon Question," *Mississippi Valley Historical Review* 36.4 (1950).

Richardson, David. *Pig War Islands.* Eastsound, Washington: Orcas Publishing, 1971.

Robbins, William G., ed. *The Great Northwest: The Search for Regional Identity.* Corvallis: Oregon State University Press, 2001.

Schwantes, Carlos. *The Pacific Northwest: An Interpretive History.* Lincoln: University of Nebraska Press, 1989, rev. 1996.

Shepard, Cyrus. *Diary of Cyrus Shepard, March 4, 1834–December 20, 1985.* Vancouver, Washington: Clark County Genealogical Society, 1969.

Shi, David E. "Seward's Attempt to Annex British Columbia, 1865–1869," *Pacific Historical Review 47* (1978).

Silver, Shirley and Wick R. Miller. *American Indian Languages: Cultural and Social Contexts.* Tucson: University of Arizona Press, 1997.

Smith, Dorothy Blakey, ed. *The Reminiscences of Doctor John Sebastian Helmcken.* Vancouver: UBC Press 1975.

Smith, Patrick J. "Cascading Concepts of Cascadia: A Territory or a Nation?" *International Journal of Canadian Studies* 25 (May 2002).

Sparke, Matthew. "Excavating the Future in Cascadia: Geoeconomics and the Imagined Geographies of a Cross-Border Region," *BC Studies* 127 (Autumn 2000).

Starr, Frederick, ed. *Russia's American Colony.* Durham: Duke University Press, 1987.

Thompson, Laurence C. "Salishan and the Northeast," in *The Languages of Native America: Historical and Comparative Assessment,* edited by Lyle Clement and Marianne Mithun. Austin: University of Texas, 1979.

CHAPTER FIVE: MARK SILK (PAGES 105–114)

Works Cited

Brebner, J. Bartlet. *Canada: A Modern History.* Ann Arbor: University of Michigan Press, 1970.

Gentile, Emilio. *Politics as Religion.* Princeton: Princeton University Press, 2006.

Herberg, Will. *Protestant Catholic Jew.* Chicago: University of Chicago Press, 1955.

Killen, Patricia O'Connell and Mark Silk, eds. *Religion and Public Life in the Pacific Northwest: The None Zone.* New York: AltaMira Press, 2004.

Kim, Andrew E. "The Absence of Pan-Canadian Civil Religion: Plurality, Duality, and Conflict in Symbols of Canadian Culture," *Sociology of Religion* 54.3 (Fall 1993): 257–275.

Lathem, Edward Connery, ed. *The Poetry of Robert Frost.* New York: Holt, Rinehart and Winston, 1967.

Notes

1. Cf. the article on the Las Casas–Sepulveda controversy by Bonar Ludwig Hernandez, http://userwww.sfsu.edu/~epf/2001/hernandez.html (accessed July 2, 2008) or the shorter article on de las Casas in the Catholic Encyclopedia: www.newadvent.org/cathen/03397a.html (accessed July 2, 2008).

2. "European men, institutions, and ideas were lodged in the American wilderness, and the great American West took them to her bosom, taught them a new way of looking upon the destiny of the common man, trained them in adaptation to the conditions of the New World, to the creation of new institutions to meet new needs." Frederick Jackson Turner, "The Frontier in American History," *American Social and Political Thought: A Reader*, edited by Andreas Hess. Edinburgh: Edinburgh University Press, 2002.

3. Jo Grimmond, former leader of the British Liberal party, speaking of the region in the 1950s, cited by Shelley Scales, "Progressives' Progress Lost," *Seattle Weekly*, April 28, 1999.

4. Euan Ferguson's interview with Douglas Coupland, "Generation next," *The Observer*, May 28, 2006.

5. "Habermas versus the Pope," *Prospect Magazine*, November 2005. www.prospect-magazine.co.uk/article_details.php?id=7084 (accessed July 2, 2008).

Works Cited

Cherry, Conrad. *God's New Israel: Religious Interpretations of American Destiny*, cited in Kevin Phillips, *American Theocracy*, N.Y.: Viking, 2006.

de Place, Eric. "This Land is My Land," *Washington Law and Politics*, October/November 2005.

Ferguson, Euan. "Generation Next," *The Observer*, May 28, 2006. Interview with Douglas Coupland.

Hess, Andreas, ed. *American Social and Political Thought: A Reader*. Edinburgh: Edinburgh University Press, 2002.

Hollinger, David A. and Charles Capper, eds. *The American Intellectual Tradition*, Volume 1, 1620–1865. Oxford University Press, 1989.

Magnusson, Warren et al., eds. *The New Reality: The Politics of Restraint in B.C.* Vancouver: New Star, 1984.

Mate, Reyes. *Memory of the West*. Amsterdam: Rodopi, 2004.

Scales, Shelley. "Progressives' Progress Lost," *Seattle Weekly*, April 28, 1999.

Schell, Paul and John Chapman, cited in Matthew Sparke, "Excavating the Future in Cascadia Geoeconomics and the Imagined Geographies of a Cross-Border Region," *B.C. Studies* 127 (Autumn 2000).

CHAPTER SEVEN: MIKE CARR (PAGES 127–142)

Works Cited

Abram, David. *The Spell of the Sensuous.* New York: Vintage Books, 1997.

Andruss, Van, Christopher Plant, Judith Plant and Eleanor Wright. *Home! A Bioregional Reader.* Gabriola Island, B.C.: New Society Publishers, 1990.

Armstrong, Jeannette. "I Stand With You Against the Disorder," www.yes magazine.org/article.asp?ID=1346 1999 (accessed July 2, 2008).

Bateson, Gregory. *Steps to an Ecology of Mind.* New York: Ballantine Books, 1972.

Berg, Peter and Raymond Dasmann. "Reinhabiting California," *Reinhabiting a Separate Country: A Bioregional Anthology of Northern California,* edited by Peter Berg. San Francisco: Planet Drum Foundation, 1978.

Berg, Peter. "More Than Just Saving What's Left." *Raise the Stakes* 8: 1–2 (1983).

Berry, Thomas. *The Dream of the Earth.* San Francisco: Sierra Club Books, 1988.

British Columbia Environmental Network. "Helping the Land Heal: Ecological Restoration in British Columbia:" Conference Proceedings. Victoria, B.C.: B.C. Environmental Network, 1988.

Carlson, Keith, ed. *You Are Asked to Witness: The Sto:lo in Canada's Pacific Coast History.* Chilliwack, B.C.: Sto:lo Heritage Trust, 1997.

Carr, Mike. *Bioregionalism and Civil Society: Democratic Challenges to Corporate Globalism.* Vancouver: UBC Press, 2004.

City Repair Project. *Placemaking Guidebook: Neighbourhood Placemaking in the Public Right-of-Way,* 2nd Edition. Portland, Oregon: City Repair Project, 2006.

Ecotrust, Pacific GIS and Conservation International. *The Rain Forests of Home: An Atlas of People and Place.* Portland, Oregon, 1995.

Heiltsuk Tribal Council. *Heiltsuk Land Use Plan Executive Summary.* Waglisla, B.C: Heiltsuk Tribal Council (no date).

LaChapelle, Dolores. *Sacred Land, Sacred Sex, Rapture of the Deep: Concerning Deep Ecology and Celebrating Life.* Silverton, Colorado: Finn Hill Arts, 1988.

MacPherson, Duncan. *Democratic Theory: Essays in Retrieval*. Oxford: Clarendon Press, 1973.

Martinez, Dennis. "Managing a Precarious Balance: Wilderness vs Sustainable Forestry," *Winds of Change* (Summer 1993): 23–28.

Suttles, Wayne. "Central Coast Salish," in *Handbook of North American Indians*. Vol. 7. Washington: Smithsonian Institute, 1990.

Todd, John and Nancy Todd. *Bioshelters, Ocean Arks, City Farming: Ecology as the Basis of Design*. San Francisco: Sierra Club Books, 1984.

Todd, John and George Tukel. *Reinhabiting Cities and Towns: Designing for Sustainability*. San Francisco: Planet Drum Foundations, 1981.

Wackernagle, Mathis and William Rees. *Our Ecological Footprint: Reducing Human Impact on the Earth*. Gabriola Island, B.C.: New Society Publishers, 1996.

Walkem, Ardith and Haile Bruce. *Box of Treasures or Empty Box? Twenty Years of Section 35*. Penticton, B.C.: Theytus Books, 2003.

World Conservation Monitoring Centre. *Global Biodiversity*. London: World Conservation Monitoring Centre, 1992.

CHAPTER NINE: SALLIE MCFAGUE (PAGES 157–172)

Notes

1. For further elaboration, see Sallie McFague, *The Body of God: An Ecological Theology* (Minneapolis: Fortress Press, 1993).

2. For discussion of the epistemological and theological role of metaphor and model, see Sallie McFague, *Metaphorical Theology: Models of God in Religious Language* (Minneapolis: Fortress Press, 1982) and *Models of God: Theology for an Ecological, Nuclear Age* (Minneapolis: Fortress Press, 1987).

3. For further elaboration of this and related issues, see Sallie McFague, *Life Abundant: Rethinking Theology and Economy for a Planet in Peril* (Minneapolis: Fortress Press, 2000).

4. For an overview, see John B. Cobb Jr. and David Ray Griffin, *Process Theology: An Introductory Exposition* (Philadelphia: Westminster Press, 1976).

5. See, for instance, Arthur Peacocke, "Mammalian females . . . create within themselves and the growing embryo resides within the female body and this is a proper corrective to the masculine picture — it is an analogy of God creating the world within herself. . . . God creatures a world that

is, in principle and in origin, other than him/herself but creates it, the world, within him/herself" (*Creation and the World of Science* [Oxford: Clarendon Press, 1979], 142).

6. The natural theology tradition of Roman Catholicism, epitomized by Thomas Aquinas, sees creation as a reflection of God. It is not just human beings who are made in the image of God; rather, all creatures are. As Thomas expresses it: "But creatures cannot attain to any perfect likeness of God so long as they are confined to one species of creatures; because, since the cause exceeds the effect in a composite and manifold way. . . . Multiplicity, therefore, and variety, was needful in the creation, to the end that the perfect likeness of God might be found in things according to their measure" (as quoted in Arthur O. Lovejoy, *The Great Chain of Being: A Study in the History of an Idea* [Cambridge, MA: Harvard University Press, 1933], 76).

7. See, for instance, George F.R. Ellis, "Kenosis as a Unifying Theme for Life and Cosmology"; Keith Ward, "Cosmos and Kenosis"; and Jurgen Moltman, "God's Kenosis in the Creation and the Consummation of the World," *The Work of Love: Creation and Kenosis*, edited by John Polkinghorne (Grand Rapids: Eerdmans, 2001).

Works Cited

Cobb, John B. Jr and Christopher Ives, eds. *The Emptying God: A Buddhist-Jewish-Christian Conversation*. New York: Orbis Books, 1998.

Cobb, John B. Jr and Ray Griffin. *Process Theology: An Introductory Exposition*. Philadelphia: Westminster Press, 1976.

Cook, J. "Environmentally Benign Architecture," *Global Warming and the Built Environment*, edited by R. Samuels and D. Prasad. London: Spon, 1994.

Derrida, Jacques. "White Mythology: Metaphor in the Text of Philosophy," *New Literary History* 6 (1974).

"Government Efforts to Push Conservation Ineffective." *Globe and Mail* July 13, 2006.

Harvey, David. *Justice, Nature and the Geography of Difference*. Oxford: Blackwell, 1996.

Harvey, David. *Spaces of Hope*. Berkeley: University of California Press, 2000.

Hume, Stephen. "We are seeing the urban future and it is slums — slums on a frightening scale," *Vancouver Sun*, June 21, 2006. See also UN report

"State of the World Cities: Globalization and Urban Culture," 2004–2005.

Kjellberg, S. *Urban Eco Theology*. Utrecht: International Books, 2000.

McFague, Sallie. *The Body of God: An Ecological Theology*. Minneapolis: Fortress Press, 1993.

——. *Life Abundant: Rethinking Theology and Economy for a Planet in Peril*. Minneapolis: Fortress Press, 2000.

——. *Metaphorical Theology: Models of God in Religious Language*. Minneapolis: Fortress Press, 1982.

——. *Models of God: Theology for an Ecological, Nuclear Age*. Minneapolis: Fortress Press, 1987.

Merchant, Carolyn. *The Death of Nature: Women, Ecology and the Scientific Revolution*. San Francisco: Harper and Row, 1983.

Murdoch, Iris. "The Sublime and the Good," *Chicago Review* 13 (Autumn 1959).

Pollan, Michael. *The Omnivore's Dilemma: A Natural History of Four Meals*. New York: Penguin Press, 2006.

Raven, Peter. "The Sustainability of the Earth." Draft paper for University of Chicago conference, "Without Nature," October 2006.

Soja, Edward. "Seeing Nature Spatially." Draft paper for University of Chicago Conference, "Without Nature," October 2006.

Todd, Douglas. Draft Overview Paper for SFU Symposium: *Cascadia Spirituality, Geography and Social Change*. SFU, August 2006.

UNEP. Millennium Ecosystem Assessment, Statement from the Board: "Living Beyond Our Means: Natural Assets and Human Well-being."

CHAPTER 10: PAULO LEMOS HORTA (PAGES 175–193)

Notes

1. I would like to acknowledge a Library Research Grant from the J.P. Getty Research Institute, in Los Angeles, which allowed me to probe the genealogies of magic realism. I wish also to acknowledge the work of my research assistants Lauren Gabriel and Victoria Haynes, the comments of Douglas Todd and the two readers for Ronsdale press, the generous answers of George Bowering, Pauline Holdstock and Jack Hodgins, and finally Laurie Ricou for first interesting me in the writing of this region.

2. Jack Hodgins to the author, email July 1, 2008.

3. Jack Hodgins to the author, email July 1, 2008.

4. Jack Hodgins to the author, email July 3, 2008.

5. Jack Hodgins to the author, email July 7, 2008.

6. To borrow British Columbia author Geoff Hancock's apt definition of magic realism in Canadian letters, from his "Preface" to *Illusions Two: Fables, Fantasies and Metafictions* (Toronto: Aya Press, 1983): 6.

7. Jack Hodgins to the author, email July 7, 2008.

8. "The True World: When Consensual Reality is not Enough," *Margin: Exploring Modern Magical Realism.* Ochsner's contribution to a forum on magic realism at the 2005 conference of the Associated Writing Programs conference held in Vancouver, British Columbia. Note that there are no page numbers for this online essay, http://www.angelfire.com/wa2/margin/pcp2.html (accessed July 1, 2008).

9. Qtd. "The True World."

10. "The True World."

11. Franco Moretti, *Atlas of the European Novel 1800–1900* (New York: Verso, 1998), 3.

12. *Where the Read Fern Grows*, "a journal of personal reflections related to the Pacific Northwest region" http://fiddlehead-fern.livejournal.com.

13. "The True World."

14. See Rudy Wiebe and Andreas Schroeder's *Stories from Pacific & Arctic Canada* (Toronto: Macmillan of Canada, 1974); Jack Hodgins' *The West Coast Experience* (Toronto: Macmillan of Canada, 1976); and Laurie Ricou's *The Arbutus/Madrone Files: Reading the Pacific Northwest* (Corvallis: Oregon State University Press, 2002).

15. Geoff Hancock, *Magic Realism: An Anthology* (Toronto: Aya Press, 1980): 7.

16. Franz Roh, *Nach Expressionismus: Magischer Realismus: Probleme der neusten europäischen Malerei.* Klinkhardt, 1925.

17. George Bowering to the author, email April 30, 2008.

18. *One Hundred Years of Solitude.* New York: Harper Perennial Modern Classics, 2006.

19. For the affinities between Grass and Rushdie, see Patricia Merivale's "Saleem Fathered by Oskar: Intertextual Strategies in *Midnight's Children* and *The Tin Drum*," in *Ariel: A Review of International English Literature* 21.3 (July 1990): 5–21.

20. Mario Vargas Llosa, "Questions of Conquest: What Columbus wrought, and what he did not," *Harper's Magazine* (December 1990): 53.

21. Mario Vargas Llosa, "Questions of Conquest," 53.

22. Mario Vargas Llosa, "Questions of Conquest," 48.

23. *Burning Water*, 134.

24. Michael Ondaatje, "Introduction," *From Ink Lake* (Toronto: Knopf Canada, 1992): XIII–XIV.

25. Alejo Carpentier, *The Kingdom of this World*, Translated by Harriet de Onis (New York: Farrar, Straus and Giroux, 2006).

26. Jack Hodgins, *The West Coast Experience* (Toronto: Macmillan, 176): 114

27. Tony Tremblay, Interview, "Tall Tales from a Genteel Hoodlum: The Artful Exaggerations of Bill Gaston." *Studies in Canadian Literature*. www.lib.unb.ca/Texts/SCL/bin/get.cgi?directory=vol16_2/&filename=Tremblay.htm.

28. In particular Gail Wells faults Barry Lopez's 1986 *Arctic Dreams: Imagination and Desire in a Northern Landscape*. The quotation is from a draft of Wells' essay "Nature-Based Spirituality in Cascadia: Prospects and Pitfalls," which appears in a revised form in this volume.

29. Jack Hodgins' "empathy" proves a key value for "most" of the authors he finds representative of West Coast writing, and he urges readers to "consider too how each of these authors does much more than simply make maps" (*The West Coast Experience*, 114).

30. Hodgins to the author, email July 3, 2008.

31. Hodgins to the author, email July 3, 2008.

32. Every magic realist author claims, like Hodgins, not to be making things up but rather to be "mostly giving shape to lives that were being lived around me" (Hodgins, email to the author, July 3, 2008).

33. http://biography.jrank.org/pages/4429/Hodgins-Jack.html.

34. *One Hundred Years of Solitude*, translated by Gregory Rabassa, 1.

35. See Franco Moretti's chapter on *One Hundred Years of Solitude* in his study of the epic, *Modern Epic: The World-System from Goethe to García Márquez* (New York: Verso, 1996): 233-250.

36. Hodgins to the author, email July 1, 2008.

37. All the traits listed here are noted in Mario Vargas Llosa's seminal study *García Márquez: Historia de un Deicidio* (Barcelona: Barral, 1971) and all recur in Hodgins' *The Invention of the World*.

38. Hodgins to the author, email dated July 1, 2008.

39. My translation of Mario Vargas Llosa, *García Márquez: Historia de un Deicidio*, 470.

40. Hodgins, *The Invention of the World*, 69–70.

41. Hodgins to the author, email July 1, 2008.

42. Hodgins to the author, email July 3, 2008.

43. George Bowering to the author, email April 30, 2008.

44. See Chilean author Alberto Fuguet's "Presentación del País McOndo," the prologue for *McOndo: una antología de nueva literatura hispano-americana* (Barcelona: Grijalbo-Mondadori/Barcelona, 1996) and Mexican author Jorge Volpi's (et al) *Manifiesto Crack* (*Lateral. Revista de Cultura*. N. 70 October 2000). The *Crack Manifesto* was originally published in 1996.

45. My translation (for the original passage see Saramago, *A Caverna*, Sao Paulo: Companhia Das Letras, 2000: 82–83).

46. Gina Ochsner, "The True World: When Consensual Reality is not Enough." *Margin*. http://www.angelfire.com/wa2/ margin/pcp2.html (accessed July 1, 2008).

47. Gina Ochsner, "The True World."

48. "The True World."

49. "The True World."

50. "The True World."

51. "The True World."

52. "The True World."

53. Gina Ochsner, "Articles of Faith," *People I Wanted to Be* (New York: Mariner, 2005): 12.

54. Ochsner, "Articles of Faith," 5.

55. Ochsner, "Articles of Faith," 2.

56. Ochsner, "Articles of Faith," 5.

57. Ochsner, "The True World."

CHAPTER 11: ELEANOR J. STEBNER (PAGES 195–205)

Notes

1. Mary Douglas, *Natural Symbols* (1970).

2. Richard Clark, *Sam Hill's Peace Arch* (2005).

3. Andrew Butterfield, "Monuments and Memories," in *New Republic* 228, no. 4. Refer also to Robert Ivy, "Memorials, Monuments, and Meaning," in *Architectural Record* 190, no. 7.

4. The debate regarding the Christian cross on Mount Soledad, San Diego, a monument built to honour the American veterans of the Korean War is only the latest in a series of legal and social debates. Refer also to Sanford Levinson, *Written in Stone* (1998). Levinson notes, for example, a

proposed statue to honour women suffragists in the US capital that became controversial because it did not include an African American woman. On how monuments were used in Iraq (and by extension, by many political dictators) refer to Kanan Makiya, *Monument* (1991).

5. Lewis Mumford, *The Culture of Cities* (1938).
6. The word monument originates from the Latin *monumentum*, meaning memorial, and is related to *monêre*, meaning to remind. The English words mind, remind and remember are also evoked in the word monument.
7. Elaine Porterfield, "Geography, economy bring Northwest cities ever-closer" in *Christian Science Monitor* 91, no. 167.
8. Patricia O'Connell Killen and Mark Silk, *Religion and Public Life in the Pacific Northwest* (2004).
9. Numerous online resources exist for Sam Hill. Refer also to John E. Tuhy, *Sam Hill* (1983) and Lois Davis Plotts, *Maryhill, Sam Hill and Me* (1979).
10. Direct quotes are from Richard Clark's book.
11. Refer to Laurel Sefton MacDowell, "Paul Robeson in Canada: A Border Story," *Labour/Le Travail* Spring 2003. Available online.
12. ww2.christinaalexander.com:1975/home.htm (accessed August 19, 2008).

Works Cited

Butterfield, Andrew. "Monuments and Memories," in *New Republic* 228 (2003): 27–32 (available online).

Clark, Richard. *Sam Hill's Peace Arch: Remembrance of Dreams Past.* Bloomington, Indiana: Authorhouse, 2005.

——. "Jesus Wants Us to Be Nice: A Theological Fantasy." Unpublished manuscript, 2006.

Douglas, Mary. *Natural Symbols: Explorations in Cosmology.* London: Barrie and Rockliff, 1970.

Ivy, Robert. "Memorials, Monuments, and Meaning," *Architectural Record* 190.7 (July 2002).

Killen, Patricia O'Connell and Mark Silk. *Religion and Public Life in the Pacific Northwest: The None Zone.* Walnut Creek: California, AltaMira Press, 2004.

Levinson, Sanford. *Written in Stone: Public Monuments in Changing Societies.* Durham: Duke University Press, 1998.

Makiya, Kanan. *Monument: Art, Vulgarity, and Responsibility in Iraq.* Berkeley: University of California Press, 1991.

MacDowell, Laurel Sefton, "Paul Robeson in Canada: A Border Story," *Labour/Le Travail* (Spring 2003).

Means, Benjamin. "Monuments to the Past in a Leveling Wind," *Michigan Law Review* 97.6 (May 1999).

Mumford, Lewis. *The Culture of Cities*. New York: Harcourt Brace and Co., 1938.

Nietzsche, Friedrich. *The Use and Abuse of History for Life*. Whitefish, Montana: Kessinger Publishing, 2004 [1873].

Plotts, Davis. *Maryhill, Sam Hill and Me*. Camas, Washington: Post Publications, 1979.

Porterfield, Elaine. "Geography, economy bring Northwest cities ever-closer," *Christian Science Monitor* 91.167 (July 26, 1999).

Tuhy, John E. *Sam Hill: The Prince of Castle Nowhere*. Portland: Timber Press, 1983

CHAPTER 13: MARK WEXLER (PAGES 215–239)

Notes

1. I would like to thank Douglas Todd, Jean Donald, Anthony Chan and Judy Oberlander for their indispensable assistance in the writing of this paper. I would also like to thank the Social Sciences and Humanities Research Council of Canada for their ongoing support of my work on governance and business ethics.

CHAPTER 14: GAIL WELLS (PAGES 241–262)

Notes

1. Another way to look at this, as a nature-loving spiritual friend of mine pointed out, is that mini-mansions and SUVs are far more conspicuous in many other parts of the country, and so perhaps nature-based spirituality is exerting a corrective influence on consumption in the Northwest.

2. In *The Real Work: Interviews and Talks, 1964–1979* (New York: New Directions, 1980), the poet and bioregionalist Gary Snyder uses this same biblical language to describe what must happen to non-Native Americans if they are ever to be at home on the Earth: "He or she must be *born again* in this hemisphere, on this continent, properly called Turtle Island."

Works Cited

"Abraham Lincoln on slavery." Wikipedia online encyclopedia. http://en. wikipedia.org/wki/ (accessed September 16, 2008).

Beard, Mary, John North and Simon Price. *Religions of Rome*. Cambridge, UK: Press Syndicate of the University of Cambridge, 1998.

Brinkley, Douglas. "Vonnegut's Apocalypse," *Rolling Stone* (August 9, 2006).

Callenbach, Ernest. *Ecotopia: The Notebooks and Reports of William Weston*. Berkeley, CA: Banyan Tree Books, 1975.

Carson. Rachel. *The Sea Around Us*. New York: Oxford University Press, 1951.

Corinthians (First) 13:11. *The New Oxford Annotated Bible* (revised standard version). New York: Oxford University Press, 1973.

Dunlap, Thomas R. *Faith in Nature: Environmentalism as Religious Quest*. Seattle, Washington: University of Washington Press, 2004.

"Ecology Hall of Fame: Julia Butterfly Hill." www.ecotopia.org/ehof/hill/index.html (accessed September 16, 2008).

Goodenough, Ursula. *The Sacred Depths of Nature*. New York: Oxford University Press, 1998.

Guha Ramachandra. "Radical American Environmentalism and Wilderness Preservation: A Third World Critique," *Environmental Ethics* 11.1 (Spring 1989).

James, William. *The Varieties of Religious Experience: A Study in Human Nature*. New York, NY: The Modern Library, 1936.

Lopez, Barry. *Arctic Dreams: Imagination and Desire in a Northern Landscape*. New York: Scribner, 1986.

Moore, Thomas. *The Soul of Sex: Cultivating Life as an Act of Love*. New York: Harper Collins, 1998.

Oregon Historical Quarterly 108.2 (Summer 2007).

Orsi, Robert A. "When 2 + 2 = 5." *American Scholar* 76.2 (Spring 2007).

Sightline Institute. *Cascadia Scorecard: Seven Key Trends Shaping the Northwest*. Seattle: Sightline Institute, 2007.

Snyder Gary. *The Real Work: Interviews and Talks, 1964–1979*. New York: New Directions, 1980.

Stegner, Wallace. *Where the Bluebird Sings to the Lemonade Springs: Living and Writing in the West*. New York: Random House, 1992.

White, Lynn. "The Historical Roots of Our Ecological Crisis," *Science* 155 (March 10, 1967).

INDEX

⁓

Benedict, Pope XVI, 123
Bennett, W.A.C., 23
Berg, Peter, 132, 139, 140
Berry, Thomas, 21–22, 132, 141
Beyond Measure (Holdstock), 187
Bibby, Reginald, 12
Bible, 55, 56, 109, 168, 170, 274
Bill and Melinda Gates Foundation, 23, 226
binationalism, 5, 8, 106, 110, 113, 199
bioregional Earth-centered spirituality, 129, 131–32, 134–40
See also nature-based spirituality
bioregionalism
defined, 129–32
and myth, 217
and place, 139–40, 216
protecting, 21
spirituality, 131–32, 134–40
tools for, 140–41
Bioregionalism and Civil Society: Democratic Challenges to Corporate Globalism (Carr), 130
Black Elk, 48
Blaine, Washington, 199, 204
See also International Peace Arch
Blanchet, Bishop Francis Norbert, 78
"body" as metaphor, 160, 163–71
Boeing Company, 7, 119
bonding, ecological, 133, 136
boomers, 244
border, international, US-Canada, 3, 6, 58, 89, 90, 119, 143–44, 197–98
See also International Peace Arch
borders, 54, 90, 143

See also International Peace Arch; rivers
born-again experience. *See* spiritual experience
bottles, recycling, 10, 18, 144, 253
boundaries. *See* border, international, US-Canada; borders; rivers
Bowering, George, 18–19, 28, 179, 180–81, 186, 192, 267–68, 275–76
British Columbian newspaper, 101
British Columbians
and aboriginals, 24–26
alienation from Canada, 112–13, 117–18, 120
economy and demographics, 14–15, 25–26, 78–79, 84–85, 119, 122–23, 147
environmental stewardship, 148
evangelicals and Nones in, 75
health, 147
morality issues and drugs, 24, 57, 73
politics and society, 76–77, 118, 122–23
religion, spirituality and liberalism, 12, 15–16, 23–24, 26, 34, 66–80, 74, 75, 122
See also literature, regional
Brother Twelve, 9, 175–76, 184
Buddhism (Zen), 13, 14, 17, 26, 131, 151, 171
built environment (second nature), 158–61, 171–72, 212, 219
Burning Winter (Bowering), 180–81, 186
Bush, George W., 22, 109, 110
Butterfield, Andrew, 198

Calgary, Alberta, 6
California, 37, 43, 90, 108, 117
Callenbach, Ernest, 8, 33, 244
Camp Brotherhood, 73
Campbell, Gordon, 46
Canada
    civil religion in, 112, 117
    inventing and documenting,
        181–82
    politics in, 117–18
Canadian River Expeditions, 19
Canadians, 3, 7, 12, 75, 111
cannabis. *See* marijuana
capitalism, 11, 118, 130, 162, 163, 166,
    171
car crashes, 147, 149
Carpentier, Alejo, 182
Carr, Emily, 20
Carr, Mike, 21, 25, 27–28, 70, 127–28,
    255, 276
Carson, Rachel, 261
Casares, Adolfo Bioy, 186
Cascade Curtain, 119, 250
Cascade-Siskiyou National
    Monument, 43–45
Cascadia
    the big picture, 58–60
    bioregion, 216
    defined, 1–3, 144–45, 215–17,
        248–49
    demographics, 78–79, 100, 113,
        144, 146, 216–17
    do-it-yourself mentality, 23,
        58–59, 62
    economy, 6–7, 14, 23–24, 51–52,
        94–96, 119, 146–47, 219
    geography, 4–5, 127–29, 236
    history, 3, 89–104, 218

human rights in, 24, 25, 26, 57, 71
independent, 3, 5, 144
and individualism, 10–11, 16, 58
lifestyle, 90
links among residents, 4–7
mission statement, 50–52
mythic, 217
nature and environmental
    stewardship, 19–20, 144,
    147–48, 252–54
past and future, 48–50, 218–19
polarized, 10, 23, 61, 75, 118,
    250–51
a social spiritual "map," 55, 56
spirituality, 3–4, 8–15, 23–26
a sustainable, 46–52, 140–42
the ties that bind, 4–8, 26–29
as utopia, 16–19
See also Pacific Northwest
Cascadia Center. *See* Discovery
    Institute Cascadia Center
Cascadia Scorecard (Durning),
    27–28, 149, 248
Cascadian Bioregionalism, 7
Cascadian mountain range, 11, 59,
    89, 90, 127, 143–44, 195
Cascadian Nationalist Party, 7
Casey family foundations, 23
Catholic bishops' "letter" on the
    Columbia River, 74
Catholics. *See* Roman Catholics
Cave, The (Saramago), 188–89
CCF (Canadian Commonwealth
    Federation), 117, 118
census, religious, 12, 34
ceremonies and rituals, 25, 129, 133,
    137, 140, 164, 217
channelling, 36

building, 140–42
and consumerism, 130
empowering, 211
health, 49, 232, 238
identity and, 66
Midwestern, 108
more-than-human, 84
planning, 148
sustainable, 66–67
vision, 131, 138–39, 141
compassion, 62, 171, 238
conflict, 46, 60–61, 109
connectedness, 19, 133, 140, 211
Connecticut, 110–11
consciousness, 62, 81, 83–84, 161, 249
consensus building, 11, 140
conservation and conservationists, 22, 28, 144, 149, 254
conservatives, 15, 22, 118
consumerism, 130, 141, 153
contemplation, 83–84
Continental Congress of the North American Bioregional movement, 127
Conversations with God (Walsch), 21, 35, 39
Coos Bay, 250
Coupland, Douglas, 21, 82–84, 120–21, 283
creation, honouring, 84, 210
creation stories, 135–37, 168–69, 170
creativity, 79–80
    See also workplace spirituality
Cripple and His Talismans, The (Irani), 187
Crist, Charlie, 113
Croake, Fr. James, 78

Cronon, William, 44–45
Crossroads ecumenical fundamentalism, 108–14
culture
    clashes and challenges, 46
    and creativity, 33–34, 49
    distinct and dominant, 47, 58–59, 245
    evolution and adaptation, 33–35, 38, 141–42, 231–32, 238
    indigenous. *See* indigenous peoples: culture
    landscape and, 40, 105–6
    overview, 28
    regional, 119
    religious. *See* civil religion; *other religion headings*
    shaping political, 106–9
    sustainable, 47–49
    and symbols, 50, 195–97
    ties and individualism, 4–8, 10–11
    and wilderness, 44–45
Cure for Death by Lightning, The (Anderson-Dargatz), 186

Danby, Ken, 179
David Suzuki Foundation, 49, 247
De las Casas, Bartolomé, 116
Dean, Howard, 107
decriminalization, 18, 24, 56–57
Defenders of the Earth, 247
density, 61, 151, 169–70, 235
Derrida, Jacques, 164–65
destiny. *See* Manifest Destiny
DeVoto, Bernard, 250
Discovery Institute Cascadia Center, 6

energy consumption, 146, 147, 148, 149–50, 153, 158, 160

Enns, Eli Bliss, 25, 70, 207–213, 277

entrepreneurs, 23–24, 35, 39, 74–75, 221, 223, 251

environment
    built, 160, 171, 196, 212, 219
    religious, 73–78, 80
    scorecard, 145–47
    spiritual, 74

environmentalists and environmentalism
    Christian, 148, 255–56
    in civil religion, 112
    divided, 118
    and faith, 260–61
    grassroots movements, 80, 147–48
    hardcore, 21
    and nature-based spirituality, 251–55
    non-religious, 246–48
    and older faith traditions, 259–62
    radical, 234–35, 244–45
    and science and religion, 258
    and spiritual seekers, 237–38
    stewardship, 74, 84, 210, 212–13, 254

epiphany
    geographic, 250
    mountain, 40

Episcopalians, 13, 116–17
    See also Anglicans

Esowista War, 209–10

Esquivel, Laura, 186, 192

ethics, 137, 150–55, 162, 254

ethnicity and religious plurality, 107

Eucharist, 164

euthanasia. *See* physician-assisted suicide

evangelicalism, 13–14, 22, 23, 37–38, 74–75, 75, 122

Evergreen State College, 17

evolution, 43, 258

explorers, New World, 180–82

faith
    born-again, 260–61
    Christian, 13, 15–16
    and environmentalism, 258, 260–61
    in the individual, 59
    in nature, 243
    "Range of," 56–58
    in systems, 225
    and utopia, 176
    and vision, 261
    See also magic realism
    See also workplace spirituality

Faith in Nature (Dunlap), 245

Farley, Edward, 81–82

Farley, Jim, 117–18

farmer-based movements, 117

farmland protection, 10, 18

feminists, 131, 167

festivals, New Spirituality, 38

fiction. *See* magic realism

Fire and Ice (Adams), 23

First Nations peoples. *See* indigenous peoples

first nature, 158–61, 168, 171–72

fishing, a story, 2, 190–91

flag, Cascadian, 5, 195–96

flakiness, of Cascadians, 10–11, 18, 265

prophetic, 169–72

public, 8, 38, 73

relevance of, 56

science and, 17, 258, 261–62

spirituality and, 9, 228, 229, 245

utopian, 16–17

See also civil religion; nature-based spirituality; organized religion

Religion by Region Series (Silk), 106

religions, major. *See names of individual faiths and Protestant denominations*

religious configurations, 67–72

religious expression, 254–55

Religious Society of Friends. *See* Quakers

Republic of Cascadia, 7, 196

Republic of the Pacific, 2

Resnick, Philip, 18–19, 20, 21, 28, 250, 256–57, 269–72, 280–81

Restoring Eden: Christians for Environmental Stewardship, 22

Resurrection of Joseph Bourne, The (Hodgins), 186

revelation, historicizing and de-mythologizing, 188

Revelation Colony, 175–76

reverence, for all life, 25, 44, 171, 172, 256

revolution, quiet, 140–41

Rhinestone Button, A (Anderson-Dargatz), 187

Ricou, Laurie, 178

rights, human and civil, 27, 44, 57, 81, 148, 237, 255

See also indigenous peoples: rights

Rilke, Rainer Maria, 172

Rite of Christian Initiation for Adults, 80

rituals. *See* ceremonies and rituals

rivers, 46, 50, 128, 129, 137, 248

See also: names of individual rivers

Robeson, Paul, 203

Rocky Mountains, 90

Roh, Franz, 179

Roman Catholics

activists, 27

Cascadian style, 79

dominance, 72

early American, 77–78, 115, 116–17

identifiers, 68

inter-faith activities, 73, 74

liberal, 13

and nature, 116, 151

public role, 70–71, 72, 75, 107

spiritual practice, 151

theology, 167–69

traditionalist, 109–10

romanticism, 25, 50, 244, 256, 260

Roof, Wade Clark, 109

rootlessness, 10, 233

Royal Commission on Aboriginal Peoples (1996), 134

Rushdie, Salman, 178, 179, 186, 187, 188, 192

Russia, 94

Sabbath, observing, 153

sacralization, 110, 111, 258

sacred, the, 21, 34, 36, 41, 133, 137

Sacred Depths of Nature, The (Goodenough), 261

sacred space, 48, 203

Sacred Tree, The (Thomas), 41–43

sacredness, ecological, 137

social change, 130, 159, 203, 255

social control, 67, 72

Social Credit Party, 117

social ethic, 137, 140

social movements, 13, 38, 71–72, 255
    See also grassroots movements

social services, 80

Social/Spiritual Map of Cascadia
    (Clegg-Brown), 54

Socialist Party of Canada, 118

Sointula Finnish Community, 184

Solidarity Movement, B.C., 118

Soul of Sex, The (Moore), 245

Southern Crossroads region, 108–9

sovereignty, 94–103, 112

Spain, 94

spirit presences, 132

Spirits of the Ordinary (Alcalá),
    187

spiritual cinema, 38–39

spiritual experience, 15–16, 36, 40,
    42, 245–46, 259–60, 260–61

spiritual expression, 243–44

spiritual practice, 34–38, 151, 153,
    243, 244

spiritual shopping center, 36

spirituality
    alternative, 16–19
    defined, 2, 208
    environmental. See nature-
        based spirituality
    and ethics, 150–51, 153–54
    Ignatian, 83–84
    and magic realism, 177–78, 198
    "mapping" and values, 54–63
    and morality, 23–24
    nature-based. See nature-based
        spirituality

new age. See New Age
    spirituality
    religiosity and, 11–14
    sacred self, 36–39
    secular, 14, 20–21, 33–52.
        See also apocalyptic groups;
        nature-based spirituality;
        New Age spirituality
    shaping public life, 8–11
    and social change, 26–29, 127–42
    and sustainability, 143–55
    women's, 36–37
    workplace. See workplace
        spirituality
    See also indigenous peoples:
        spirituality

Spring Creek Project for Ideas,
    Nature and the Written Word,
    249–50

Starbucks Coffee Company, 7, 23,
    119, 197, 225

"State of Jefferson," 41, 43, 45

Stebner, Eleanor, 5, 217, 282–83

Stegner, Wallace, 244, 249, 250

stewardship, 20, 21–22, 22, 74, 84,
    150–51, 210, 212–13, 254

Sto:lo Nation, 136

subduction zone, 4, 54, 241, 248

success, 130, 160

suicide, physician-assisted, 24, 112

Super, Natural Christians
    (McFague), 157

supernatural, the, and faith, 177, 180

survivalists. See apocalyptic groups

sustainability
    common good and, 78
    and globalization, 27–28, 130–31,
        140–41